THE
COOK'S
BOOK OF
Essential
Information

THE
COOK'S
BOOK OF
Essential
Information
A KITCHEN HANDBOOK

by Barbara Hill

A DELL TRADE PAPERBACK

A DELL TRADE PAPERBACK

Published by
Dell Publishing
a division of
Bantam Doubleday Dell Publishing Group, Inc.
666 Fifth Avenue
New York, New York 10103

Although the author and publisher have exhaustively researched all sources to ensure the accuracy and completeness of the information contained in this book, we assume no responsibility for errors, inaccuracies, omissions, or any inconsistency herein. Any slights of people or organizations are unintentional. Readers should use their own judgment and/or consult their personal physician or a nutritional counselor for specific application of the nutritional information included.

For information address: Sumner House Press, Kennewick, Washington.

The trademark Dell® is registered in the U.S. Patent and Trademark Office.

ISBN: 0-440-50263-2

Reprinted by arrangement with Sumner House Press

Printed in the United States of America

Published simultaneously in Canada

December 1990

10 9 8 7 6 5 4 3 2 1

BVG

Contents

CHAPTER 4

What Every Cook Needs • 106

Every cook has a unique cooking style and unique requirements for foods, supplies, and equipment in the kitchen. This chapter not only has guidelines for things used by most cooks under most circumstances but also includes descriptions of various materials used in making kitchen tools, descriptions of tools available to you, and advice about the kind of care that will allow your kitchen equipment to last a long time.

CHAPTER 5

Cook Until Done • 139

How do you know how long something should be cooked? What causes food to cook? What are the real reasons for cooking food in the first place? This chapter is filled with information and many timetables that will give you the information you need to be able to cook every dish to perfection.

CHAPTER 6

How to Store (Just About) Everything • 172

Safe food storage is not just a matter of convenience, it is also a matter of good health. Save time, protect the nutritive value of food, prevent food poisoning, and cut food costs by following these simple food storage methods.

CHAPTER 7

Nutrition Is Where You Find It • 198

It is now generally agreed that nearly everyone needs more calcium—and it turns up in some unexpected places. It is also widely agreed that nearly everyone needs less salt—and it turns up in some unexpected places too. Here is a brief guide to what foods give us things we need, and what foods give us things we might well do without.

APPENDIX

Food Additives • 243

The idea of substances being added to foods to help preserve, color, or flavor them is not new. It has been going on for centuries. What is new is a growing reliance on preprocessed foods as a significant portion of the daily diet. The additives in these convenience foods go far beyond simple seasonings and raise questions about the long-term safety of their use. The appendix describes additives from "Acacia" to "Zingerone."

List of Tables

CHAPTER 1

The Cook's Dictionary

It should not be surprising that cooking has its own vocabulary—it is one of the most ancient arts or technologies, depending on the way you view it, of humankind. Words used in everyday English language cookbooks come from the French, the Italian, the Spanish, the Chinese, and many other cultures. Words come from techniques, old and new, and ingredients, common and uncommon.

The list that follows makes no pretense of being an absolute and definitive culinary vocabulary. It is just a collection of definitions of words related to cooking ... words that are sometimes puzzling, sometimes ambiguous, sometimes simply unfamiliar.

The definitions come from a variety of sources, both formal and informal. Some of the definitions are open to discussion because different regions use the words differently, but in general these are the widely agreed upon definitions and explanations for the terms noted.

AL DENTE. From the Italian term meaning "to the tooth," this term describes the texture of pasta when it is cooked just enough. It is the point at which your front teeth can easily bite through a piece, but there is still a touch of firmness to it.

When the pasta reaches this point, it should be taken from the heat immediately, drained, and perhaps plunged into cold water if it is not to be served right away. The cold water stops the cooking. If the pasta is left in the hot water or even drained but not cooled, it will continue to cook.

ASPIC.   An aspic is a broth or juice that has been thickened and stiffened with gelatin. It can be used in several ways: a mold can be filled with aspic and vegetables, meats, or fish and served as a salad; it can be poured over cold food to form a "mask" or coating; it can also be poured into a shallow pan and later cut into small squares and used to garnish cold meats.

AU GRATIN.   From the French, "to a thin crust." In culinary usage it means a mixture of crumbs and grated cheese with enough butter to hold it in small lumps. The mixture is spread on food (usually a casserole) and baked or broiled until brown and crisp. If the crust is to be formed by broiling, it is a good idea to put the casserole in a dish half filled with water. This prevents the sauce on the casserole from separating by keeping it a little cooler than the surface that is being broiled.

AU JUS.   From the French, "with gravy." Normally refers to roasted beef and means to serve the meat in or with its own juices. The "au jus" commonly served in restaurants has no relation to true roast beef "juice." This spurious liquid is a substance made of hot water and beef-flavored granules. It is extremely salty, and usually loaded with preservatives.

AU LAIT.   In French, *lait* means milk and this term refers to a food or beverage served with, or prepared with, milk. Most commonly seen in the phrase "café au lait," a European morning beverage made with hot milk and hot coffee in equal parts.

BAIN-MARIE.   This phrase has its origin in the alchemy of the Middle Ages. Literally it means Mary's bath and it has, as you might expect, an interesting linguistic history. Bain-marie came into modern French from the Medieval Latin *balneum Mariae* (Mary's bath). Tradition has it that the "Mary" referred to was the sister of Moses and, allegedly, an alchemist.

In the modern kitchen, a bain-marie is comprised of two pans designed to fit together so that simmering water in the lower will gently cook the contents of the upper. This system is important for sauces that are heat-sensitive, such as hollandaise. In baking, a simple bain-marie is used for custards or other delicate foods. The custard cups or baking dish is put in a larger container and water added to half fill the outer dish. Because the mixture being cooked is not in direct contact with the heat source, separation (curdling) can be avoided.

BAKE.   To bake is to cook in an open cavity filled with heat. It is a dry cooking method (only the fluid contained in the food itself is present during cooking). When it is a meat that is being cooked, the technique is called roasting.

BASTE.   When foods, particularly meats, are cooked in the dry heat of a conventional oven, they are susceptible to drying out and becoming tough and unpalatable. This can be avoided by pouring the liquids that accumulate in the bottom of the pan over the top of the meat from time to time. This process is called basting. A spoon may be used for the process, or a tool that looks like a giant medicine dropper with which the liquid is sucked up and then squeezed out over the meat. The liquid used for basting can also include leftover marinade in which the meat has seasoned, wine, or tomato juice. The slight acid quality of wine or tomato juice also produces a modest tenderizing effect.

BATTER.   A combination of ingredients based on a mixture of flour and water, which is ultimately cooked. A thick batter is about the consistency of mashed potatoes, a medium batter is about the consistency of commercial sour cream, and a thin batter is about the consistency of commercial buttermilk.

BEAT. To beat is to mix ingredients together thoroughly using a circular motion. Beating can be accomplished by hand or by using an appliance. In general, beating by hand for about 300 strokes equals mixing with a small hand mixer at medium speed for about two minutes (at the end of several hundred strokes by hand you appreciate the benefits of electric appliances). Unless you are using a full-size mixer or food processor, it is helpful to put the mixing bowl on a damp towel to hold it steady while beating.

BÉCHAMEL. Named for Louis de Béchamel, Marquis de Nointel, gourmet, financier, and honorary lord steward of the royal household of Louis XIV, béchamel is basically an enriched white sauce. That is, milk thickened with a mixture of flour and butter, to which beaten eggs are added.

BEURRE MANIE. From the French for "kneaded butter." Similar to the idea of roux (defined below), this is a thickening material usually composed of two parts butter to one part flour (which gives it twice as much butter per volume as roux). The butter and flour are either kneaded together by hand or mixed together in a food processor, blender, or mixer, much as butter and sugar are creamed together to make a cake. In beurre manie the mixture is not cooked. It may be made up in advance, stored in the refrigerator, and used as required to thicken soups and sauces.

BIND. To bind ingredients together is to add some item that causes the rest to gain cohesiveness. This added ingredient can either be a semiliquid such as beaten eggs or mayonnaise or a dry ingredient such as crumbs or flour.

BISQUE. This is a thick creamed soup. The important word here is *thick* and that is what differentiates a bisque from a typical creamed soup or chowder. Bisques are usually based on seafood but can also be made with vegetables, particularly colorful vegetables such as carrots or broccoli. This rich soup is served either as a main dish or in very small quantities as a "before."

BLANCH.   Generally speaking, to blanch is to cook some-thing very lightly. Food may be blanched by being submerged in simmering water or by being steamed over boiling water. Blanching is used most commonly with vegetables, and its purpose is to stop the ripening enzyme action that eventually causes the produce to become tough and lose its flavor. It is important to blanch both vegetables and fruits before freezing and before drying as well.

BLANQUETTE.   Meat is usually seared (browned) before add-ing liquids and cooking to make a stew. In a blanquette the initial browning process is omitted. Skipping this step causes the finished product to be light in color (*blanquette* comes from the French word that means white). In addition, the meat used in a blanquette is usually light in color as well, such as veal.

BOIL.   Water at sea level "boils" at 212 degrees in the Fahr-enheit system (100 degrees in the centigrade system). Without a thermometer, you can judge liquid to have reached the boiling point when you see bubbles consistently forming across the surface. When the liquid is boiling so vigorously that it cannot be stirred down, it is called a rolling boil. For all but very special instances (such as jelly making) a slow boil is just as effective for cooking as a hard rolling boil.

Liquids boil at lower temperatures as altitude increases, because the higher the altitude, the less the atmospheric pressure. The less pressure there is, the easier it is for mole-cules to escape from the surface of the liquid, and hence to boil. For each thousand feet above sea level, the boiling point of water drops about two degrees Fahrenheit. Because the liquid boils at a lower temperature, food cooked at high alti-tudes must be cooked a little longer than the same food cooked at sea level.

Salt or sugar added to water will raise the temperature at which it boils (one teaspoon of salt in one quart of water will raise boiling temperature one to two degrees Fahrenheit).

Hard water (water with naturally dissolved minerals) also boils at one to two degrees higher than soft water.

BOMBE. Probably so named because its traditional globular shape is similar to an old-fashioned comic-strip bomb, a culinary bombe is a dessert made of ice cream, sherbets, cream custards, fruit, and/or whipped cream. A bombe is made in a mold (either a deep round bowl or a specially shaped mold) by layering these ingredients. The layers can be as simple as a ball of orange sherbet embedded in a covering of vanilla ice cream or as elaborate as sequential layers of ice cream, fruit, whipped cream, and so on, with a final elaborate decoration of piped-on whipped cream, candied flowers, cake-decorating candies, or whatever strikes the cook's fancy.

BONE. In cooking, to bone really means to debone—to remove the bones from the piece of red meat, poultry, or fish. Removing bones makes the meats much easier to deal with both in cooking and eating. It is sometimes necessary to tie such things as boneless roasts or stuffed chicken breasts so that they will keep their shape while being cooked.

BOUILLON. This is a clear broth made by cooking meat, fish, or vegetables in liquid and then straining the liquid off. To strengthen the flavor the broth is reduced in volume by boiling. Dried granules and cubes of bouillon are also available but they are heavily salted (the salt acts as a preservative) and they produce a different broth than real bouillon.

BOUQUET GARNI. This is an assortment of herbs and spices tied in a piece of cheesecloth with a long piece of cotton string so that it may be easily removed from the food. Traditionally several stems of fresh parsley, a bay leaf, two or three stems of fresh thyme (or a teaspoon of dried thyme), and celery tops form the basis for a bouquet garni used with meat, but depending on taste and stock being seasoned, other herbs and spices such as rosemary, tarragon, marjoram, or even fennel may be added.

For hot punches and spiced wines, tie up one or two broken cinnamon sticks, five or six whole cloves, a teaspoon of whole allspice, and two or three pieces of lemon zest carefully taken from the length of a lemon.

Add the bouquet garni no sooner than the last hour of cooking time and taste occasionally so that you can take it out when the food is properly seasoned.

BRAISE. Braising is a technique to use with less-than-tender meats. To cook by braising, toss pieces of meat in a bowl with flour seasoned with salt until the meat is well floured, then brown quickly in a small amount of oil until a lightly browned crust has formed on all sides. If the skillet does not have a lid, transfer the meat to a pot that has a tight-fitting cover. Put in enough liquid (stock, wine, tomato juice, or water) to just cover the meat. Lower the heat to the lowest point that will maintain a simmer in the pot. Cover and cook until tender. Check the pot occasionally and add more liquid if needed.

BREAD. To bread means to cover portions of food with crumbs. The crumbs may literally be bread crumbs (coarse or fine, from dry or fresh bread), but may also be made from crackers, dry cereal, cornmeal, or you may even use just flour if that is all that is available.

To make a crisp crust, set out three shallow bowls with flour in the first, lightly beaten whole egg in the second, and crumbs seasoned with salt, paprika, or whatever you like in the third. Roll each portion first in flour, then dip in the egg, and finally pat the crumbs firmly over the food. Put the pieces on a rack for 15 to 30 minutes before frying or baking. The crust will quickly cook into a shell that keeps the fish or meat or vegetable from drying out and gives a nice contrast between crisp outside and tender inside.

BRINE. Brine is a saline (salt and water) solution primarily used to preserve certain kinds of food (pickles, some fish, and some cheeses, for example). Because of the salt, the brine changes the flavor of the food as well as preserving it. If the pickled food seems too salty, rinse (refresh) it in clear water.

BROCHETTE. Taken from the French, *brochette* means a small spit or skewer. Meat and sometimes vegetables are threaded onto a rod or thin swordlike implement and either broiled in an oven or cooked over the direct heat of a barbecue. Prepared this way, the food is served "en brochette." For a change try making fish kebabs using scallops, prawns, and pieces of firm fish such as halibut mixed with cherry tomatoes, green pepper, and mushrooms.

An ancient way of cooking meat, its success depends upon using pieces not more than an inch and a half in any dimension, using tender meat, and spacing the meat on the brochette so that all sides are open to the heat. The Middle Eastern term for this style is kebab or kebap. In that part of the world vegetables are not cooked with the meat but are grilled separately.

BROIL. A dry-heat cooking method whereby the food is cooked with direct heat either under an oven broiler or over coals in a barbecue. It is important to preheat the broiler or have the coals hot before starting to cook, so that the food will cook quickly. (In effect, the meat is cooked by searing.) Food should be placed three to six inches from the heat source. The thinner the food being cooked, the closer it can be placed to the heat. Thick pieces placed too close to the heat source will char on the outside while leaving the inside not rare but raw.

CALORIE. For all the talk about it, what is a calorie? The original concept of calorie meant "gram calorie" and is the amount of heat needed to raise the temperature of one gram of water from 14.5 to 15.5 degrees in the Celsius temperature measurement system.

Because a gram calorie is a very small unit, the kilocalorie (1,000 gram calories) has become the standard unit of measurement used by researchers and it is this measurement that is almost always meant when you see the term "calorie" used regarding diet.

Strictly speaking, then, a calorie is a measure of heat and not directly related to nutrition. It comes into kitchen terminology because our bodies use the food taken in as a fuel (energy). Although the theories regarding weight gain and loss become steadily more complex, there seems to be agreement that an excessive intake of fuel, as measured by the calories represented in food eaten, will result in the body storing the excess for use later. From a simplistic view, it is this storage procedure that adds undesirable inches in the form of body fat.

CANDY.   To candy something means to coat it with a sweet covering. This may be done either by cooking it in a sugar-and-water syrup or by dipping it in lightly beaten egg whites, then in granulated sugar, and then allowing it to dry on a rack.

CARAMELIZE.   To caramelize is to heat white or brown sugar in a heavy pan or, best of all, a cast iron skillet until it melts and browns (about 330 degrees Fahrenheit). It is a term also used to indicate the glazing of a sugar topping, usually by placing the dish under the broiler for a short while (often a custard as in crème brûlée). To do this successfully, have the food to be glazed very cold and place it in a pan partly filled with very cold water. These two things will keep the custard from overheating during the glazing process.

Caramelizing is a procedure that must be watched closely because the sugar can pass from granular to charred in less time than would seem possible. Caramelized sugar also sets up very quickly when it is removed from the heat, so if you are going to make some specific use of it (such as caramelizing the bottom of custard cups before pouring the custard in), be prepared to work quickly. If the phone rings, don't answer it unless you are prepared to start over.

CASSEROLE. From the French term for saucepan, taken from the Old Provençal word *cassa* and the Medieval Latin *cattia,* both of which meant dipper or small ladle. In the present day, the term refers both to the container (heatproof pan or bowl) and the container's contents (a combination of protein, carbohydrate, and sauce, which is frequently topped with something crunchy for contrast). Casseroles are usually served directly from the container in which they were cooked.

CHIFFONADE. A term used to describe green leafy herbs (such as sorrel, lettuce, or endive) cut into thin strips, usually lightly cooked in butter and used as an addition to soups, salads, or salad dressings.

CHOP. To chop, hold a large kitchen knife at a 90-degree angle to your cutting board and plunge the edge of the blade repeatedly through the food until the pieces reach the desired size. If you are using a French chef's knife, a slight rocking motion can be used. If you are using an Oriental square cleaver, whack the food in a straight-down motion. There are also small devices for chopping that use a group of spring-loaded knives attached to the lid of a small container. The food is added, the lid tightened, and the center rod pushed down repeatedly. These gadgets are worthless because they do not hold enough for most purposes and are hard to clean and maintain.

CLARIFIED (DRAWN) BUTTER. Butter is made clear by separating out the milk solids that were in the original cream. This is done by slowly melting the butter over low heat so that the milk solids settle to the bottom. Next, very carefully pour off the yellow liquid on top. This liquid is clarified or drawn butter and it has a flavor even more delicate than whole butter. It also has a higher smoking point and so can be used for sautéing at temperatures that would cause whole butter to burn. Always use clarified butter to sauté such things as boned chicken breasts or beef tournedos.

CLARIFY.   To clarify something is to make it clear by removing bits of food and other cloudiness. If you add a mixture of lightly beaten egg white and crushed egg shell to a broth and whisk it together briskly over a medium heat, the bits and pieces will adhere to the egg and shell. When the liquid is the strained through a wire sieve, it should be completely clear.

COAT.   Depending on what is being coated with what, putting a coating on portions of food can be achieved in a variety of ways. It is handy to have a shaker can filled with sugar or seasoned flour that can be used to simply shake over the food to be coated. The food can also be rolled in the coating medium. The food pieces can be added, a few at a time, to a paper or plastic bag that contains the coating and given a vigorous shake until adequately coated.

CODDLE.   This term is most frequently used to describe a method for cooking eggs, although the method can be used for other foods as well. To coddle something, you place it in a small container with or without a cover and place it in a pan of simmering water. The food is cooked by the gentle heat being applied to the outside of the container. The result, in eggs for instance, is most like poaching (but without the possibility of the white running out of control).

COMPOTE.   A compote is a combination of cooked fruits, usually served in the winter when fresh fruits are not easily available. Sometimes sweet spices or wines are used in the poaching liquid. Compotes are best when not more than three or four fruits are used and they are allowed to marinate together long enough to blend the flavors.

CONVECTION OVEN.   Basically all dry-heat ovens work on the principle of convection heating, by which heat is naturally circulated with the hot air rising and the cooler air falling to produce a circular movement. A convection oven merely accelerates this natural phenomenon by introducing moving air into the oven chamber. The air movement tends to distribute the heat more evenly throughout the oven and by doing so cooks and browns the food more evenly. Lower heat settings may be used, which reduces power usage and also reduces the natural shrinking of meats. The convection oven may be thought of as a superefficient traditional oven.

COOL.   Cool in the culinary sense means that the temperature of the food has dropped until it is no longer warm to the touch. (A key to guaranteed success with soufflés is to cool the cream sauce mixture before adding the egg yolks. The cream sauce has reached the right temperature for mixing when you can comfortably rest the bottom of the pan holding the sauce in the palm of your hand.) If you must cool something quickly, use the refrigerator, but stir occasionally and closely cover the food with plastic wrap so that it does not dry out as the steam escapes during the cooling process.

COURT BOUILLON.   This is liquid used traditionally for poaching fish or seafood. It is prepared by sticking a few whole cloves into a small onion, adding some celery and carrots, and a bouquet garni to about two quarts of water. You can use half white wine and half water if you like. Simmer the broth for about a half hour, then cool without removing the vegetables. Drain off and use to gently simmer the fish.

CREAM.   To cream is to soften butter or shortening and mix it with sugar or flour. Although it is possible to do it by hand, this is one of those jobs ideally suited to some kitchen appliance; even a small mixer will do it quite adequately. The trick is to mix the dry ingredient and the fat product until they are truly inseparable. Flour and butter mixed this way form a beurre manie. Sugar and butter are creamed together as a first step in many cake and cookie recipes.

CRIMP.   This graphic word comes from the Middle English word *crimper,* which meant to wrinkle, and from the Old English word *gecrympan,* which meant to curl. In the modern kitchen, crimping is used to seal something. The thing sealed is most commonly a two-crust pie when the top is applied. The crimping may be accomplished either by hand (pinch the two pieces of dough together gently to form a wrinkle), or by using one of the various crimping tools that are available. Crimping is also what seals the various ravioli-type foods that appear in all cultures from China to Poland.

CROQUETTES. One of the many ways to use leftovers. In this method, minced or ground cooked foods (meat or vegetables) are mixed with either a thick white sauce or a combination of beaten eggs and bread crumbs to form flattened patties, logs, cones, or balls. These are then dipped in beaten egg and then in dry crumbs and either deep-fried or pan-fried.

CROUTONS. Croutons are small cubes of bread. It is possible to buy croutons, plain or seasoned, but they are so simple and inexpensive to make that it seems pointless to buy them unless time is just too short. They are made by cutting any semistale bread (three or four days old at least) into cubes about a half inch on a side. Some cooks deep-fry the cubes to brown them, but that seems to add excessive calories without any real gain in quality. If you butter the bread lightly and sprinkle it with some herbs or other seasonings before cutting into cubes, you can simply spread the cubes on a cookie sheet and put them in a 200-degree oven until they are completely dried and browned. The length of time it takes depends on the freshness of the bread (the fresher it is, the longer it takes).

CRUDITÉS. From the French term for raw vegetable, these are the dieter's salvation at parties. Served as appetizers and cocktail-party nibblers, crudités are attractively cut pieces of a variety of vegetables arranged on a tray and usually served with a low-cal dip. The most popular vegetables for this purpose are celery, carrots, broccoli flowers (and strips cut from broccoli stems), cauliflower pieces, and mushrooms, but any vegetable that can be managed by hand and is not starchy can be used (that means omitting peas, corn, potatoes, etc.).

CUBE/DICE/MINCE. These are the three terms used to describe the process of cutting food into square bits. To cube is to cut the food into pieces about a half inch on a side. To dice is to cut the food into pieces smaller than this but still recognizably cubelike in shape. To mince is to cut food into the smallest portion of all ... but cut, not grind.

CURDLE. This is a word that a cook would prefer never to have to use, because it means that things have gone wrong ... not irretrievably wrong, but wrong nevertheless. To curdle means to cause curds to form, to coagulate. This is fine when cheese is being made but definitely not good when the end product is to be, for instance, a hollandaise sauce. Egg sauces are particularly susceptible to curdling, which occurs because the very delicate egg has encountered something entirely too hot. The protein molecules in the egg bind themselves together and tend to stay that way (think of scrambled eggs in this connection).

The second reason for curdling is that the fat (usually melted butter) is added too quickly and the protein molecules of the eggs are unable to disperse among the fat molecules to make the emulsion that is the goal. If the oil or melted butter is added very slowly in a thin stream (almost but not quite drop by drop) while you stir constantly, your sauce will not curdle.

CURE. To cure means to preserve. It is a term usually applied to meat products and may involve brining, pickling, drying, or smoking, or some combination of these techniques.

CUT IN. In the culinary sense this means to mix solid fats such as shortening or butter with dry ingredients such as flour. Most commonly this term is used to describe the initial mixing step when making pie pastry. The trick is to start with the shortening very cold and to avoid prolonged contact with your hands, which tends to warm it. To mix the two ingredients, use two knives (cut them past each other through the mixture) or one of the pastry blenders designed for the purpose. The reason for doing this is to cut the shortening into tiny bits so that when the pastry is placed in a hot oven the fat will melt and, being encased in flour, form pockets. These tiny pockets are what make pie pastry flaky and tender.

DEGLAZE.   If you pour a little water or wine into a pan in which meat has cooked and swirl it around to pick up the bits and pieces of meat that are left, you have deglazed the pan. This simple sauce can then be poured over the meat to return some of the flavor that has been lost in cooking. Be sure to use only enough liquid to clear the pan (usually around a half cup, but let your eye be the final judge). If the sauce seems too thin, allow it to boil for a moment and reduce the volume slightly.

DEEP-FAT FRYING.   The reason for cooking in deep fat is to seal the food and cause it to be crisp on the outside while staying tender and moist inside. Using the correct temperature is essential in deep-fat frying, and there is a chart in Chapter 5 that describes the correct temperatures for most foods. Be careful not to add too many pieces at one time, as the cool food will quickly lower the temperature of the fat. When this happens the oil does not seal the food but rather is absorbed by it. This is the reason for greasy fried foods. If you use the correct temperature and cooking time for deep-fat frying, you will be surprised at how little oil is actually missing from the fryer when you finish. This is also sometimes referred to as *French frying*.

DEVILED.   Deviled foods are spiced, usually with hot spices such as pepper, chili powder, cumin, Tabasco sauce, and so forth. Deviled foods can be either cold (such as deviled eggs) or hot (such as deviled seafood casseroles). Deviling is a technique to cut blandness or richness in foods and make the flavor more interesting.

DISJOINT.   To disjoint meat means to separate it into pieces at the joints. For instance, in disjointing a chicken the pieces would be separated at the shoulder, hip, and knee.

DISSOLVE.   To dissolve is to cause a dry ingredient to become inseparably mixed with a liquid in a solution. Yeast and gelatin are two dry ingredients usually dissolved in liquid before being added to the other ingredient. If the recipe calls for dissolving one thing into another, be sure that you can no longer see bits of the dry ingredients in the liquid before adding it to anything else.

DOT.   This means to scatter some ingredient, frequently butter, on top of other ingredients by making "dots." The easiest way to do this is to scoop up the ingredient to be dotted in a spoon and then use a second spoon to scrape small bits off onto the food. It is important to scatter the bits evenly over the surface so that the ingredient will be spread evenly as it cooks.

DRAWN BUTTERS.   See *Clarified Butter.*

DREDGE.   In the kitchen, to dredge means to coat a portion of food with seasoned flour, or sometimes something like cornmeal. If crumbs are to be used, the recipe will usually say to "bread" rather than to "dredge."

DRESS.   In the culinary lexicon this means to prepare a fish or animal to be cooked—in other words, the messy job of "cleaning" it. With fish this involves removing the head, tail, innards, and scales at least, and sometimes boning (filleting) as well. With animals and birds, dressing means about the same; however, here you must remove the feathers or fur to get down to the meat. Dressing is a job few if any cooks cherish, a job most cooks feel should be the responsibility of the catcher not the cooker.

DRIPPINGS.   Drippings are what a cooking piece of meat or poultry excretes as it cooks. Drippings are made up of melted fat, fluid called myoglobin (a liquid that heat frees from the muscle portion of the meat), and browned bits. Drippings collect in the bottom of the roasting pan and are usually used in making a sauce to accompany the meat. If not used for that, they can be refrigerated and used to flavor soups or other sauces later.

DUST. To dust is to very lightly cover a piece of food with some sort of powder. Flour seasoned with salt and pepper is used to dust food to be sautéed, for instance, while powdered sugar can be "dusted" on the top of a cake instead of a frosting. Dusting is facilitated by the use of a large shaker can, which distributes the powdery ingredient evenly.

D'UXELLES. Created by a classic chef, LaVarenne of the household of the French Marquis d'Uxelles, this is a mixture of mushrooms, shallots, and butter. The mushrooms are chopped into very fine pieces, then placed between two paper towels and pressed to absorb all possible liquid. The shallots are similarly treated. The proportions are generally one part butter to one part shallots and three parts mushrooms. First clarify the butter, then add the mushrooms and shallots, season with salt, pepper, and nutmeg, and sauté over a moderately high heat until all the liquid has evaporated.

ENTRÉE. Taken from the French and literally meaning "the beginning." But the entrée has never been the first course of the meal. In the days when the classic French dinner menu included multiple courses, the entrée course was the third course, usually between the fish and the meat courses, and was a dish served in a white or brown sauce. Today, it means the main dish and can be anything from steak to a tofu casserole.

ESPAGNOLE. Another term from the classic French cuisine, which is used to describe a basic brown sauce made of meat (usually beef) drippings, liquid, and thickening of some sort.

FILLET/FILET.   These are the English and French spellings for the same concept. To fillet is to debone (or "bone" in the culinary sense) a piece of meat. When a piece of meat is without bones it is called a fillet. Fillet of beef is also referred to as a tenderloin. When the tenderloin is cut into individual-sized portions, the portions are commonly called filet mignon.

FINES HERBES.   A French term used to describe a combination of green herbs that are minced and left in the dish being prepared (unlike bouquet garni, which is removed from the food before serving). Herbs commonly used in this way include parsley, chervil, chives, and sometimes tarragon or basil. Fines herbes are used in such things as omelets, salad dressings, and some sauces.

FLAKE.   The most common method for telling if a piece of fish is done is to see if it flakes. This is done by putting a fork into the piece along one of the grain separations and gently pulling. If the piece starts to separate, it is "flaking easily," as most recipes say, and is done. If you sense resistance, the fish should cook for a while longer.

FLAMBÉ.   Means to serve something in flames (on purpose). Almost anything except salad can be served flambé and add a spectacular note to any meal. The technique involves burning some sort of potable alcohol on the food. The higher the proof (alcohol content) of the liquid, the quicker it will ignite. For sure-fire results, however, the trick, is to warm the alcohol to about 130 degrees F before you try to light it, and remember that room temperature foods and serving dishes quickly cool the alcohol even if it is prewarmed. It is quite pretty to soak cubes of sugar in the liquor and arrange the cubes on top of a cake or pudding, then ignite. Skewered meat can also be served aflame, but this is a procedure that you would be wise to rehearse before performing for guests.

FLUTE.   To flute is to make a decorative pattern on something. The something can be the edge of a pie shell (in which case the fluting is generally done by crimping the pastry between thumb and index finger to make a sort of scallop pattern) or vegetables to be served as crudités (by cutting a pattern of grooves on mushroom caps, or making radish "flowers" by fluting the edges).

FOLD. This is one of the most important techniques a cook can learn. It is primarily used to incorporate materials that have been whipped (most commonly egg white or cream) when they are added to produce greater volume and to leaven the food, but it is also used whenever the ingredients being mixed are delicate.

The lighter ingredient is always poured onto the heavier ingredients to form a layer on the top. Use a big spoon or rubber spatula and starting at one side of the bowl, make a U-shaped movement. You will come down one side of the bowl, across the bottom, and up the other side. As you come up the second side some of the heavier material will be pulled up over the whipped material. Turn the bowl as you go so that the heavy material will be pulled from all sides.

Be careful not to simply stir the mixture together, because that will negate all the benefits of adding the air to the whipped ingredient. Continue to fold the two materials together only long enough to distribute the whipped ingredient evenly throughout. Gently, gently is the keynote here.

FONDUE. This is a word with two quite different culinary meanings. The most common contemporary one means to cook or dip small portions of food in some hot liquid. This can be cubes of bread dipped in seasoned cheese sauce, cubes of beef in hot oil, cubes of chicken breast in seasoned chicken broth, strawberries in chocolate sauce, or some variation on one of these. The term is also used in an older sense, which means to make a sort of casserole based on bread slices or crumbs, some protein (usually cheese), with an egg mixture poured over all then baked.

FORCEMEAT.   This is a rather old-fashioned term but still is seen from time to time. It means a thick puree or paste of meat, poultry, or seafood, which is bound with egg white or butter for consistency and then piped onto other food such as casseroles or soups as a decoration.

FRAPPÉ.   Related to the French verb meaning to strike, frappé is used to describe finely crushed ice with some flavoring, liquor, or fruit juice poured over it. It can also describe a juice frozen to the point of being slushy. In either case a cool and elegant ending to a summer meal.

FRICASSEE.   To fricassee is basically to braise, and the term is most commonly used to describe a method for cooking chicken. The resultant sauce is much lighter in color than the sauce that results from braising red meat.

FRY.   To fry means to cook in hot oil. For specific types of frying, read the entries for sauté, deep-fat frying, and stir-fry.

FUMET.   Although the term is taken from the French verb "to smoke," no smoke is involved in making a fumet in the kitchen, because it is a concentrated stock or broth. Although most commonly used to describe a fish-based stock, it can be made of other basic stocks as well.

GLAZE.   Based on the French word for "ice," to glaze is to cover with some sort of shiny coating. For meat dishes this is done with a very concentrated meat stock made by boiling the liquid in which meat and meat bones were cooked until it is reduced to about one-tenth the original volume.

Glaze is also used to describe a final coating put on some desserts. The glazing of cakes is done with a thin powdered-sugar frosting that is poured (not spread) on the pastry. Fruit tarts are glazed with a sweet coating made either by adding a tablespoon of water to a half cup of jelly and melting it together or by using arrowroot to thicken a sweet fruit juice such as apple juice. (When using arrowroot be sure not to let the mixture boil or it will not thicken properly.) There are also commercial mixes available. Tarts are glazed over the top surface of the filling but not over the pastry.

GRATE.   To grate something is to shred it by using a metal device that has holes of varying sizes to accomplish a variety of purposes (tiny holes for grating the peel from citrus fruits, slightly larger holes for cheese, medium holes for firm vegetables such as carrots, larger holes for cabbage). Food processors and some mixers also have grater attachments, but if you have only a little grating to do, it is always a question whether it is worth all the setting up and cleaning afterward. A small tool that no kitchen should be without is a nutmeg grater, because no preground nutmeg can ever equal the flavor of nutmeg that is freshly grated.

GRILL.   To grill is to cook over direct heat. Grilling may be done with the food or a barbecue grate, or in a flat open pan with little if any oil. It is a dry, non-oven cooking technique.

GRIND.   The only way to grind something is to pass it either through a hand grinder or through a grinding device on your mixer or food processor. The technique pushes the food (using a broad screw-shaped device) through a cruciform knife, then through a plate with round holes. The combination of pressure (from the pushing) and cutting tends to squash the food together and produces a unique texture.

HULL.   The hull is the outside layer of certain vegetables, nuts, or seeds. It is normally not edible because of its fibrous consistency. To hull something is to remove this outside covering. Peanuts, for instance, are hulled by removing their outside shells.

HUSK.   This is a term normally limited to describing the outer green leaves that cover an ear of corn. To husk the corn is to remove this nonedible layer and the corn silk threads as well.

JULIENNE. The technique of cutting an ingredient length-wise into long slivers. It can be used with raw or cooked vegetables, fruit, cooked meat, or cheese. It is a graceful way to add meat and cheese to a summer salad. It also produces attractive vegetable servings, especially with firm vegetables such as potatoes, turnips, carrots, and so forth.

KNEAD. Normally associated with bread making, there are some other times when kneading is used, but whenever used the same method is employed.

Stand facing the food to be kneaded. With your arms bent at the wrist and the food at a comfortable height, press the heel of your hand into the dough with as much pressure as you can reasonably exert. Turn the dough a quarter turn, then fold the dough over from the top and press again. Repeat this folding and pressing until the dough is smooth and resilient (for bread dough this takes about ten to fifteen minutes ... of which the last three or four will seem very long indeed). Some cooks find kneading tiresome, others find it satisfying, but in either case, kneading should not be skimped on.

Kneading is the key to good texture in your bread be-cause it distributes the yeast evenly throughout the dough and also softens the gluten (a protein found in grains), which allows the gluten to form a good structure for supporting the expanded dough as the bread bakes. Heavy, dense loaves are usually a result of inadequate kneading.

Some mixers and food processors are strong enough to take over the kneading process and make the whole job one of observation rather than participation.

LARD. As a noun, lard refers to animal fat that is rendered from the meat of certain parts of the animal carcass. Lard usually refers to fat from pork, while suet is fat from beef. As a verb, to lard is to put pieces of fat on top of or in slashes cut into pieces of meat or fish to provide additional moisture, add flavor, and prevent drying out during roasting. Be aware that animal fat is a saturated fat and among the various types of fats is the least desirable from a nutrition standpoint.

LEAVEN. Leaven is a term used to describe the process of causing bread dough to expand or rise. It is accomplished by the use of a leavening agent such as yeast or baking powder, and its purpose is to make the bread easier to eat because more air is incorporated into the dough. There are also unleavened breads (matzo, for instance), which are baked to be thin enough to eat easily.

MACERATE. This term means to soften. In cooking, to macerate usually means to soak some ingredient in a liquid, either to soften the ingredient or to flavor the liquid. For instance, dried fruit can be macerated in a semisweet wine. The wine softens the fruit, the fruit flavors the wine, and both benefit from the relationship. Allow several hours for the best results.

MARINADE. Although we usually think of a marinade as a liquid in which a piece of meat soaks to become tender and absorb flavor, there are also dry marinades, which are mixtures of herbs and spices rubbed into a piece of meat several hours before cooking.

The liquid marinade usually contains some slightly acid ingredient such as wine, vinegar, or tomato juice to tenderize the meat, plus whatever seasonings go with the meat. Many culinary reputations have been based on a unique marinade concoction, and you should feel free to improvise and develop your own. If you soak the meat at room temperature it will absorb the marinade quickest, but you should not leave it unrefrigerated for more than two hours. For longer soaking, keep it in the refrigerator. In either case turn the meat frequently.

MASK. When food is masked, it is completely covered with something thick enough to stick to it. This covering can be a gelatin mixture (semiset before applying), mayonnaise, jelly (melted slightly), or whipped cream (usually stabilized with softened gelatin at the ratio of one teaspoon gelatin dissolved in warm water to one cup of cream, added before the cream is quite whipped).

MEUNIÈRE. From the French term for a miller's wife, this is a style of cooking whereby the food is dredged in flour and then sautéed in butter. A little lemon juice and a sprinkle of chopped parsley finishes the dish. This technique is used most commonly for preparing fish fillets.

MICROWAVE. Cooking by microwave is achieved by electromagnetic waves in frequencies above the audible range, which are generated by a part in the microwave oven called a magnetron. These waves are distributed in the oven cavity by a fanlike device called a stirrer. When these electromagnetic waves come into contact with the liquid molecules in the food, the molecules are caused to go into motion, and it is this motion (which causes friction, which causes heat) that ultimately cooks the food. Because the plate or bowl containing the food is solid, there are no liquids to be agitated and thus the container stays cool. (If it becomes hot, it is from the heat of the food it contains.) Metal containers cannot be used in a microwave oven, because the electromagnetic waves can cause an electrical arcing to take place, which can damage the magnetron.

Microwave cooking has some advantages (notably the speed with which some foods are cooked), but it is not suitable for all foods nor is it always faster than traditional cooking techniques. Foods that are rehydrated during cooking—pasta, for example—cook in about the same time either way.

MIREPOIX. This is a combination of minced vegetables used to season soups or sauces. The vegetables traditionally include carrots, onions, and celery, with others added depending on the food to which the mirepoix is to be added. Unlike a bouquet garni, it is part of the final product and not removed before serving, and unlike fines herbes, it is made up of firm vegetables and not leafy herbs.

MOUSSE.   Taken from the French word for froth, there are entrée mousses and dessert mousses. Entrée mousses frequently contain gelatin, mayonnaise, and minced fish, poultry, or meat plus some agreeable vegetables and seasonings to enhance the texture and flavor of the dish. An entrée mousse makes a perfect summer luncheon dish. Dessert mousses are based on sweetened whipped cream, which is given firmness either by adding gelatin or by freezing. Dessert mousses frequently have fruit and/or flavorings added and are a spectacular end to any meal.

MULL.   An archaic term that is now used almost exclusively to describe a method of making a warmed, spiced beverage, usually cider or wine.

PAPILLOTE.   From the French word for curled paper, papillote originally referred to the trim used to decorate some foods (such as lamb chops), but now is used to describe a cooking technique. Paper is the operative word, however, and the technique is one in which baking parchment paper is wrapped around meat, poultry, or fish before baking. The food is placed in the center of the paper and two sides are drawn up and matched, then folded down until the food is reached. The open ends are then folded and fastened (stapled or pinned), and sometimes a lightly beaten egg is spread over the paper to seal it completely. Before serving cut off the fastened ends with kitchen shears and also make a cut along the center fold of paper, but leave the food paper-wrapped to present at table for serving.

PARBOIL.   To parboil is to partially cook. It means to cook the food (usually vegetables) a little more than you would when blanching, but not to full tenderness. Parboiled foods are usually incorporated into another dish to complete their cooking. It is a technique used mainly to ensure that everything in a combination dish has finished cooking at the same time. When preparing a stir-fry meal, it is often a good idea to slightly precook dense ingredients (such as root vegetables).

PARE/PEEL. Both terms mean to remove the outer layer from a piece of food. Scraping is also sometimes recommended in recipes but unless carefully done can result in a rather ragged-looking piece of vegetable. Since many of the most important nutrients are located in or just below the outer covering of the vegetable or fruit, from a nutritional standpoint the less peeling the better. There are, however, times when there is no substitute for paring/peeling. Strictly speaking, to pare is to cut the outer layer with a knife, while to peel is to pull the covering off by hand. You would, to be precise, pare an apple but peel an orange.

PICKLE. Pickling is a technique used to preserve foods of various sorts. The food is soaked, and usually also cooked as well, in a solution of water, vinegar, salt, and spices in varying proportions. Unless it is to be kept in the refrigerator until used, the food then must be properly canned. There are traditional methods for making sauerkraut and some kinds of cucumber pickles that do not call for canning, but these techniques must be carefully monitored for signs of spoilage (see Chapter 6 for more information on pickling).

PIPE. To pipe means to force a stiff paste through a tube (either a metal cylinder or a cone of paper or coated cloth) and then through a nozzle that produces a shaped product. It is the technique used by bakers to decorate cakes and cookies, but it is also used to make attractive hors d'oeuvres and decorated main dishes. With a few nozzles and a little practice, the imaginative cook can develop a reputation for artistic expertise. Try covering an ordinary meat loaf with mashed potatoes, then piping a design across the top before putting it into the oven to brown ... meat and potatoes, but with a definite difference.

PIT. The pit is the seed of a fruit and is usually, but not always, removed before cooking. Sometimes the pit is left in to maintain the shape of a fruit, such as an apricot, which softens greatly during cooking. To pit is, as you might expect, the process of removing the pits.

PITH. Pith is a word used to describe the white fibrous part of some vegetables. Although usually tasteless, in citrus fruits the pith (the portion of the fruit between the colored rind and the fruit itself) is quite bitter and should not be used in food preparation unless the bitterness is desirable (as in citrus marmalades).

PLUMP. In the kitchen this means to increase the dimensions of something by soaking it in liquid. In this case you are not softening it (as in macerating) so much as rehydrating it and letting it assume its former dimensions. It is a term most frequently encountered with regard to raisins.

POACH. To poach is not to cook in boiling water. To poach is to very gently cook in water that is just about, but not quite, boiling. It is a cooking technique used for delicate foods (eggs and fillet of sole come to mind) that may either toughen (as in eggs) or fall apart (as in sole) if cooked too fast at too high a temperature. The finished product of poaching may be improved by adding a little acid to the water, about a tablespoon of white vinegar to a pint of water. The acid relaxes the structure of the protein molecules and allows them to bind together more effectively.

PREHEAT. To preheat means to bring the oven or other appliance up to the recommended cooking temperature before putting the food in to be cooked. Most electric ovens preheat by turning on both the top element (the broiler) and the bottom element at the same time until the set temperature is reached. Heat is then maintained by using the bottom element only. If you have this sort of system and you put food in before the correct temperature is reached, the food will be seared on the top before it has really started to cook, something you probably do not want to have happen. On the other hand, some foods are not bothered by the over/under heat; potatoes, for instance, frequently can be put in before the oven is heated, with no negative results.

PRESSURE COOKING. Top-of-the-stove pressure cooking has been around for several decades. For normal meal preparation it is used primarily as a timesaver and nutrient preserver (shorter cooking times keep nutrients from dissipating). For home-canners it is an essential technique for preserving any low-acid food—that is to say, all vegetables (except certain varieties of tomato), meats, and combination foods such as soups and other prepared dishes. The higher temperature that can be reached inside a pressure cooker is the only way that the home-canner can be assured of destroying the toxic *Clostridium botulinum* bacteria.

PROOF. This is a somewhat archaic term that means to activate yeast and "prove" it is viable. Yeast is mixed with water and a little sugar and shortly thereafter will begin to bubble and expand. The temperature of the water used to dissolve the yeast, and sugar is very important because if too hot, it will kill the yeast, and if too cool, it will slow the growth process. The water should be between 105 and 115 degrees Fahrenheit (just comfortable against your inside wrist). Remember, too, that the water will lose some heat as it comes in contact with the bowl. In making bread, the yeast-sugar-water mixture is then incorporated into the dry ingredients, which are primarily carbohydrates (flour). As the yeast feeds on the carbohydrates it produces carbon dioxide as a byproduct. It is this carbon dioxide gas that causes the dough to rise.

PUREE. From the French verb that means to purify or put through a sieve, to puree is to make a smooth mash out of one or more ingredients. Classically it was done by running the food through a sieve or food mill several times, but fortunately we now have blenders and food processors that do the job not only more quickly but also better than the old methods. Purees may be made of any food: fish, meat, vegetables, or fruit.

RANCID.   Rancid is a word used to describe a fat or fat product that has spoiled. The state of spoilage is easily identifiable by the distinctive and extremely unpleasant odor that comes from the food. It should, of course, not be consumed by either people or pets.

RECONSTITUTE.   To reconstitute is to bring a product back to its original consistency, normally by adding water to a dried product. Most commonly come across when referring to dry milk but also applied to many other food items such as the great variety of freeze-dried foods now available.

REDUCE.   To reduce means to condense a liquid by boiling away much of the original fluid volume. It is done to concentrate the flavor in less volume and should be done over a high heat. Frequently the technique is used to produce a quick sauce after deglazing a pan in which meat has been cooked. The meat is kept waiting (in a warm place) until the sauce is ready, so it should be done as speedily as possible.

REFRESH.   When food has been parboiled or blanched, the process by which the cooking is stopped involves dunking the food into iced water. To do this is to refresh the food. The term is also used to describe rinsing brined food in cold water.

RENDER.   To render is to pull all of the fat out of pieces of meat. Meats most commonly rendered are bacon, short ribs, or beef suet (beef fat chunks). Rendered fat has the flavor of the original meat and can be useful in cooking if calorie counting and dietary saturated fat are not considerations. (A quarter cup of bacon renderings added to a batter for an eight-inch pan of cornbread adds wonderfully to the flavor.) Rendering is sometimes referred to as "trying out."

RICE. Rice, of course, is a cereal grain. To rice something means to make it look like that grain. The technique involves using a sievelike device with round holes in it. A lever pushes the food through the holes and it does, in fact, come out looking something like rice. Most commonly used as a technique for serving cooked potatoes, other root vegetables can also be riced for a slightly different look. It does take a special ricer, however, which is just one more special tool to store when not being used.

ROAST. To roast is to cook in an uncovered pan with dry heat. Roasting produces a crisp, dark surface and a moist interior. If the surface of the meat starts to dry out during the cooking time, baste with pan juices but do not cover, because meat will steam in moist heat if covered and the surface will be soft. Roasting is a term used to describe cooking a whole piece of meat although what is done is, strictly speaking, baking. Traditionally, however, one bakes meatloaf but roasts a standing rib. Interestingly, hams are "baked" rather than "roasted."

ROUX. In French, the word *roux* describes a particular color, reddish or sandy, and is usually used to refer to a certain color hair. In food preparation, a roux is a cooked mixture of flour and butter or some other solid fat used to thicken a sauce. The cooking is what differentiates roux from beurre manie. A light-colored sauce is produced when the roux is cooked only slightly so that the flour does not darken, but for a darker sauce the mixture is allowed to brown evenly.

SAUTÉ. To sauté is to cook food in oil over high heat while stirring and turning it frequently to brown evenly on all sides. This is one of the basic cooking techniques that all cooks should learn. It is not necessary to use a lot of oil when sautéing, only enough to keep the food from sticking to the pan. Frequently a recipe will call for onions and other ingredients to be sautéed before being added to a sauce. The reason for doing this is not only to soften the vegetables by precooking but also to smooth out and blend the flavor so that it will not be too harsh.

SCALD. To heat to just below the boiling point. Tiny bubbles appearing around the edge of the liquid indicate scalding. Sometimes also used to mean the process of blanching.

SCALLOP. In cooking you will find this word used in two quite different ways. As a food, a scallop is a sea animal of the mollusk phylum whose edible muscle is prepared in a variety of delectable ways. As a process, to scallop a dish means to layer solid ingredients with a cream sauce and usually top the whole thing off with a crumb topping. Although most commonly used as a method for preparing a potato casserole, almost any firm vegetable can be substituted for the potato.

SCORE. To score in the kitchen has nothing to do with sporting events but rather with making shallow cuts into meat or a large piece of fish, usually in a diamond pattern. The effect is decorative and also allows seasonings to penetrate into the meat. Scoring also refers to cutting the fat along the edge of a steak, chop, or bacon so that it will not curl up as it cooks. This curling is caused because the outer edge cooks faster and sets up before the inner portion of the meat cooks.

SEAR. When you sear you very quickly brown all sides of a piece of meat in fat or oil. The purpose of searing is to seal the juices in the meat, and it is usually done before some long cooking method (such as braising or stewing). By keeping the moisture in, the meat does not become stringy as it is cooked.

SEASON. The derivation of this word in the culinary sense is rather interesting, as it comes from the Old French word *seson,* which derives from the Latin verb *serere,* to sow or plant. In the kitchen, it would seem flavorings are sown into the food . . . not a bad description.

The most common seasoning is salt, with sugar coming in a close second. The whole range of culinary herbs and spices come into use at some time or another as seasonings. Certain ones seem to form natural families: Italian herbs, for instance, typically are basil and oregano, while Mexican food calls for dried chili peppers and cumin, and Scandinavian for cardamom and caraway. Certain seasonings seem to group themselves together because of the way they are used. Cinnamon, nutmeg, cloves, and allspice tend to be "sweet" seasonings used in desserts and sweet drinks (although certainly not limited to those categories), while garlic, thyme, savory, tarragon, and such are thought of as "savory" seasonings and usually used in main dishes and appetizers.

SHELL.   The shell is the outer covering of something. It may be a mollusk such as a scallop, or it may be a vegetable such as green peas or nuts. To shell something is to remove this hard, inedible covering.

SIFT.   To sift is to pass dry ingredients through a metal sieve. The purpose of sifting is not only to remove any unacceptably large pieces but also to mix some air into the dry ingredient. Although almost always specified in older recipes, it is seldom suggested in modern cooking directions, because the flour is so uniform and a good stirring is sufficient to "unpack" the flour before measuring.

SIMMER.   Simmering is an important concept to understand. Simmering is not the same as boiling. To simmer means to keep the food at the scalding point (just below the true boiling point of the food) for an extended period of time. The reason for simmering instead of cooking at a higher temperature usually has to do with preserving the consistency of the food being prepared, or it may be to allow seasonings to evenly penetrate the food.

SKIM.   To skim is to remove something from the surface of a liquid. In dairy foods it means to remove the cream from the milk. The term can also be used to describe the process by which fat is removed from soups or stews. This latter technique is a valuable thing to keep in mind because animal fats are saturated and it is generally recommended that they be avoided whenever possible. The easiest way to skim a stock or other liquid is to chill it. As it cools, the fats rise to the surface where they can easily be removed.

STEAM. Steaming is an excellent method for cooking not only fruits and vegetables but also fish and poultry. It is most effectively accomplished by using a steamer, which is either a three-part pot (bottom to contain liquid, a perforated middle section to hold food, and a cover) or a metal basket on short legs that is placed in a pan containing the water (the legs keep the food above the level of the liquid). The cover is important to keep the water or other liquid from evaporating. Steaming chicken or fish also gives a fringe benefit in the form of excellently flavored liquid stock, which can be used as a basis for sauce or soup. Steaming is highly recommended as a healthful way to cook as it allows important nutrients to be retained in the vegetables instead of dissolving into the cooking liquid.

STEEP. In steeping, ingredients repose in liquid, usually a hot liquid, either to extract flavor from the liquid or to add flavor to it. In the latter case the process is also called infusion.

STEW. To stew is to cook meat and vegetables together in a seasoned liquid over a low heat or in a slow oven for a long period of time. It is one of the elementary ways of food preparation and can be found in virtually every culture ... ragout, goulash, call it what you will. It is filling, flavorful, and a universal favorite.

STIR-FRY. This is a technique that has been brought into Western cooking from the Oriental kitchen. To stir-fry, a variety of vegetables (with or without meats) are quickly sautéed in a large fry pan with oil. It is best to use peanut oil alone or mixed with salad oil (two parts peanut oil with one part salad oil), because peanut oil has a very high smoking point and it is important to have the oil very hot before adding the vegetables.

Good results can be achieved if you steam-blanch all but the leafy vegetables (time depends on size of pieces and type of vegetable), then dump them into a colander submerged in a big bowl of ice water for two to three minutes to stop the cooking. Drain and put on doubled paper towels to remove all water. Cook the stir-fry by putting the vegetables that require the most cooking in the pan first (carrots, green peppers, celery, broccoli stem strips, etc.), then add quick-cooking vegetables and vegetables that have been previously frozen, and last of all add slivered cooked meat, poultry, fish, seafood, and leafy vegetables. Stir-fry seasonings are usually, but not necessarily, Oriental in character.

STOCK. Any good dictionary will list twenty or more definitions of this word, but in the kitchen, stock is the liquid that results from the cooking of any meat or vegetable. It is the basis for virtually all soups and most sauces. Reduced stock in the freezer is like money in the bank for a cook because it opens the possibility of a variety of meals on a moment's notice. Stock is reduced by simply boiling it until part of the liquid has evaporated, and therefore there is less volume to store. It can be reconstituted to its original volume or used as is in sauces. One efficient way of storing reduced stock is to freeze it in ice cube trays, then remove the cubes and store them in the freezer in airtight plastic bags until needed.

SUET. Suet is animal, usually beef, fat. Seldom used in its natural condition, it is sometimes melted down and used as a basis for bird food during the winter. There are also some recipes that call for suet to be inserted into large roasts, but with current methods for producing fat-laden table beef, this tenderizing method is no longer meaningful.

TOSS.   Tossing is just what it would seem: mixing something (usually salad, but also other things such as shrimp or other small seafood) with something else by lifting and turning the solid portions to evenly distribute the other ingredient. A surprisingly small amount of dressing will quite nicely season a salad if it is tossed adequately.

TRUSS.   To truss is to tie something. Frequently it is a term used to describe the manner of tying the appendages of a bird close to its body before cooking, so that the ends of the wings and legs do not overcook. To truss a bird, draw a loop of string around first one wing and then the other and then draw the two wings together over the breast. Tie the legs together in a similar manner. If the bird is not trussed, the legs and wings will not only cook too fast but the tightening of the muscles during the cooking process will tend to make the legs and wings splay out in a rather unattractive manner.

WHIP.   The purpose of whipping is to add air to a liquid in order to increase its volume and give it a semisolid quality. When cream is being whipped, remember that overwhipping will produce butter, usually not the desired result, while over-whipping egg whites will make the protein in the white toughen and the whites far less stable while being mixed into the other part of the food being prepared. Start the whipping process with the beater at a slow speed until the liquid becomes frothy, then increase to a fast beating speed to complete the process. Cream will whip best when beaters and bowl as well as cream are very cold. Egg whites will whip best when they are at room temperature.

ZEST.   The zest is the outermost rind of a citrus fruit. Do not confuse zest with the whole peel, which includes the bitter white pith portion. Typically the zest is obtained by fine grating, but for use in drinks it can be made by carefully cutting long strips from the fruit with a paring knife.

CHAPTER 2

Strategic and Tactical Meal Planning

Meals occur through two methods: they are planned or they just happen.

The busy cook is not unlike the military commander who has to have a good idea how the battle is going to progress both from an overall (strategic) viewpoint and from a detail-oriented (tactical) viewpoint.

No matter how much you might enjoy it, you do not have unlimited time to devote to meal preparation. You have your regular job, your outside responsibilities, your children, your friends, your recreation activities. In other words, you have the rest of your life going on, so a strategic and tactical approach to meal planning is as useful for you as it is for any commanding general.

The strategy involves putting together an overview of the kinds of meals you and your family like and making sure that you have everything on hand to prepare those meals.

The tactics involve actually planning what will be eaten when.

One of the first things to do is to make a general plan for a month's meals. Don't think this is an impossibility ... it definitely is not. When you stop to analyze it you will see that there are only a limited number of things that your family has most of the time. Use this knowledge to make your plan.

Start with dinners first. Take a piece of paper and make an outline something like this:

DINNER SCHEDULE

	Week 1	Week 2	Week 3	Week 4
Day 1				
Day 2				
Day 3				
Day 4				
Day 5				
Day 6				
Day 7				

Depending on what day you normally do your weekly shopping (yes, with this system you shop only once a week), designate the various days of the week. (For the example, shopping is done on Friday.)

DINNER SCHEDULE

	Week 1	Week 2	Week 3	Week 4
Friday				
Saturday				
Sunday				
Monday				
Tuesday				
Wednesday				
Thursday				

Next you enter the main ingredient in the entrees, starting with the ingredients that must be used while they are very fresh. Here's an example:

DINNER SCHEDULE

	Week 1	Week 2	Week 3	Week 4
Friday	fish	seafood	fish	seafood
Saturday	beef	chicken	beef	chicken
Sunday	s&s*	s&s	s&s	s&s
Monday	pork	lamb	ham	liver
Tuesday	veg	chicken	veg	chicken
Wednesday	soufflé	quiche	omelet	cheese
Thursday	pasta	pasta	pasta	pasta

*s&s = soup-and-sandwich in the winter or salad-and-sandwich in the summer

Now you have an idea where you are heading through the month. Obviously the people you cook for may have preferences other than those shown above, but try to include some non-red-meat dinners and even some completely vegetarian dinners if you can. Tofu is a good vegetarian main ingredient that can substitute surprisingly well for hamburger or other ground meats, in a casserole for example.

With this month-long chart as your strategy, next you need the tactics for the week ahead. Let's start with week 3 and plan the week's dinners.

Friday:
Baked fish fillets with lemon butter sauce
Fresh rolls (from the bakery, reheated in the oven)
Green salad
Steamed sliced carrots (with some of the sauce)
Fresh fruit and cookies

Saturday:
Broiled steaks
Baked potatoes
Broiled Parmesan tomatoes
Green salad
Cake (bakery or one you make on Saturday)

Sunday:
(winter)
Vegetable soup (homemade, maybe?)
Open-faced toasted cheese sandwiches
Cake

Monday:
Baked ham slice
Spinach or broccoli soufflé
Potatoes au gratin
Baked apples

Tuesday:
Stir-fry vegetables topped with shredded ham on brown rice
Gelatin with fruit and whipped topping

Wednesday: Cheese and mushroom omelet
     Green salad
     Garlic toast
     Sherbet or ice cream

Thursday: Spaghetti with meat sauce
     Green salad
     Vanilla pudding

Obviously these are simple meals, but an adequate supply of both nutrition and calories for most of us. Each has a protein source, carbohydrates, and fat. Green vegetables appear either in salad or in a cooked vegetable. Desserts are light.

You will notice that the sequence of the meals depends not only on the day you shop but also on preceding meals ... the ham that tops the stir-fry vegetables on Tuesday is left over from Monday's baked ham, for instance.

Another thing to notice is that much of the preparation can be done at one time and simply wait in the refrigerator until time to heat and serve. If you are able to shop near the end of the week, this preparation time can be over the weekend, but one day a week, whenever you can arrange it, should be plenty of time to fix the week's meals.

So much for dinners ... now what about the rest of the meals? Lunch is different in each family. Sometimes everyone is there for lunch, sometimes lunches are taken to work or school, sometimes lunches are eaten in restaurants or lunchrooms.

If all lunches are eaten at home you should treat them much as you do dinners ... usually lighter, including more salads, sandwiches, soups, and other light dishes.

If lunches are packed, don't limit them to sandwiches-and-fruit-and-cookies ... think in terms of the meals during the day and try to contribute to the day's nutrition by what you make up. A small wide-mouth thermos opens up the world not only of soups, stews, and chili but also of salads, yogurt, and cottage cheese.

If lunches are usually eaten away from home, you need only think about weekends and the occasional at-home midday meal on holidays. Your pantry should be able to cope with all these situations.

Which brings us to breakfast.

For most people on most days, breakfast is not a leisurely meal. It is eaten with a timetable in mind and there is little time for either preparation or participation. Given that this is the case, make out a list of breakfast menus that fit your family's preferences and the time available. Have about ten or twelve different meals on your list and then simply rotate through the list one by one. This system will break the monotony of the same things every morning but not call upon you to come up with something original every day either. When you have your weekday breakfast list complete, make another list for weekend brunches to be enjoyed when you have more time and inclination to cook and eat in a leisurely manner.

Here is a possible list of weekday breakfasts:

1. Orange juice
   Dry cereal with bananas and milk
   Buttered whole wheat toast

2. Tomato juice
   Scrambled egg
   Toasted English muffin or bagel

3. Grapefruit juice
   Lean beef patty
   Buttered whole wheat toast

4. Orange slices
   Poached egg on toasted English muffin

5. Applesauce
   Toast with cream cheese and jelly

6. Mixed-vegetable juice
   Bacon
   Rye toast

7. Orange juice
   Peanut butter on whole wheat toast

8. Fruited yogurt over fresh fruit
   Crackers

You can see what the general pattern is ... some sort of fruit or juice, some protein source, and some carbohydrate for early morning energy. None of these meals is high in calories or time-consuming in preparation.

Weekend brunches give you the time and opportunity to fix the waffles, omelets, and quiches that everyone enjoys.

STRATEGIC AND TACTICAL SHOPPING

Whether you enjoy shopping for food or not, it is something that must be done regularly. However, with the storage facilities that are available to any cook in the latter part of the twentieth century, there is no reason to shop more than once a week unless you have an uncontrollable urge for something or an emergency arises.

The keys to efficient and effective shopping are two: know what you need and know where it is in the store.

Let's start with the second thought first since it is the simplest. You can save yourself untold hours and, considering the size of most supermarkets, miles of walking if you shop at the same store most of the time. There are several aspects to this recommendation.

The first, and by far the most important, is that you can arrange your shopping list so that it follows the layout of the store.

The second is that you can become acquainted with the store personnel. This not only makes your shopping trip more pleasant, it can also make it possible to ask for small special services occasionally.

The third is that you develop an awareness of prices and variety so that when you see something advertised somewhere else that is significantly different you can recognize it and decide whether you want to follow up on the ad or not.

Your shopping list is the real key, however. It should be developed from two sources ... things you run out of as the week progresses and that need to be replaced, and things that you are going to need to fix the menus you have planned for the week ahead.

If you have access to a copy machine you can make up a preprinted and prearranged list that makes it easy to keep track of both.

Here is an example of what it might look like:

SHOPPING LIST FOR WEEK OF _____

Meat and Fish	Beverages, etc.
_____	_____
_____	_____
Dairy Products	**Canned Products**
_____	_____
_____	_____
_____	_____
Frozen Foods	**Household Supplies**
_____	_____
_____	_____
_____	**Staples**
Fresh Produce	_____
_____	_____
_____	_____
_____	

Miscellaneous   _____

_____   _____

_____   _____

_____   _____

This, is, of course, just a suggestion. What sections you would include and how you would arrange them would be in line with your particular shopping needs. If you shop at more than one place during a shopping expedition, you might list reminders on the back ... *dry cleaning, bank, post office, hardware store, drugstore,* and the other regular stops you make.

The important thing is to have a list and stick to it, unless you find some incredible bargain for something you buy regularly or unless you see something new that is so intriguing that you want to try it for yourself.

Here are the things to keep in mind that will make your shopping efficient, effective, cost-conscious, and perhaps even fun:

1. Shop with a list.

2. Try to finish your grocery shopping within a half hour. Studies have suggested that the longer you stay in the store the more money per minute you spend.

3. Shop alone if you can. Helpers, whether children, spouse, roommate, or friends, can help you to buy things that you would not buy if you were alone. There are plenty of opportunities for social occasions ... shopping probably should not be one of them.

4. Try to control your own impulse buying. This goes back to number 1, but it really means more than that. Studies of shoppers indicate that as much as half of the purchases are bought on impulse (one wonders how many of the purchases linger on cupboard shelves). The time shoppers are most vulnerable to impulse buying is at the

beginning when the cart is empty ... store designers are not unaware of this phenomenon!

5. Don't shop when you are hungry. Everything looks just wonderful and buying small amounts seems to be a ridiculous idea.

6. Keep an eye on the unit-price stickers. You'll find some surprises if you do ... "economy"-size packages sometimes are the highest price per ounce. Boxed products in particular can deceive the eye.

7. In general avoid individual-serving packages unless you are shopping and cooking just for yourself. It stands to reason that it costs manufacturers more to offer products this way and that cost will be passed along. Sometimes it is worth the extra cost ... that is something you have to determine personally.

8. If you use coupons, use them with common sense. You make no saving if you buy something that you will not use in a reasonable time. Be sure that you have matched the coupon with the exact product, because it can really slow down your checkout time if you have picked up the wrong size, one of the product when the coupon was for two, and so forth. Also check the "cents off" price with the price on comparable items; often you'll find that there is no particular saving.

9. Consider generics and bulk foods. Some shoppers are brand loyal, others are more experimental or more cost-conscious. Some generics are the same product as the brand-name products ... others, however, are not. The only way to find if the generic is satisfactory is to try it for yourself. The same applies to bulk foods. "Bag-it-yourself" can save money in most cases ... some shoppers object to the open-to-everyone aspect of bulk-food departments. Again a matter of personal preference.

10. Be a seasonal shopper for fresh produce. The best produce and the best prices are available during the time

that it is being harvested. This is particularly true of fruits. We have an amazing transportation and distribution potential in this country ... all you have to do is look at the produce section in February to realize just how good it is. Nevertheless, the best-tasting produce at the best prices is available during harvest. (From a nutrition standpoint, you are probably better off with frozen vegetables at other times of the year, because produce to be frozen is usually processed directly from the fields.)

The following chart indicates the availability of most commonly purchased fruits and vegetables on a month-by-month basis.

HARVEST CHART

A = Peak to good supply; B = Fair supply; C = Low supply—not available

Month	J	F	M	A	M	J	J	A	S	O	N	D
APPLES	B	B	B	B	B	C	C	C	A	A	A	A
APRICOTS	C	C	C	C	C	A	A	C	C	C	C	C
ASPARAGUS	C	C	A	A	A	B	C	C	C	C	C	C
BANANAS	A	A	A	A	A	A	A	B	B	A	A	A
BEANS, GREEN	B	B	B	B	A	A	A	A	B	B	B	B
BEETS	C	C	B	B	B	A	A	A	A	A	B	C
BLUEBERRIES	C	C	C	C	C	A	A	A	C	C	C	C
BROCCOLI	A	A	A	A	B	B	C	C	B	B	A	A
BRUSSELS SPROUTS	A	A	B	B	C	C	C	C	B	A	A	A
CABBAGE	A	A	A	A	A	A	A	B	A	A	A	A
CANTALOUPE	C	C	C	C	B	A	A	A	A	C	C	C
CARROTS	A	A	A	A	A	A	B	B	A	A	A	A
CAULIFLOWER	B	B	B	B	C	C	C	C	A	A	A	B
CELERY	A	A	A	A	A	A	A	B	B	A	A	A
CHERRIES	C	C	C	C	B	A	A	B	C	C	C	C

Month	J	F	M	A	M	J	J	A	S	O	N	D
CORN	C	C	C	B	A	A	A	A	A	A	C	C
CRANBERRIES	C	C	C	C	C	C	C	C	B	A	A	A
CUCUMBERS	C	C	C	B	A	A	A	A	B	B	B	B
GRAPEFRUIT	A	A	A	A	B	B	C	C	C	B	A	A
GRAPES	C	C	C	C	C	B	A	A	A	A	A	B
HONEYDEWS	C	C	B	B	B	A	A	A	A	A	C	C
LEMONS	B	B	B	B	A	A	A	A	B	B	B	B
LETTUCE	A	A	A	A	A	A	A	A	A	A	B	A
LIMES	C	C	C	C	B	A	A	A	B	B	B	B
MUSHROOMS	A	A	A	A	A	A	B	B	B	A	A	A
NECTARINES	C	C	C	C	C	A	A	A	A	C	C	C
ONIONS, DRY	A	B	A	A	A	A	A	A	A	A	A	A
ORANGES	A	A	A	A	A	B	C	C	C	C	B	A
PEACHES	C	C	C	C	C	A	A	A	A	C	C	C
PEARS	B	B	B	B	C	C	C	A	A	A	A	B
PEAS	B	A	A	A	A	A	A	B	B	C	C	C
PEPPERS, BELL	B	B	B	B	B	A	A	A	A	B	B	B
PINEAPPLES	B	B	A	A	A	A	A	A	C	C	B	B
PLUMS	C	C	C	C	C	A	A	A	A	C	C	C
POTATOES	A	A	A	A	A	A	A	A	A	A	A	A
PUMPKINS	C	C	C	C	C	C	C	C	C	A	C	C
RADISHES	B	B	A	A	A	A	A	B	B	B	B	B
SPINACH	A	A	A	A	B	B	B	C	B	B	B	B
SQUASH	B	B	B	B	B	A	A	A	A	A	A	B
STRAWBERRIES	C	C	B	A	A	A	B	C	C	C	C	C
SWEET POTATOES	B	B	B	B	C	C	C	C	A	A	A	A
TOMATOES	B	B	B	B	A	A	A	A	B	B	B	B
WATERMELONS	C	C	C	C	A	A	A	A	B	C	C	C

LABELS TELL THE TALE

To be a good shopper, it is important that you read and understand the labels that appear on processed foods. The Food and Drug Administration and the U.S. Department of

Agriculture oversee the food-processing industries and require that labels give information regarding the contents of the food in the container.

There are certain types of information that must appear on all labels:

First, the label must clearly say what the food product is, giving its common name (such as carrots, not *Daucus carota,* which is the botanical term for the common carrot).

Second, if the product is commonly available in a number of ways (for instance, canned carrots can be purchased whole, sliced, or diced), the label must say which form the container holds (unless the product can be easily seen through the container).

Third, the label must say how much the package contains. The net weight on canned food normally includes the liquid in which the product is packed unless otherwise specified. For packages weighing more than a pound but less than four pounds, the label must give the weight in both ounces and in a combination of pounds and ounces—for example: 24 ounces (1½ pounds or 1.5 pounds).

Fourth, the label must include the name, place of business (at least the city), and zip code for the manufacturer, packer, or distributor of the food product. (If you have to contact the food processor for some reason, you can obtain the full address, phone, and often the appropriate department to contact by calling the reference department of your local public library.)

Fifth, the label must list the ingredients. Ingredients are listed by volume, starting with whatever the food contains most of and ending with whatever it contains least of. If you see canned corned beef hash, for example, that lists potatoes first, then water, then corned beef, don't be surprised if you find precious little meat when you open the can.

Watch for the indications of the amounts of salt and sugar (in all their forms). Salt and sugar are by far the most common of the ingredients known as "food additives." They are, however, only the tip of the iceberg. In the Appendix you will find a list of common food additives, what they do, where they are found, and what the U.S. Food and Drug Administration thinks of them. If you are concerned about the place of additives, both natural and synthetic, in the food you serve—and we all should be—this list should give you some guidelines of value.

If the ingredients are not listed on the label it is because the product is considered a "standard food" by the FDA.

"Food standard of identity" applies to food products that have been determined by the FDA to follow standard manufacturing processes and include standard ingredients. To use the name of one of these foods on the label, the manufacturer must conform to this standard list of ingredients.

Some of the kinds of foods that are considered to be standard in their ingredients are bakery products, canned fruits and juices, cheeses and cheese products, dressings for foods, egg products, frozen desserts, fruit pies, macaroni and noodle products, milk and cream products, nutritive sweeteners, margarines, fruit preserves, rice and related products, tomato products, and wheat flour and related products. This list is not complete but only indicative of the kinds of foods that are considered to be in the standard-food category.

The FDA has carefully defined descriptions for the ingredients allowed in each of the standard-food classes, and if a particular product does not meet the description exactly, it must be called something else. (Mayonnaise, for instance, is on the standard list; consequently the low-calorie version, which contains a significant amount of water and other ingredients, must be called "imitation mayonnaise.")

These standard tables also act as a consumer protection service. If the food name is used by a manufacturer, the contents must be as required in the description. For instance, "chili con carne" must have at least 40 percent meat, while "chili con carne with beans" can cut the required meat to 25 percent meat, and if it is labeled as "chili sauce with meat" it can have as little as 6 percent meat. If you are interested in having more information about standard foods and what they contain, write to Consumer Information, Pueblo, Colorado 81002, and ask for a list of foods and food product standard guides. From the list you will be able to choose the particular foods that are of interest to you and write for the descriptive information you need.

One case of special labeling requirements that is interesting to know about is that for frozen dinners. In order to be called a "frozen dinner" the product must include at least three separate dishes selected from meat, poultry, fish, cheeses, eggs, vegetables, potatoes, rice or other cereal-based products.

There are also some ingredients that are allowed to be grouped together ... spices, flavorings, and colors may be listed without giving the specific ingredient. "Vegetable oil" means that one or more of a variety of vegetable oils may be included. These concessions allow food processors to use, within certain guidelines, the most easily available product.

HOW OLD IS IT?

Many food-product manufacturers date their products. This service, called open dating in the industry, is voluntary under federal regulations but many states require it. There are three kinds of dating that are commonly seen:

> **EXPIRATION DATE.** The final date on which you should serve the food. It is most usually printed as "Do not use after ..."
>
> **PULL DATE, FRESHNESS DATE, OR SELL DATE.** The date by which the food should be removed from the shelves. This date allows for a certain amount of storage time at home before being used.
>
> **PACK DATE.** The date on which the food was packaged.

The only problem as far as the shopper is concerned is that frequently there is simply a date and no way to tell which date it is. Only meat and poultry labels are required to explain the meanings of the printed dates.

UPC MARKS

Other information on the package includes the UPC (Universal Product Code), which has come into being since the introduction of computers into food retail sales. The black vertical lines represent a code that is unique to the product. The UPC codes benefit the retailers by allowing them to use computer check-out systems and also as a means of good inventory control. The consumer benefits by quicker and more accurate checkout and possible cost savings because of the improved inventory.

WHAT ELSE DOES THE LABEL TELL?

In the area of special notations on labels, there are a few others that you will see from time to time. "K" indicates that the food is kosher, that is that it has been prepared in accordance with Jewish dietary laws and under the supervision of a rabbi. ("U" has a similar meaning in that the food has been approved by the Union of Orthodox Jewish Congregations of America.) "C" indicates a copyright on the design of the label. "TM" or "R" means that the trademark has been registered with the U.S. Patent and Trademark Office.

In Chapter 7, the portions of labels that cover nutrition are discussed in detail.

U.S. DEPARTMENT OF AGRICULTURE FOOD GRADES

If you understand how the USDA assigns grades to food products, you can use the knowledge to save money and improve nutrition. Although certain changes are being contemplated to the current system, which some consumer advocates feel is too complicated for the average shopper, there is no estimated date for any change, so it is worth learning about the current standards.

Grading of food is voluntary and is paid for by the food processor who requests it. Grade labeling is not required by federal law. When applied, grading services are provided by the USDA's Food Safety and Quality Service and/or state Departments of Agriculture.

DAIRY PRODUCTS

USDA Quality Approved stamps may be found on such things as cottage cheese and other cheese, and sour cream. This means that the processing plants have been inspected and approved by USDA inspectors.

In butter, USDA grade AA is assigned to butter with a sweet flavor, pleasing aroma, and smooth texture. Grade A butter may lack the smoothness of Grade AA but be entirely suitable for cooking. Grade B butter may have a slightly off taste.

Nonfat dry milk must dissolve quickly and completely in water and have a pleasant taste to receive the USDA Extra Grade designation.

Eggs are commonly graded AA, A, or B. The grading is based on the height of the yolk when the egg is broken onto a plate (the higher the yolk, the higher the grade), on how much the white spreads out (the less it spreads the higher the grade), and on the condition of the shell. Grade A is not very different from AA, but the yolks are usually not quite as high and the whites are a little less viscous. Grades AA and A are best for use when the egg is going to be poached, fried, or boiled. Grade B eggs are not usually found in retail stores. However, although the Grade B egg may not be as attractive as Grades AA and A, if it is to be used in the preparation of another dish such as a custard, Grade B can be quite acceptable.

MEATS AND POULTRY

USDA Grading of Red Meat

Beef, veal, and lamb are all graded according to the following standards:

Prime: very tender, juicy, flavorful, and highest in fat. Most commonly served in restaurants, not typically for sale in retail stores.

Choice: quite tender, juicy, and flavorful. Highest grade commonly available in retail stores and also quite high in fat content.

Good: leaner, lower calorie and cholesterol count, somewhat less juicy (because of less fat). Should still be quite tender and often is an excellent buy.

Standard: very lean with little fat, so needs to be cooked with liquid (braised, stewed). Usually from young animals and so reasonably tender. Not commonly seen in retail stores.

Commercial: usually from older animals. It has adequate fat but because of age may be best cooked in a slow method. Not commonly seen in retail stores.

Pork is graded in a slightly different way from the meats noted above. It has only two classifications: acceptable and unacceptable. Unacceptable pork tends to be soft and watery and is not available for retail purchase. There are, in fact, four lean meat (yield) levels that are used to describe pork carcasses, but again they are not identified at the retail level. If you should purchase whole porks, however, you should be aware that the grades run from No. 1 (53 percent or more of the weight is lean meat) to No. 4 (less than 47 percent of the weight is lean meat).

The important things to consider when choosing meat grade are: 1) your nutritional goals (less fat, for instance) and 2) how the meat is to be cooked.

SAVE MONEY BY BUYING LARGE CUTS OF MEAT

If you have adequate storage facilities, you might consider the advantages of buying larger cuts of meat: the cost per pound is less, you can have the meat cut and packaged appropriately for your own use, and you can plan meals based on meat you know you have on hand.

"Subprimal" is a term used to describe a large cut of fresh processed meat that is available for sale through retail meat outlets. An animal carcass is usually divided into four or five major parts (or "primal" cuts) by the meat wholesaler. When these large cuts are further divided the pieces are called subprimal. Subprimals have had excess fat and bone removed and run between five and thirty pounds. The retail butcher cuts these pieces into the type and size most commonly seen for sale at the meat counter and repackages them.

Subprimal cuts are almost always vacuum-packed at the meat packer's plant and because of the vacuum-packing have a rather purplish color. The bright red color you associate with fresh meat comes about because of the meat's exposure to the air. The red color will appear shortly after you open the package.

Many meat sellers will custom-cut the piece to your requirements and wrap it for use or for freezing at no charge. If there is a charge it is usually minimal, and even with service charge included, your overall cost per pound is less.

The three most common subprimal cuts of beef are the whole bottom round, the whole round tip, and the whole top round. Occasionally you will also see (or you can special order) the strip loin, the rib-eye roll, the tenderloin, or the sirloin butt.

Whole Bottom Round. This is the largest subprimal cut. It can weigh between eighteen and thirty pounds. Overall it is not a particularly tender cut, but there are pieces that can be taken from it that are suitable for broiling or barbecuing. The piece consists of an eye-of-round roast, a rump roast, and pieces for top-quality ground beef. Its cost per pound will probably be about what you would pay for the ground beef per pound. The "roast" pieces can also be cut into steaks.

Whole Top Round. This subprimal weighs in at around twenty pounds. The first few inches are tender enough to slice and then broil or barbecue. This is the meat often used in preparing a London broil, instead of flank steak. The remainder of the top round can be cut to use for pot roast, stew meat, or steaks to braise (Swiss steak). Portions can also be made into ground beef.

Whole Round Tip. This is the most tender of the three beef round subprimal cuts. It weighs around ten to twelve pounds. If you are entertaining or particularly like roasted beef, the whole piece can be cooked at one time. If not, it can be divided into steaks, roasts, or cubes for shish kebab.

Whole Pork Loin. Pork is also available in a subprimal cut, most commonly as the whole pork loin. It will weigh between fifteen and twenty pounds and will be the piece of meat that runs from shoulder to hip on the pork carcass. It can be cut into roasts and a variety of styles of pork chops. You may also have the tenderloin cut out separately if you wish.

If you decide to try using these large cuts and will be storing them in your freezer, remember to wrap them carefully and date the packages. Chapter 6 describes the proper technique for freezer-wrapping and also gives details on how long various cuts should be stored.

MORE ABOUT SHOPPING FOR BEEF AND VEAL

Both beef and veal come from cattle. Veal is from the young animal (usually less than three months old). Beef comes from the mature animal (usually fifteen to thirty months old). Occasionally you will see something designated as "baby beef." This is meat from animals in the seven-to-ten-month age range.

A new trend in the retail sale of beef is brand-name labeling, something that is standard in most other food areas but has been missing from the meat department except in poultry and ham sales. Certain beef growers are making an effort to gain brand identification for their products by selling in their own retail stores, by mail order, and by highly visible packaging in regular supermarkets.

Cuts of meat, particularly cuts of beef and veal, vary in what they are called in different parts of the country. If you move from Boston to San Diego you may find that a very familiar-looking cut is called something you have never heard of before. There are, however, certain universal terms that you can use when you ask the butcher for help.

Common Retail Cuts of Beef and Veal

Anatomical Part	Retail Beef Cut	Retail Veal Cut
Shoulder	Chuck Roast	Shoulder Roast
Ribs	Rib Roast, Steaks	Rib Roast, Rib Steaks
Loin	Club, T-bone, Por- terhouse Steaks	Loin Roast, Loin Chops
Sirloin	Sirloin Steaks	Sirloin Roast, Sirloin Steaks
Round (Rump)	Rump Roasts, Round Steaks	Round (Rump) Roasts Round Steaks, Cutlets
Foreshank (Foreleg)	Shank Crosscuts	Whole Shank and Shank Crosscuts
Brisket (just behind shank)	Brisket	Brisket
Short Plate (be- tween Brisket and Flank)	Short Ribs	Breast of Veal, Riblets
Flank	Flank Steak	Not normally used
Liver	Beef Liver	Veal or Baby Beef Liver
Heart	Beef Heart	Baby Beef Heart
Kidneys	Beef Kidneys	Baby Beef Kidneys
Brains	Brains	Brains
Sweetbreads (Thymus Glands)	Not present in mature animals	Sweetbreads
Tripe (Stomach Parts)	Honeycomb Tripe	Tripe

Some other common cuts you will find for sale are:

Fillet of Beef is the whole tenderloin.

Filet Mignon is the whole tenderloin or steaks cut from it.

Delmonico Steak is the center of the rib steak.

Boneless Brisket is a flat boneless piece cut from the brisket that is often used to make corned beef.

Crown Roast of Veal is a circle made from the rib section. Usually the meat is removed from the pointed end of the rib chop to accentuate the crown look.

Veal Kidney Chops are loin chops presented with a slice of kidney.

Ground beef or **veal** is sold according to the amount of fat present. Standard Ground Beef or hamburger can be up to 30 percent fat, Lean Ground Beef or hamburger can be up to 18 percent fat, Extra Lean can contain no more than 14 percent fat. Meat labeled as "ground beef" must contain only beef, while meat labeled as hamburger can contain extra fat from other sources (most commonly pork).

Stew Meat is usually made from trimmings from the tender cuts. The pieces are usually roughly cube-shaped and run from one to two inches on a side.

PROCESSING BEEF TO MAKE IT MORE PALATABLE

Aging. If you buy "fresh cut" meat, it has probably been about six to ten days since the animal was slaughtered. Sometimes you will see the designation "Aged Beef" used in ads or on the meat label. Aging tenderizes the meat by allowing certain bacterial action to take place. This bacterial action softens the muscle fibers and makes the meat more tender.

Aging is accomplished in two ways: either the meat is held at temperatures in the mid-30-degree-Fahrenheit range for three to six weeks, or else it is kept for about two days at nearly seventy degrees Fahrenheit. In this latter method ultraviolet light is used to keep bacterial growth under control. These aging techniques must be done under careful control and so are really not something you should try to do at home.

Cured Meat. Curing takes place by allowing the meat to absorb some mixture of ingredients; usually the mixture contains salt, sugar, and seasonings. The curing can be done with a dry mixture or in a brine solution. Sometimes the cured meat is also smoked. Some typical cured meats include corned beef, beef sausages, dried beef, and cold cuts.

Pretenderized Beef. Meat can be tenderized either chemically (in the packing plant before the animal is slaughtered or at home with powdered meat tenderizers) or mechanically (by pounding or scoring the surface, as in cubed steak for instance).

MORE ABOUT SHOPPING FOR PORK

The good news about pork is that not only is it generally less expensive per pound than beef, but also that in response to demand farmers are breeding leaner and leaner pigs all the time.

Pigs are usually matured only about a year before slaughtering, which means that there is less investment for the livestock producer in terms of facilities and feed. Pork is available as fresh pork, cured, or cured and smoked. There are also many processed and canned pork products on the market.

The most common cuts of pork are:

Chops cut from the loin or shoulder.
Roasts cut from loin or shoulder.
Ham made from the hip-to-knee hind legs.
Bacon made from the sides and sometimes back of the pig.

In addition to these familiar cuts, you may also see some that are not so familiar:

Center-cut Pork Chops are cut from the whole loin.
Butterfly Chops are made from a pair of boned loin chops cut not quite all the way through and then pressed open.
Country Ribs (Back Ribs) are made by splitting the loin lengthwise through the rib section near the backbone.
Crown Roast is made by bending two rib sections to form a circle and fastening them together, then trimming the "points" of the crown.

Side Pork is taken from the side of the carcass and generally trimmed to a roughly rectangular shape. It alternates layers of fat and lean (something like a big piece of bacon).

Canadian Bacon is a lean cut from the loin, cured and smoked.

Pork Cushion is made from a shoulder with the bone removed (the resulting space makes a place for a stuffing to go).

Pigs' Feet are usually sold as "pickled." They are mostly bones and tendons and have little actual meat.

Chitterlings are the small and large intestines of hogs, which have been cleaned and processed.

Pork variety meats (liver, heart, brains, kidneys, and tongue) are slightly different from their beef and veal counterparts in flavor but similar in texture.

MORE ABOUT SHOPPING FOR LAMB

Among Americans, lamb is not nearly as popular as beef and pork. This is unfortunate, because lamb meat is usually tender and flavorful and an excellent source of lean protein. It is unfortunate that in most parts of the country lamb is more expensive than either beef or pork. Some of the cost differential is accounted for because not all meat-packing plants are set up to handle sheep, and this means that in some areas the meat must be shipped in from distant meat packers. The cost plus unfamiliarity keeps many cooks from trying lamb, to their loss.

Sheep are usually less than a year old when slaughtered. The meat is most commonly available as leg of lamb, lamb chops (both rib and shoulder), lamb steaks (usually from the shoulder, sometimes from the leg), and lamb roasts (again usually shoulder pieces). Lamb is also available in stewing pieces and ground. Organ meat from lamb is also excellent, including the sweetbreads.

MORE ABOUT SHOPPING FOR CHICKEN

Chickens are in abundant supply year-round and are very economical. The youngest chickens are marked as broilers or fryers, while the older birds are designated as roasting or stewing hens. Capons, which are castrated male chickens, are also available for roasting.

In most instances the best way to buy chickens is to buy the whole bird. This is because by doing so you are able to cut the chicken up as you personally choose to have it, you have all of the bones to go into your stockpot, and you get the best price per pound. Chicken is, of course, also available in a wide variety of packaged parts: breast, wings, legs, thighs, cut-up chickens (sometimes packed with extra legs), necks and backs, and halved or quartered.

The following chart will give you some general idea how the price of packaged parts compares on a per-pound basis with meat available from whole birds:

Whole Chicken Price per lb.		Boneless Breast	Breast with Bone	Thigh	Thigh & Leg	Leg	Wing
.59	=	.80	.78	.66	.63	.61	.48
.65	=	.89	.86	.72	.70	.67	.52
.69	=	.94	.91	.77	.74	.71	.56
.75	=	1.02	.99	.84	.81	.77	.60
.79	=	1.08	1.04	.88	.85	.81	.64
.85	=	1.16	1.12	.95	.91	.87	.69
.89	=	1.21	1.18	.99	.95	.91	.72
.95	=	1.30	1.26	1.06	1.02	.98	.77
.99	=	1.35	1.31	1.10	1.06	1.02	.80
1.05	=	1.43	1.39	1.18	1.10	1.09	.85
1.09	=	1.49	1.44	1.22	1.16	1.13	.89
1.15	=	1.57	1.52	1.29	1.23	1.19	.94
1.19	=	1.62	1.57	1.33	1.27	1.23	.97
1.25	=	1.71	1.65	1.40	1.33	1.29	1.02

Whole Chicken Price per lb		Boneless Breast	Breast with Bone	Thigh	Thigh & Leg	Leg	Wing
1.29	=	1.76	1.71	1.44	1.38	1.33	1.05
1.35	=	1.84	1.79	1.51	1.44	1.40	1.10
1.39	=	1.90	1.84	1.56	1.48	1.44	1.13

SHOPPING FOR FISH AND SEAFOOD

Fish is available in a variety of forms ... understanding what each is will help you to select the one that is best for your needs.

Round Fish. This term is used to describe the whole fish just as it is taken from the water. To make it ready for cooking you will need to "clean" it ... that is, remove the head, tail, and fins and also the internal organs. The fish needs to have the scales removed before cooking as well. Round or whole fish are usually available only in locations near the point where the fish are taken, so you should look for the traditional signs of freshness: pinkness behind the gills, globular eyes (not flattened), and of course an absence of a fishy smell. Round fish may be cooked whole by grilling or baking or may be cut into smaller pieces if the fish is large. Fish most commonly available in round are trout, salmon, smelt, and sometimes red snapper.

Drawn Fish. Drawn fish are whole but have had their internal organs removed. Head, tail, and fins remain attached. Scales need to be removed before cooking.

Dressed (or Pan Dressed) Fish. Here much of the work has been done for you. The fish has had internal organs and usually scales removed as well. Sometimes in smaller fish such as trout the head and tail will be left on, but on larger fish head, tail, and fins are removed to shrink the fish to a size that will cook easily in a conventional pan.

Steaks. Fish steaks are cross-section cuts taken from large fish such as salmon and halibut. You will find the spine and rib bones in most steaks. These may be removed, but the piece will not hold its shape during cooking as well as it will if they are left in. Once the fish is cooked, the bones are easily removed either by the cook or the person eating the fish.

Fillets. Fish fillet pieces are taken from the sides of the fish. When carefully done, there should be no bones in a fillet. The filleting knife is drawn between the meat and the rib bones and the whole side is lifted off. In a small fish such as sole the fillets are most often used whole; in larger fish such as salmon they may be cut into serving-size pieces before or after cooking. Butterfly fillets are made by leaving the skin across the belly of the fish intact while removing the spine and ribs.

Fish Sticks (Cutlets, Portions). These are prepared, frozen pieces of fish that have been coated with some sort of batter or crumb coating. Frequently you will find there is more coating than fish, that the coating is quite salty, and that on a per pound basis the price is very high to say the least.

WHAT ABOUT PARASITES IN FRESH FISH?

The popularity of raw fish served in the Japanese manner has raised the question of parasite infestation. In truth, parasites are a consideration not only in raw fish but also in undercooked fish. To avoid problems keep these things in mind:

1. Cook fish until the interior reaches 140 degrees F.

2. If you have reason for particular concern about parasites, soak the fish in a solution of two tablespoons salt per quart of cold water for about five minutes before cooking. The brine will bring out the parasites. Rinse fish before cooking.

3. Remember that ocean fish are far less likely to have parasites than fresh-water fish, and fish caught in cold water during nonsummer months are also less likely to be infested.

HANDLING FROZEN FISH FILLETS

Frozen fish fillets are a great convenience to the cook, and a wide variety of fish are available in this form. You should remember, however, that it is important to store frozen fish at minus ten degrees Fahrenheit or lower until you are ready to cook them. Fish should be partially thawed before cooking (until it is slightly pliable). Once thawed, fish should never be refrozen in its raw state. It may be refrozen after cooking.

CANNED FISH

Quite a few popular fish are available canned: salmon, tuna, sardines, and mackerel, to name a few.

Several varieties of salmon are available in cans and the price goes up as the color deepens, that is, the redder the salmon, the higher the price and the higher the oil content. Protein availability is the same whatever variety you choose.

Canned tuna is either white meat (taken only from albacore) or light meat (which comes from yellowfin, bluefin, and skipjack). Furthermore, tuna is available either in the traditional oil pack or packed in water for those who are calorie conscious. If the water-pack style seems too salty, simply rinse under cool water before using.

Sardines are normally found in flat cans packed in oil or some seasoned sauce (such as tomato or mustard). They are usually packed whole (except for heads).

Mackerel is a fishier-tasting fish than tuna or salmon, but it is also much less expensive and just as good a protein source. It is usually packed in water.

SEAFOOD

Seafood is the broad category of water-dwelling creatures that are not fish. Included are such things as shrimp, scallops, oysters, mussels, clams, crab, lobster, and squid. Typically seafood is sold whole although it is also possible to buy crab and lobster "meat."

Shrimp (Scampi, Prawns). Shrimp are available in a variety of sizes, from the tiny Alaskan shrimp, which is suitable for salads and sandwiches and is usually sold already cooked, frozen, and ready to use—to the very large scampi and prawns, two or three of which can make a generous serving. Shrimp are usually sold headless and are sometimes called "green shrimp" if they have not been cooked. It is necessary for the cook to remove the thin shell and legs that are attached to the shell and also to remove the black vein that runs down the back of the shrimp. This "vein" is the shrimp's intestinal tract. It is easiest to remove it under running water.

Scallops. There are two kinds of scallops: sea scallops, which are about an inch and a half across and up to an inch thick, and bay scallops, which are about half that size. The bay scallops are more tender and very delicately flavored. They are also usually in limited supply and not available in all parts of the country. Sea scallops are taken from the deeper parts of the ocean. They are quite plentiful and more easily available. Sea scallops can be so large that you may prefer to cut them into smaller pieces before using.

Oysters. Oysters are available in three ways: live in the shell, removed from the shell (shucked) either fresh or frozen, and canned. The flavor and texture of oysters varies considerably depending on where they come from. If you buy oysters fresh and in the shell, make sure that the shells are tightly closed, because that indicates that they are still alive. If the shells are open, the oysters are dead and not fit to be eaten. Oysters can be kept alive for several days in the refrigerator at 40 degrees Fahrenheit or lower. Shucked oysters should be plump and the liquid should be clear. Properly refrigerated, they can be kept from seven to ten days after shucking.

Clams (and Mussels). These mollusks can also be purchased alive and in the shell, shucked (fresh or frozen), or canned. Like oysters, you should not purchase clams in the shell if the shell is not closed, because that means that the clam is dead and not edible. Sometimes you can detect life by just touching the siphon: it should twitch or retract if the clam is still alive. Clams will remain alive for several days if kept at 40 degrees Fahrenheit or lower. Shucked fresh clams should be plump and the liquid with them clear. They may be kept shucked from seven to ten days if properly refrigerated. Frozen clams should be kept frozen until ready to use and not refrozen once thawed.

Crab. There are several varieties of crab available in different parts of the country. Along the Atlantic seacoast the blue crab is the most common, while in the West the Dungeness is found from Washington south to California and the king crab is taken in the waters off the coast of Alaska. Near fishing grounds the crabs are usually sold either alive (there is no question about whether a crab is alive or not!) or fresh-cooked. Inland crab is most commonly available fresh-cooked or frozen. "Soft-shell" crabs are actually blue crabs that are caught between the moulting of one shell and the complete development of another.

Lobster. Like the others, lobsters are available either live, fresh-cooked, frozen, or canned. Live lobsters are taken from the waters off the coast of New England and shipped live all over the country. They weigh from just under one pound to as much as three pounds, and the meat comes from both the tail and the claws. A cousin of the lobster, the crayfish, is also available in some parts of the country. Quite commonly available is the large species of the crayfish called "rock lobster." These are in fact not lobsters at all but very large crayfish that come from the waters around Australia and South Africa. Only the tails of rock lobster are eaten.

Squid. The squid is a relative newcomer to American tables, although it has been a traditional mainstay protein source in Mediterranean countries and in Asia. Where it is available, the squid is sold whole, fresh or frozen. Properly cooked (that is, not overcooked), it is tender and tasty.

Imitation Shellfish. In recent years a new fish product has appeared in supermarkets—a substitute for real shellfish that is called "imitation" lobster, shrimp, scallops, crab, and so forth. This product is an amazing look-, taste-, and smell-alike for the real thing ... at a half to a third of the cost. The process originated in Japan, where it has been used for a long time. The imitations are made with a mild-flavored white fish like pollock, which is processed to remove all possible color and odor. The result of this is an odorless, tasteless fish protein paste that the Japanese call *surimi.* This paste is then colored and flavored to simulate the more expensive shellfish. Various texturizers are used to imitate the consistency of the shellfish being manufactured. Nutritionally these products are the same as the fish from which they are made. People on a sodium-restricted diet should be aware that the sodium count is rather high, however.

SHOPPING FOR EGGS

Eggs available in most retail outlets are graded either by the USDA or by state Department of Agriculture inspection. The grade and size is displayed on the carton.

Egg Sizes

Size is determined by the weight of the eggs required to make up a dozen, not the physical size of the eggs.
A dozen extralarge eggs must weigh at least 27 oz.
A dozen large eggs at least 24 oz.
A dozen medium eggs 21 oz.
A dozen small eggs 18 oz.

Because of this method of sizing, it is possible for the careful shopper to determine which size is the best value on a particular day. The chart that follows shows how to figure the per pound value of various sizes.

EGG PRICES PER POUND

Small	Medium	This Price per Dozen Large	ExLarge	Equals This Price per Pound
$ .41	$ .48	$ .55	$ .62	$ .36
.45	.52	.60	.67	.40
.49	.57	.65	.73	.43
.52	.61	.70	.79	.46
.56	.65	.75	.84	.50
.60	.70	.80	.90	.53
.64	.74	.85	.95	.56
.67	.79	.90	1.01	.60
.71	.83	.95	1.07	.63
.75	.87	1.00	1.12	.66
.79	.92	1.05	1.18	.70
.82	.96	1.10	1.24	.73
.86	1.00	1.15	1.29	.76
.90	1.05	1.20	1.35	.80
.94	1.09	1.25	1.40	.83
1.00	1.15	1.31	1.48	.86
1.05	1.20	1.38	1.55	.90

Small	Medium	This Price per Dozen Large	ExLarge	Equals This Price per Pound
1.09	1.24	1.42	1.60	.93
1.12	1.28	1.47	1.65	.96
1.17	1.33	1.53	1.72	1.00

SHOPPING FOR CHEESE

Cheese making is an ancient technology first developed as a means of preserving animal milk for later use. The differences in taste, texture, and appearance are brought about by the differences in the milk from which the cheese is made, the way the milk is curdled and processed, the kind of bacteria or molds used in the ripening process, the conditions used for ripening, and finally the additional seasonings that are added to the milk base.

Natural cheeses are categorized by their state of "ripening" and their consistency. The following are the categories most commonly used to describe individual cheese types.

Soft Unripened. (Cottage Cheese, Cream Cheese, Neufchâtel, Ricotta). High in moisture. Not ripened at all. Meant to be eaten soon after being made. Usually made of cow's milk. Mild or slightly acidic flavor.

Firm Unripened. (Gjetost, Mozzarella, Mysost.) Low moisture. Not ripened at all. Will keep for several months. Some varieties are made of cow's milk, others of goat's milk. Mild, somewhat sweet flavor.

Soft Ripened. (Brie, Camembert, Limburger.) Slightly moist. Ripening takes place from the outside of the cheese toward the middle in about four to eight weeks. Specialized bacteria are used to produce distinctive flavors and texture. Usually made of cow's milk. Mild to very pungent flavors.

Semisoft ripened. (Bel Paese, Muenster, Port du Salut.) Less moisture than the soft ripened cheeses noted before. Ripened equally throughout the cheese. Ripening takes from one to eight weeks depending on variety. Specialized bacteria and molds are used to produce distinctive flavors and texture. Usually made of cow's milk. Mellow to robust flavors.

Firm Ripened. (Cheddar, Colby, Edam, Feta, Gouda, Provolone, Swiss.) Relatively low in moisture content. Ripened equally throughout the cheese. Ripening takes from one to twelve months depending on variety. Ripening due to special bacteria. Usually made of cow's milk (feta is usually made of goat's milk). Mild to very sharp flavors.

Very Hard Ripened. (Parmesan, Romano, Sapsago.) Very low moisture content. Ripened equally throughout the cheese. Ripening takes from five months to as much as two years because of the low moisture content. Usually made of skimmed or low-fat cow's milk. Sharp flavor.

Blue-vein Mold Ripened. (Roquefort, Bleu, Stilton, Gorgonzola.) Semisoft and crumbly. Ripened with bacteria and mold cultures. Ripening takes from two to twelve months. Made of cow's or a combination of cow's and goat's milk. Slightly sharp to peppery flavor.

SHOPPING FOR FRUITS

Americans are eating more fruits than ever before. They are eating a far greater variety of fruits. Produce departments in supermarkets offer shoppers everything from Bosc pears to mangoes to kiwi fruit. The apple section alone often presents six or seven varieties to choose from. To help you get the best value for your shopping dollar, here are some things to look for.

CHOOSING FRESH FRUITS

Apples. There are basically two kinds of apples: those that are best eaten raw and those that are best when cooked. If you shop at farmers' markets or buy directly from growers, you may find some uncommon varieties available, but if you do most of your shopping in grocery-store produce departments, the most common eating apples are Red and Golden Delicious, McIntosh, Stayman, Jonathan, and Winesap. Golden Delicious also cook well, as do Gravenstein, Jonathan, and Newton. Cooking apples are usually slightly more tart than eating apples and also keep their shape when cooked. For baking look for Rome Beauty, Northern Spy, Winesap, and York Imperial. These varieties are flavorful and firm when baked.

Look for: Firm, well-colored apples. Apples are picked when mature and held in special humidity- and temperature-controlled warehouses until sold. Don't buy apples that are slightly shriveled or bruised. Also watch out for apples that have been frozen (they will be soft and look slightly bruised because the internal cells have been broken down) and apples that are overripe (you will feel a softness when you press). Occasionally you may see "scald" on apples (irregularly shaped, dry-feeling tan area on the skin); this usually does not affect the taste of the apple. Grades used on apples are U.S. Extra Fancy, U.S. Fancy, U.S. No. 1, and occasionally U.S. No. 2, running from the best quality to the least acceptable. Grading is not required and in western states the grading is sometimes done by state rather than federal standards.

Apricots. Apricots are available only during the harvest season because they are picked when ripe but still firm and do not keep well. In this country most of the fresh apricots come from the states of California, Washington, and Utah. Some varieties are best for eating fresh, canning, or cooking (Castlebrite, Derby-Royal, Royal Blenheim), others are best when canned (Tilton), while still other varieties are best for home-drying (Royal Blenheim, Patterson).

Look for: Apricots that are plump and well formed with a uniform golden-orange color and a slight yielding when pressed. Fruit that is greenish and very firm or dull-colored and soft indicates underripe and overripe fruits respectively, and neither will be satisfactory.

Avocados. Avocados are available most of the year and are grown primarily in California and Florida. Although there are many varieties of avocado, the two most common types are the rough-skinned and the smooth-skinned. Avocados are usually pear shaped; avocados that are almost spherical are occasionally available. When purchased, avocados are usually not ripened but will complete their ripening process in three to five days if kept at room temperature (keeping in the refrigerator will slow this process down).

Look for: If you want to use the avocado immediately look for one that is slightly soft near the stem end. The longer it will be before you plan to use the avocado, the firmer it can be when you buy it. Occasionally avocados will have irregular surface markings in a tannish color, which do not affect the taste or texture of the fruit. Do not buy avocados that have a cracked or broken surface or dark sunken spots, which indicate internal decay.

Avocados have a great tendency to darken after cutting. This can be avoided if you brush the cut surface with lemon juice and tightly wrap the remaining avocado in plastic wrap before storing in the refrigerator.

Bananas. Certainly one of the three most popular fruits (apples and oranges being the other two), bananas are available year-round. Unlike other fruits, bananas are picked and shipped green and develop their best flavor after being harvested. Bananas do not keep well below 55 degrees (the skins will darken); the ideal temperature to complete the ripening process is between 60 and 70 degrees.

Look for: Bananas should be firm and free from bruises. Choose slightly green bananas if they are to be kept for several days. For eating immediately choose fruit that is completely yellow with some brown flecks. Do not choose fruit that is obviously bruised or that has discolored skin, which can indicate decay.

Blueberries. Fresh blueberries are available from mid-May through the end of September in most parts of the country. Stores usually stock cultivated varieties, which are quite a bit larger than the wild blueberries that grow in some parts of the country. The flavor of the cultivated varieties is also more mellow than the wild strains.

Look for: Blueberries should look blue with a haze of silver. This silver overlay is a natural waxy coating that protects the berries. Blueberries should be plump, firm, and similar in size. They should be kept dry until you wash them at home just before using.

Cherries. Most of the commercially available cherries are grown in the western states and are available in markets from May through mid-August. There are basically two types: the sweet dark cherries that are eaten fresh or cooked, and the tart light-colored cherries that are used primarily in cooked desserts such as pies and cobblers. Popular varieties for eating fresh are Bing, Lambert, and Rainier, and these varieties are also suitable for canning or cooking. Bing cherries are the best variety to use for drying.

Look for: In sweet cherries the color must be dark, almost maroon, to indicate ripeness. Sour cherries are bright red when ready to use. Both types should be bright, glossy, and plump-looking, and there should be stems attached. Watch out for brownish spots, which are sometimes hard to see on the dark-colored cherries but which indicate bruising and decay. Also look out for shriveled fruit and overly dried-out stems. Cherries take on a dull appearance if they are overripe and ready to spoil and they should not be purchased.

Cranberries. Sold fresh only during the fall and winter months of September through January, cranberries are often associated with holiday meals. They are grown in the cooler climates of New England and the Northwest and are available in all parts of the country during that period. Although there are several varieties of cranberries grown, the varieties are not usually named on the cranberries available in stores.

Look for: Cranberries should be plump and firm with a bright, dark red color. Since cranberries are shipped great distances, always pour them into a bowl of water and sort out the few that might have spoiled in transit before you use them.

Grapefruit. Grapefruit is available year-round in most stores and is grown in Florida, Texas, Arizona, and California. Grapefruit varieties have two differentiations: seedless and those with seeds, and yellow- or pink-colored sections. Stores usually indicate these differences in the fruit they have available. Grapefruit is ready to eat when you purchase it.

Look for: The fruit should feel heavy, be well shaped and firm. In general, thin-skinned fruit is juicier than fruit with thick skin. One clue to skin thickness is the fruit's shape: Thick-skinned fruit tends to be somewhat pointed at the stem end. Do not buy grapefruit that has soft or discolored areas or indications of water-soaking.

Grapes. Table grapes available in this country are either those that have been grown from European stock (Thompson Seedless, Tokay, Cardinal, and Emperor), which are firm and have a high sugar content, or those that are native to North America (Concord, Delaware, or Catawba), which are softer and juicier than the European strains.

Look for: Grapes should be firm, well colored (depending on their variety), and attached to stem. Beware of purchasing soft or wrinkled grapes, or grapes that seem to be leaking juice, because these are signs of poor handling during shipment.

Lemons. Like its citrus cousins the orange and the grapefruit, lemons are available year-round. They are grown primarily in California and Arizona.

Look for: Lemons should be a bright, rich yellow color and feel heavy. A smooth skin indicates a juicier fruit while a rough skin means that the skin is thicker and the fruit drier. Do not buy lemons that have soft spots or any sign of mold; look out, too, for lemons with hard skins, because that is a sign that they have not been stored properly.

Limes. You may see both truly green limes and limes that are slightly yellow. The former are sometimes called Persian limes while the yellowish ones are sometimes designated as Key limes.

Look for: As with lemons, limes should be bright-colored and feel heavy. Dry skins should be avoided as should soft or molded skins. Occasionally limes will be marked with a "scald," which is a brownish dry patch. As long as these spots are relatively small they do not affect the quality of the lime.

Melons. The methods for choosing a good melon are part of the folk wisdom of the kitchen. Here are some ways to be successful every time. Start by sniffing the melon (does it have a true melony aroma?). Next press the stem end (does it yield to gentle pressure?). Finally lift the melon in one hand (does it feel heavy for its size?). If the answer is "yes" to these three questions, the chances are you have chosen a sweet, juicy melon.

Look for: Each melon has its own distinctive signs of ripeness.

Cantaloupes or muskmelons should be golden-colored, the skin with a uniform webbing, and the stem joint indented.

Casabas will be bright yellow with distinct furrows running from end to end and the blossom end (instead of the stem end) should be slightly soft.

Crenshaws are large with quite smooth skin and only shallow furrows. The rind should be deep yellow, the surface should yield slightly when pressed, and there should be a melony aroma.

Honeydew melons are quite large and oval in shape. A ripe honeydew will have a soft feel to the rind with a slight softness at the blossom end and be a creamy-white color.

Icebox melons are very spherical in shape and should have dark green rind and a crisp red interior.

Persian melons are similar to cantaloupes but more spherical; they also have a finer webbing than cantaloupes. Their ripeness can be tested in the same way you would test a cantaloupe.

Tiger melons are striped light and dark green on the outside and have bright yellow flesh.

Watermelons are very hard to judge before cutting, but some of the things you can try include thumping the melon to see if it has a hollow sound, making sure that the underside has a rich, creamy color and that the ends are filled out. Given all these things it is still possible to choose a melon that isn't all it might be, so just be philosophical if that happens and hope that your next choice will be better.

Nectarines. This fruit is a man-made blending of peaches and plums and has the best qualities of both. Nectarines are grown commercially primarily in the western states and are available from mid-June through early September. All varieties of nectarines are good for eating fresh. Firebrite, Spring Red, and Red Diamond are specially good for canning while Firebrite, Spring Red, Red Diamond, and Red Gold are recommended for drying. Nectarines are easy to peel if they are placed briefly in hot water.

Look for: Golden-orange color with red highlights and a slight yielding to pressure. If the fruit seems a little firm, keep it at room temperature for a day or two and it will ripen completely. Don't buy fruit that is just plain hard, because it has been picked too early and will never attain a good flavor. Overly soft fruit should also be avoided. Occasionally you will find nectarines with a brownish stain on the skin but this staining will not affect the fruit's quality.

Oranges. The final member of the citrus family and certainly a mainstay among fruits, oranges are available year-round in all locations. Although there are a number of varieties grown, the two varieties most commonly seen are Navel and Valencia. Navel oranges (available November till mid-May) have a thicker and rougher skin; however, they are easy to peel and segment. The Valencias are available from late April through the end of October and are smoother and thinner-skinned, very juicy, and good for slicing. Both of these varieties are grown in California and Arizona. Florida produces Temple oranges, available from December through early March. Both Florida and Texas grow Parson Brown and Hamlin varieties, which are in the stores from November through March.

Look for: Firm fruit that feels heavy and has a bright-looking peel. Color is not a reliable characteristic of ripeness or quality because completely ripe oranges can have a greenish cast and also because the FDA allows artificial coloring of oranges. Watch out for very rough peel, which means the peel is thick and there will be less fruit beneath it. Spongy or soft oranges should also be avoided because they are at the least overripe and at the most decayed.

Peaches. Like apples, there are many varieties of peaches available in markets and from growers. Basically they fall into two broad categories: those whose seeds release from the flesh easily (freestone) and those whose flesh sticks to the seed (clingstone). The best varieties for eating fresh include Redhaven, O'Henry, Rio Oso Gem, and Yakima Hale. For canning consider Redhaven or Yakima Hales and for drying the best varieties are Angelus, Fay Elberta, and O'Henry.

Look for: Peaches should be just barely softening when you buy them. The skin color should have no green spots but be orangy-yellow with some red areas. Do not buy peaches that are obviously green, because they will not ripen properly. Soft fruits should also be avoided because they are too ripe and will not hold their shape or flavor. If there is a visible bruise on the surface you can be sure there is a large discolored area below in the fruit.

Pears. There are quite different fruits that belong to the pear family. The most popular is, of course, the Bartlett, which is available from early August through mid-November and is grown primarily in Washington, Oregon, and California. This is an excellent variety for eating fresh or for canning. In the fall and winter months you will see Anjou, Bosc, Winter Nellis, and Comice pears. These varieties are firm and keep well.

Look for: Pears should be firm when you buy them, with perhaps just a hint of yielding to pressure. Bartletts should have a good yellow color. Anjou and Comice will be yellowish green. Bosc will be greenish yellow to brownish yellow. Winter Nellis will be medium to light green. Do not buy pears of any variety that are wilted or shriveled-looking or have spots on the sides or near the blossom ends.

Pineapples. Pineapples are most plentiful in the late spring but are usually available year-round. They come to your market not only from Hawaii but also from Puerto Rico and Mexico. When picked, the pineapples are fully grown but not ripened. In choosing pineapple to be eaten right away, be guided by your nose. Sniff the stem end and if there is a sweet pineapple aroma it is probably ready to eat. Another guide to ripeness is whether you can easily pull one of the "leaves" away from the fruit.

Look for: Pineapple should be plump, feel heavy, and have a rich golden or reddish-gold color. Don't buy fruit that is obviously bruised or has soft spots or "eyes" that are soft and moist.

Plums and Prunes. Like peaches, plums are classified as either freestone or clingstone. They are on the market from June through mid-September and available in several varieties to suit several purposes. For eating fresh, Santa Rosa, Laroda, and Elephant Heart are recommended. Best for canning are Santa Rosa, Laroda, Friar, Casselman, and Italian prunes, while Friar and Elephant Heart are the best to use for drying.

Look for: Plums and prunes should have a good color for the variety. They should be fairly firm but with a slight yielding to pressure. Fruit that has broken skin or discolorations should be avoided.

Raspberries. (Boysenberries, blackberries, dewberries, loganberries, and youngberries.) All these berry types are similar in structure although they have slightly different size, colors, and flavors.

Look for: Berries should be clean and uniform in appearance. These berries have a tendency to mold easily and do not ship well. Look at them carefully and do not buy any that show signs of mushiness or mold. If the container has stain or moisture marks, the berries inside are probably overripe.

Strawberries. Although strawberries are available from early February through late summer, the best berries are in the stores from late May through mid-July.

Look for: Strawberries should be bright red in color. The best flavor will be found in berries that are not too large. Look through the carton to make sure that there are not less desirable berries in the lower layers. Like other berries, strawberries are susceptible to molding, so make sure that none of the berries you buy show mold, because it can quickly spread throughout the carton. Don't wash strawberries until just before you plan to use them.

FINAL ADVICE

Finally, as an overall guide to economical shopping, here is a month-by-month list of best buys in various food categories. This list will help you not only get the best value for your food dollar, but will also give you a way to give good variety to your monthly menu plan.

Protein	Vegetables	Fruit	Other
January			
pork, eggs, beef, ham, fryer chickens, turkey	broccoli, onions, potatoes, turnips, lettuce, eggplant	apples & citrus	nuts, honey, raisins
February			
eggs	broccoli, Brussels sprouts, lettuce, potatoes, cabbage, spinach, parsnips	citrus, bananas, avocado, apples	nuts, honey, raisins

Protein	Vegetables	Fruit	Other
March			
fryer chicken, eggs, beef	radishes, spinach, carrots, potatoes, broccoli, cabbage, artichokes	citrus, pineapples, bananas, apples	raisins, prunes
April			
fryer chicken, pork, eggs, ham	mushrooms, carrots, spring greens, peas, early potatoes, artichokes, celery	pineapple, bananas, citrus	raisins, prunes
May			
fryer chicken, eggs	asparagus, spinach, lettuce, tomatoes, potatoes, cucumber, mushrooms, peas	strawberries, rhubarb, pineapple	
June			
chicken, fish	tomatoes, potatoes, asparagus, lettuce, peas, cucumbers, greens, beets, beans	berries, citrus, cherries, nectarines, apricots	frozen foods
July			
fryer chicken, turkey	cabbage, tomatoes, corn, squash, green beans, peppers, potatoes, cucumbers	berries, pears, melons, peaches, plums, grapes	canned goods, frozen foods
August			
fish	beans, beets, squash, carrots,	grapes, peaches,	canned goods,

Protein	Vegetables	Fruit	Other
	chard, eggplant, peppers, corn, onions, tomatoes	melons, pears	honey
September			
lamb, stewing chicken	onions, cabbage, beets, tomatoes, corn, peppers, squash, beets	apples, melons, pears, grapes	grains, honey
October			
lamb, stewing chicken, pork, veal, turkey	sweet potatoes, potatoes, onions, cauliflower, peppers, turnips	apples, bananas, cranberries, avocados, pomegranates, pears	grains, honey
November			
turkey, pork, veal	sweet potatoes, potatoes, onions, cauliflower, squash, broccoli, celery	bananas, citrus, apples, cranberries, avocados	nuts, grains, raisins
December			
turkey, pork, veal, lamb	sweet potatoes, onions, potatoes, spinach, celery, mushrooms	apples, citrus, cranberries	nuts, honey

The time you spend planning your meals, planning your food storage, and planning your shopping will save you time, will save you money, will encourage family participation in meal planning, and will give you a wider variety of nutritious meals.

CHAPTER 3

How Much of What

As a cook you are constantly confronted with two questions: **what** ingredients to use and **how much** to use.

Do you remember the first time you popped corn? Who would have thought that just a cup of dry kernels would produce a kitchen full of popped corn ... about twenty cups!

It's summer and a lemon chiffon pie sounds like a perfect dessert. You want to make a graham cracker crust for a change. How many graham crackers should you crush to make a crumb pie shell? You need to have enough to make a shell thick enough to hold together, but you would prefer not to have an extra cup of crumbs to store until the next time. Do you crush ten crackers? Twenty crackers? The whole box?

Your lemon chiffon calls for a quarter cup of freshly squeezed lemon juice and a teaspoon of grated lemon rind. Should you buy one or five lemons when you shop?

And what about substitutions? What if you have a special request not for a lemon chiffon, but for a chocolate chiffon pie instead? As you go to prepare it you find you have no un-sweetened chocolate squares ... you do, however, have some cocoa. Is there any way you can use that instead? Yes, you can! (Just add two teaspoons of shortening for each three tablespoons of cocoa.) You have saved yourself an emergency trip to the store!

In everyday meal preparation the thing to remember is that there are some ingredients of any dish that perform an absolutely essential function ... nothing substitutes for the eggs in a towering cheese soufflé, or for the yeast in a crusty loaf of French bread, or for gelatin in your frothy lemon chiffon pie.

On the other hand, there are quite a few ingredients that are not that essential. Most liquids, for instance, fill two requirements: they provide moisture and add flavor. Many times you can use a similar liquid that you have on hand instead of the one called for and have your results all that you could want. If you are in the mood for your chiffon pie but have no lemons on hand, perhaps you have an orange or two ... what about an orange chiffon pie instead?

In the case of liquid substitutions the important thing is to understand what liquids are like what other liquids. You probably wouldn't want to substitute tomato juice for milk but you could substitute tomato juice for broth in most cases, and you also can often substitute just plain water for milk.

For weight watchers, substitutions can be a key to calorie reduction. Substituting skim milk for whole milk, or even using water in some instances, can save a considerable number of calories. When making a white sauce, the amount of butter called for can usually be cut in half without affecting the quality of the sauce ... and again you have saved many calories.

A few words about the process of measuring ...

Dry ingredients should be stirred before measuring, then the appropriate-size measuring device (a measuring cup or spoon) filled, and the top leveled off with a knife.

If you are measuring **liquid ingredients** in a glass measuring cup, hold the cup up at eye level after you have poured in the liquid. Looking down on a cup placed on a counter can distort your view of the amount measured. When measuring liquids in a spoon, use the correct-size measuring spoon and fill it to the top with the liquid.

Shortening, butter, and **margarine** should be measured in a cup in the amount required, pressed firmly down, and leveled off with a knife. **Brown sugar** should be measured the same way.

Still and all, you should be aware that virtually no ingredient is so critical that absolute measurements are essential.

Train your eyes to measure ingredients. Start by measuring out a teaspoon of salt and pouring it into your hand. Look at it carefully. As you cup your hand slightly, where does the edge of the salt come? How does it feel in your hand? Practice a few times and once you have this mastered, you can measure a teaspoon of any grainy ingredient by eye. Take a pinch of pepper, then pour the pinch into a quarter-teaspoon measuring spoon. How much is a pinch? Try it with salt ... is it the same amount? If you experiment a bit you will find that you will soon be able to add ingredients without careful measuring ... and have results that you like.

Taste the dish you are preparing and adjust the seasoning as you go along. Remember that the way you would like something to taste may or may not be the way the person who created the recipe liked it. For example, most recipes for waffles do not call for vanilla flavoring, or any flavoring at all for that matter, but many cooks feel that a bit of vanilla vastly improves the flavor and you may too.

Try things out ... don't be constrained by the word printed on the page. Some of the things you try won't work out ... but you will never know unless you experiment.

A word of advice about measuring potent seasonings and flavorings, such things as Tabasco sauce or almond extract: Don't measure directly over the dish you are preparing. If your hand should slip, you may spoil something that would have been wonderful. Instead, measure the amount you think you want to use into the spoon you are using for mixing and then stir it into the dish.

Cooking is a science that involves physics and chemistry, but it is also an art that involves all five of our senses. The difference between a pedestrian food-preparer and a creative cook often falls into that gray area between kitchen science and kitchen magic ... and no one cook can tell another exactly how it is done ... only experience and desire to experiment can do that.

INGREDIENT EQUIVALENTS

Food Type	Volume Before Preparation	Weight Before Preparation	Amount After Preparation
Grains:			
Barley	1 cup	7 ounces	2 cups cooked
Bulgur wheat	1 cup	5 ounces	1½ cups cooked
Cornmeal	1 cup	6 ounces	3 cups cooked
Popcorn	¼ cup	2 ounces	5 cups popped
Rice, brown	1 cup	7 ounces	4 cups cooked
Rice, white	1 cup	8 ounces	3 cups cooked
Wheat berries	1 cup	7 ounces	2 cups cooked
Wild rice	1 cup	6 ounces	3 cups cooked
Pasta:			
Macaroni, small	1 cup	5 ounces	2 cups cooked
Macaroni, large	1 cup*	2½ ounces	1 cup cooked
Noodles, thin	1 cup*	4 ounces	3 cups cooked
Noodles, wide	1 cup*	2 ounces	1 cup cooked
Noodles, lasagna	6 6" strips	3 ounces	2 servings
Spaghetti	—	4 ounces	4 cups cooked

*It is better to measure these by weight than by volume.

Food Type	Volume Before Preparation	Weight Before Preparation	Amount After Preparation
Crumbs:			
Bread, dry	1 slice	1 ounce	3 tbsp.
Bread, soft	1 slice	1 ounce	½ cup
	1 loaf	16-oz. loaf	10 cups
Soda crackers	28 squares	—	1 cup
Rich crackers	24 crackers	—	1 cup
Graham crackers	15 squares	—	1 cup
Gingersnaps	15 cookies	—	1 cup
Vanilla wafers	28 cookies	—	1 cup
Chocolate wafers	16 cookies	—	1 cup
Dairy Products:			
Butter/margarine	1 cube	4 ounces	½ cup or 8 tbsp.
	4 cubes	1 pound	2 cups
Cheese, firm	—	4 ounces	1 cup grated
	—	1 pound	2⅔ cups cubed
Cheese, hard	—	2 ounces	½ cup
Condensed milk	large can	15 ounces	1¾ cups
	small can	6 ounces	¾ cup
Cottage cheese	pint pkg.	1 pound	2 cups pureed
Cream, whipping	1 cup	—	2 cups whipped
Cream cheese	6 tbsp.	3-oz. pkg.	—
Egg, small	1 dozen	18 ounces	6 in 1 cup
Egg, medium	1 dozen	21 ounces	5 in 1 cup
Egg, large	1 dozen	24 ounces	4 in 1 cup
Egg, extra large	1 dozen	27 ounces	3 in 1 cup
Egg white	1 large	3 tbsp.	¾ cups beaten
	7-9 whites	1 cup	4 cups beaten
Egg yolk	12-14 yolks	—	1 cup stirred

Food Type	Raw Volume	Raw Weight	Servings
Fruits:			
Apples, dried	—	8 oz.	6-8 servings
Apples, fresh	3 med.	1 pound	3 cups sliced

Food Type	Raw Volume	Raw Weight	Servings
Apricots, dried	—	8 oz.	6-8 servings
Apricots, fresh	5-6 med.	1 pound	5 cups cooked
		3 pounds	4 cups puree
Bananas	3 med.	1 pound	1 cup puree
			¾ cup sliced
Blueberries	2 cups	—	4-5 servings
Cherries	—	1 pound	2 cups pitted
Coconut, dried	—	2 oz.	1 cup grated
Coconut, fresh	—	1 pound	5 cups grated
Cranberries	4 cups	1 pound	3 cups ground
Dates	1 cup pitted	8 oz.	1⅓ cups chopped
Figs, fresh	—	1 pound	3 cups chopped
Grapes, seedless	—	1 pound	5-6 servings
Lemons	1 med.	6 oz.	3 tbsp. juice
			2 tsp. grated zest
Limes	1 med.	3 oz.	2 tbsp. juice
			1⅓ tsp. grated zest
Mixed fruit, dried	—	8 oz.	6-8 servings
Oranges	1 med.	8 oz.	1¼ to 1⅓ cup juice
			4 tsp. grated zest
Peaches, dried	—	8 oz.	6-8 servings
Peaches, fresh	1 med.	4-6 oz.	½ cup sliced
Pears, dried	—	8 ounces	4-5 servings
Pears, fresh	1 med.	4-6 oz.	½ cup sliced
Pineapple	1 med.	2 pounds	8 1-inch slices
			6-7 cups ground
Plums, fresh	—	1 pound	3-4 servings
Prunes, dried	2½ cups	1 pound	4 cups cooked
			4-5 servings
Raspberries	4 cups whole	—	8 servings
Raisins, seeded	2½ cups	1 pound	—
Raisins, seedless	3 cups (loose)	1 pound	—

Food Type	Raw Volume	Raw Weight	Servings
Strawberries	4 cups whole	—	3 cups sliced 8 servings
Canned fruit	—	1-lb. can	3-4 servings
Frozen fruit	—	10-12 oz.	3-4 servings

Food Type	Weight	Servings

Meats:

Beef

Round steak	1 pound	3-4 servings
Sirloin steak	1 pound	4 servings
Chuck roast	1 pound	2-3 servings
Rib roast (bone in)	4 pounds	8 servings
Short ribs	2 pounds	2-3 servings
Stew meat (boneless)	1 pound	4-5 servings
Ground beef (regular)	1 pound	3 servings
Ground beef (lean)	1 pound	4 servings

Lamb

Leg of lamb	5 pounds	8-10 servings
Steak/chop (shoulder)	1 pound	2 servings
Chop (loin)	1 pound	2 servings
Stew meat (neck)	2 pounds	2 servings

Pork

Steak (shoulder)	1 pound	2 servings
Chop	1 pound	2-3 servings
Roast	2 pounds	6 servings
Sausage	1 pound	3 servings
Bacon	1 pound	6-8 servings ½ cup bits
Ham, slice	1 pound	3 servings
Ham, whole, precooked	5 pounds	15-18 servings
Canadian bacon	1 pound	6-8 servings

Food Type	Weight	Servings
Veal (similar to Pork)		
Boneless raw meat	1 pound	3-4 servings
Ground raw meat	1 pound	3-4 servings
Poultry		
Chicken, whole fryer	2-3 pounds	3-5 servings
Chicken, whole roaster	3-6 pounds	4-8 servings
Breast, both sides	¾ pound	2 servings
Thighs/legs	1 pound	2 servings
Duck	3 pounds	6-7 servings
Goose	5 pounds	10-12 servings
Pheasant, dressed	3 pounds	5-6 servings
Rock Cornish game hen	1 pound	2 servings
Turkey, whole small	8 pounds	16 servings*
Turkey, whole large	15-20 pounds	20-30 servings*
Breast, half (one side)	5 pounds	8-10 servings
Leg, one	2 pounds	1-2 servings

*Servings, not people, and servings include meals made from leftovers.

Food Type	Weight	Servings
Fish:		
Whole fish	1 pound	1-2 servings
Steaks (with bones)	1 pound	3 servings
Fillets	1 pound	4 servings
Seafood/Shellfish:		
Clams, no shells	1 pound	3 servings
Lobster tails	1 pound	2 servings
Lobster meat	1 pound	4 servings
Oysters, no shells	1 pound	3 servings
Scallops, no shells	1 pound	4 servings
Shrimp, whole	1 pound	2-3 servings
Shrimp meat	1 pound	4 servings
Squid	1 pound	3 servings

Food Type	Weight	Servings
Nuts:		
Almonds	1 lb. in shell	1 cup shelled
		¾ cup sliced
		¼ cup ground
	1 lb. shelled	3 cups whole
Peanuts	1 lb. in shell	1¼ cups whole
		1 cup chopped
		⅓ cup ground
Pecans	1 lb. in shell	1⅓ cups whole
	1 lb. shelled	4 cups whole
		1¾ cups chopped
Walnuts	1 lb. in shell	1⅔ cups whole
	1 lb. shelled	1½ cups chopped

Note: Nut measurements are approximate and depend on how finely nuts are chopped and the size of the whole nuts.

Food Type	Volume	Weight
Staples and Misc.:		
Baker's chocolate	1 square	1 ounce
	5 tbsp. grated	
Baking powder	1 cup	5½ ounces
Cocoa	4 cups dry	1 pound
	25 5-oz. cups	
Coffee	80 tbsp.	1 pound
	40-50 5-oz. cups	
Cornstarch	3 cups	1 pound
Flour, cake	5 cups	1 pound
Flour, white	4 cups	1 pound
Flour, whole grain	3½ cups	1 pound
Gelatin, flavored	½ cup	3¼ ounces
Gelatin, unflavored	1 tbsp.	¼ ounce
Honey	1⅓ cups	1 pound
Marshmallows	16 large	¼ pound
	1 cup melted	

Food Type	Volume	Weight
Shortening	2 cups	1 pound
Sugar, brown, packed	2½ cups	1 pound
Sugar, cubes	100-130 cubes	1 pound
Sugar, granulated	2⅓ cups	1 pound
Sugar, powdered	4 cups	1 pound
Tea	1 tsp.	½ ounce
	1-2 cups	
Water	2 cups	1 pound

Food Type	Vol. Before Cooking	Wt. Before Cooking	Amt. After Cooking
Vegetables:			
Asparagus	—	1 pound	3-4 servings
Asparagus (f)*	—	10-oz. pkg.	2-3 servings
Beans, dry	2½ cups	1 pound	6 cups cooked
Beans, green	3 cups cut	1 pound	2½ cups cooked
Beans, green (f)	—	10-oz. pkg.	3-4 servings
Beans, lima	—	1 pound	2-3 servings
Beans, lima (f)	—	10-oz. pkg.	3-4 servings
Beets	—	1 pound	2 cups diced
Broccoli	—	1 pound	3-4 servings
Broccoli (f)	—	10-oz. pkg.	3 servings
Brussels sprouts	—	1 pound	4-5 servings
Brussels sprouts (f)	—	10-oz. pkg.	3 servings
Cabbage	1 small	1 pound	5 cups shredded
			5-6 servings
Carrots	6-8 med.	1 pound	3 cups sliced
			2 cups shredded
Cauliflower	1 small	1 pound	3 servings
Cauliflower (f)	—	10-oz. pkg.	3 servings
Celery	1 bunch	2 pounds	4 cups chopped
	1 stalk	3 ounces	½ cup chopped
Corn (f)	—	10-oz. pkg.	3 servings

*frozen

Food Type	Vol. Before Cooking	Wt. Before Cooking	Amt. After Cooking
Kale	—	1 pound	2-3 servings
Lentils, dried	2 cups	1 pound	6 servings
Mushrooms	12 large	1 pound	5 cups sliced
			4 cups chopped
			2 cups after cooking
Okra	—	1 pound	4-5 servings
Onions	med.	4 ounces	½ cup chopped
	4 med.	1 pound	3-4 cups chopped
Parsnips	3-4 med.	1 pound	3 cups sliced
			2 cups shredded
Peas, dried	2 cups dry	1 pound	6 servings
Peas, fresh green	1 cup	1 pound	2 servings
Peas (f)	—	10-oz. pkg.	3 servings
Peppers, sweet	1 med.	6 ounces	¾ cup chopped
Potatoes, sweet	3 med.	1 pound	3 cups sliced
Potatoes, white	3 med.	1 pound	2 cups diced or sliced
			2 cups mashed
Spinach	12 cups	1 pound	1½ cups
Spinach (f)	—	10-oz. pkg.	2-3 servings
Squash	—	1 pound	2 cups puree
Tomatoes	3 med.	1 pound	1 cup cooked
			1½ cups pulp
Turnips	3-4 med.	1 pound	3 cups sliced
			2 cups shredded
Zucchini	3 med.	1 pound	¾ cup sliced
			1 cup shredded
Canned vegetables	—	1-lb. can	3-4 servings

INGREDIENT SUBSTITUTIONS

Instead of:	Amount:	Use:
Arrowroot	1 tsp.	1 tbsp. flour
	2 tsp.	1 tbsp. cornstarch
Bacon bits	1 tbsp.	1 slice bacon
Baking powder	1 tsp.	¼ tsp. baking soda + ½ tsp. cream of tartar + ¼ tsp. cornstarch
Baking powder, double-acting	1 tsp.	1½ tsp. phosphate baking powder or 2 tsp. tartrate baking powder
Bay leaf, ground	⅛ tsp.	1 whole bay leaf
Bay leaf, crumbled	¼ tsp.	1 whole bay leaf
Beef soup base	1½ tsp.	1 bouillon cube
	1 tbsp. + 1 cup water	1 cup beef stock
	1 tsp.	1 tsp. beef extract
Butter	1 cup	1 cup margarine, or 1 cup shortening + butter flavoring, or ⅘ cup bacon drippings + ¼ cup liquid, or ⅞ cup vegetable oil
Buttermilk	1 cup	1 cup yogurt, or 1 cup warm milk + 1 tbsp. white vinegar or lemon juice; allow to stand for 10 mins.
Cake flour	1 cup	1 cup less 2 tbsp. white flour + 2 tbsp. cornstarch

Instead of:	Amount:	Use:
Cardamom, ground	½ tsp.	10 whole pods (pod removed, seeds crushed)
Chicken soup base	1½ tsp.	1 chicken bouillon cube
	1 tbsp. + 1 cup water	1 cup chicken stock
Chocolate, unsw.	1 square	3 tbsp. cocoa + 2 tsp. shortening
Chocolate, semisw.	1 square	3 tbsp. cocoa + 2 tsp. shortening + 3 tbsp. sugar
Cornstarch	1 tbsp.	2 tbsp. white flour, or 1 tbsp. arrowroot, or 1 tbsp. tapioca
Cracker crumbs	¾ cup	1 cup dry bread crumbs
Cream	1 cup	¾ cup milk plus ⅓ cup melted butter
Egg	1 egg	2 yolks for thickening
Flour, white	1 cup	1⅛ cup cake flour, or 1⅛ cup whole wheat flour, or 1⅓ cup rye flour
Garlic, minced	1 tsp.	1 clove fresh garlic
Garlic powder	½ tsp.	1 clove fresh garlic
Ginger, fresh chopped	1 tsp.	2 tsp. crystallized ginger (rinse off sugar coating) or ¼ tsp. ground ginger
Herbs, dried	1 tsp.	1 tbsp. fresh herb
Honey	1 cup	1 cup corn syrup, or 1¼ cup sugar + ¼ cup water
Horseradish, prepared	2 tbsp.	1 tbsp. dry horseradish + 1 tbsp. water
Lemon peel, dried	1 tsp.	1 tsp. fresh grated peel, or grated peel of 1 med. lemon, or ½ tsp. lemon extract

Instead of:	Amount:	Use:
Milk	1 cup	½ cup condensed milk + ½ cup water, or ⅓ cup dry milk + 1 cup water, or 1 cup buttermilk plus ½ tsp. baking soda, or ½ cup coffee creamer + 2 cups water* *Note: Not suitable for use in puddings or custards because it will not thicken well.
Mint, fresh chopped	¼ cup	1 tbsp. dried mint
Molasses	1 cup	1 cup honey
Mustard, prepared	1 tbsp.	1 tsp. dry mustard + 1 tbsp. water, vinegar, wine
Nutmeg, ground	2-3 tsp.	1 whole nutmeg grated
Onion, dry chopped	1 tsp.	1 tbsp. fresh chopped
	1 tbsp.	1 small onion or 2 tbsp. chopped fresh
Onion powder	1 tbsp.	1 medium fresh onion or 4 tbsp. chopped fresh
Orange peel, dried	1 tbsp.	1 tbsp. fresh grated, or grated peel of 1 med. orange, or 2 tsp. orange extract
Parsley, dried	1 tsp.	3 tsp. fresh chopped
Pepper, green, dried	1 tbsp.	3 tbsp. chopped fresh
Sour cream, cultured	1 cup	1 cup yogurt, or 6 oz. cream cheese + liquid to make 1 cup, 6 oz. cottage cheese pureed in blender with 1 tsp. lemon juice, 1 cup buttermilk

Instead of:	Amount:	Use:
Sour milk	1 cup	1 cup yogurt, or 1 cup warm milk +1 tbsp. white vinegar or lemon juice; allow to stand for 10 mins.
Sugar	1 cup	1 cup molasses + ½ tsp. baking soda, or 1 cup honey + ½ tsp. baking soda (in either case reduce liquid in recipe by ¼ cup)
Tomatoes, canned	2 cups	2½ cups peeled fresh tomatoes seasoned and cooked for 10 mins.
Vanilla bean	1-in. piece	1 tsp. pure vanilla extract

In making substitutions, and these are just to give you some ideas about what can be done, there are basically two things to keep in mind: chemistry and flavor. If the ingredient you are substituting is similar in chemical structure (liquid for liquid, acid for acid, and so forth) you should have no problems.

Similarly, if the flavors are compatible all will be well. This is another area where experience is the best teacher of all. Don't be afraid of failing ... if you are short of an ingredient and need to make a substitution, make the best guess you can and see what happens. Even if your dish is a total failure from a classical point of view, you can always say, with a straight face and complete sincerity, "Don't you think this has an interesting taste—texture—color? It's something I've developed myself."

MEASURING THINGS BY VOLUME

tsp.	teaspoon
tbsp.	tablespoon
speck	less than ⅛ tsp.
pinch	approx. ⅛ tsp.
⅛ tsp.	half of ¼ tsp.
60 drops	1 tsp.
3 tsp.	1 tbsp.
⅓ of 1 tbsp.	1 tsp.
½ of 1 tbsp.	1½ tsp.
½ of 3 tbsp.	1 tbsp. + 1½ tsp.
⅓ of 5 tbsp.	1 tbsp. + 2 tsp.
½ of 5 tbsp.	2 tbsp. + 1½ tsp.
⅓ of 7 tbsp.	2 tbsp. + 1 tsp.
½ of 7 tbsp.	3 tbsp. + 1½ tsp.
⅛ cup	2 tbsp.
¼ cup	4 tbsp.
⅓ cup	5 tbsp. + 1 tsp.
½ cup	8 tbsp.
⅔ cup	10 tbsp. + 2 tsp.
¾ cup	12 tbsp.
⅞ cup	1 cup less 2 tbsp.
1 cup	16 tbsp.
⅓ of ¼ cup	1 tbsp. + 1 tsp.
⅓ of ⅓ cup	1 tbsp. + 2¼ tsp.
⅓ of ½ cup	2 tbsp. + 2 tsp.
⅓ of ⅔ cup	3 tbsp. + 1½ tsp.
⅓ of ¾ cup	¼ cup
½ of ¼ cup	⅛ cup or 2 tbsp.
½ of ⅓ cup	2 tbsp. + 2 tsp.
½ of ½ cup	¼ cup
½ of ⅔ cup	⅓ cup
½ of ¾ cup	6 tbsp.

1 gill	½ cup
1 pint	2 cups
1 quart	2 pints or 4 cups
1 gallon	4 quarts
1 peck	8 quarts (dry measure)
1 bushel	4 pecks (dry measure)

LIQUID MEASUREMENTS

1 ounce liquid measure	⅛ cup or 2 tbsp.
2 ounces liquid measure	¼ cup
3 ounces liquid measure	¼ cup + 2 tbsp.
4 ounces liquid measure	½ cup
5 ounces liquid measure	½ cup + 2 tbsp.
6 ounces liquid measure	¾ cup
7 ounces liquid measure	1 cup less 2 tbsp.
8 ounces liquid measure	1 cup
16 ounces liquid measure	1 pint
32 ounces liquid measure	1 quart
128 ounces liquid measure	1 gallon

AVOIRDUPOIS WEIGHTS

27^{11}⁄$_{32}$ grains	1 dram
16 drams	1 ounce
16 ounces	1 pound

METRIC MEASUREMENTS

⅛ tsp.	.5 milliliters (ml)
¼ tsp.	1.5 milliliters
½ tsp.	3 milliliters

¾ tsp.	4 milliliters
1 tsp.	5 milliliters
1 tbsp.	15 milliliters
2 tbsp. (1 oz. liquid meas.)	30 milliliters
¼ cup	60 milliliters
⅓ cup	85 milliliters
½ cup	125 milliliters
⅔ cup	170 milliliters
¾ cup	180 milliliters
1 cup	240 milliliters
2 cups	480 milliliters
3 cups	720 milliliters
4 cups	960 milliliters

COMMON METRIC PACKAGE-SIZE CONVERSIONS

1 tsp. dry measure	4 grams
1 tsp. liquid measure	5 grams
1 ounce	28.35 grams
3.57 ounces	100 grams
¼ pound (4 oz.)	113 grams
½ pound (8 oz.)	225 grams
¾ pound (12 oz.)	340 grams
1 pound	450 grams
1½ pounds	675 grams
2 pounds	900 grams
3 pounds	1.4 kilogram
10 oz. (many frozen foods)	280 grams
10½ oz. (canned soups)	294 grams
15 ounces	425 grams
16 ounces	450 grams
1 lb. 24 oz. (lg. can size)	850 grams

1 microgram	1/1,000,000 gram
1,000 micrograms	1 milligram
1 milligram	1/1,000 gram

1,000 milligrams	1 gram
100 milliliters	1 deciliter (dl)
10 deciliters	1 liter (l)
1,000 grams	1 kilogram

The Cook's Guide to Metric Measurement Conversion

If the recipe calls for:	Multiply by:	To find:
teaspoons	5	milliliters
tablespoons	15	milliliters
fluid ounces	30	milliliters
cups	0.24	liters
pints	0.47	liters
quarts	0.94	liters
ounces (by weight)	28	grams
pounds	0.45	kilograms

A rule of thumb is that a kilogram is "a little more" than two pounds. For ease of figuring it is probably more convenient to round the conversions off, for instance figuring an ounce to be equivalent to about 25 grams. In cooking, absolute precision is, fortunately, not required or even desired ... a good approximation will do very nicely.

European recipes are almost always given in metric measures. If you are following a recipe from a British or other European cookbook, you can use the following table to convert those metric amounts (which are given by metric weight, not volume) into the volume amounts that American cooks are accustomed to using.

CONVERSION TABLE FOR COMMON FOODS
FROM METRIC TO AMERICAN

Ingredient	Metric Measure	American Measure
Baking powder	4 grams	1 tsp.
	30 grams	2½ tbsp.
Bread crumbs, dry	90 grams	1 cup
Bread crumbs, fresh	45 grams	1 cup
Butter, margarine,	15 grams	1 tbsp.
or shortening	125 grams	½ cup
	500 grams	2 cups
Cheese	500 grams	1.1+ pound
Cheese, grated	100 grams	1 cup
Coffee, ground	85 grams	1 cup
Cornstarch	10 grams	1 tbsp.
Cream of tartar	3-4 grams	1 tsp.
Flour, all-purpose	35 grams	¼ cup
	70 grams	½ cup
	142 grams	1 cup
	500 grams	3½ cups
Flour, cake, sifted	30 grams	¼ cup
	60 grams	½ cup
	120 grams	1 cup
Gelatin, granulated	8 grams	1 tbsp.
Gelatin, sheets	6 med sheets	2 tbsp. grains
Pepper, ground	7.5 grams	1 tbsp.
Raisins, seedless	10 grams	1 tbsp.
	160 grams	1 cup
	500 grams	3 cups
Rice	240 grams	1 cup
Salt	15 grams	1 tbsp.
Spices, ground	2.5 grams	1 tsp.
	15 grams	2 tbsp.
Sugar, brown	10 grams	1 tbsp.
	40 grams	¼ cup
	160 grams	1 cup
Sugar, granulated	5 grams	1 tsp.

Ingredient	Metric Measure	American Measure
	15 grams	1 tbsp.
	60 grams	¼ cup
	240 grams	1 cup
Sugar, powdered	35 grams	¼ cup
	140 grams	1 cup

The British and some of the Commonwealth countries use a liquid measure known as the Imperial standard. As a basic unit for comparison, consider the American pint at 16 liquid ounces while the Imperial pint is 20 liquid ounces. Other measurement units are as follows:

2 U.S. pints	1¾ Imperial pints
1¼ U.S. pints	1 Imperial pint
1 U.S. pint	¾ Imperial pint

Liquors have a set of measurements all their own.

1 pony	¾ ounce
1 shot	1 ounce
1 jigger	1½ ounces
1 split	usually about 6 ounces
1 fifth	25.6 ounces, or
	750 milliliters, or
	⅕ gallon
1 gallon	128 ounces

Champagne carries the liquor measurements on further:

1 magnum	2 quarts
1 jeroboam	.8 gallon (1.6 magnums)
1 rehoboam	3 magnums
1 methuselah	4 magnums
1 salmanazar	6 magnums
1 balthazar	8 magnums
1 nebuchadnezzar	10 magnums

AVERAGE CAN SIZES

Can Size	Weight	Volume	Typical Use
6 oz.	6 oz.	¾ cup	frozen juice concentrate
6½ oz.	6½ oz.	½ + cup	fish, seafood, meats
8 oz.	8 oz.	1 cup	fruits, vegetables
No. 1	10½ oz.	1⅓ cups	condensed soups
No. 300	15 oz.	1¾ cups	pork and beans, etc.
No. 1½	16 oz.	2 cups	pie fillings
No. 303	17 oz.	2 + cups	ready-to-serve soups
No. 2	20 oz.	2½ cups	fruits, vegetables
No. 2½	28 oz.	3½ cups	large fruits, tomatoes
No. 5	46 oz.	5¾ cups	most fruit/vegetable juices
No. 10	106 oz.	13 cups	institutional size

DECIMAL-TO-OUNCE CONVERSION

Bar-code (computer-generated) pricing labels often use the decimal system instead of ounces to compute the weight and price. The conversion is made by multiplying the decimal number by 16 (number of ounces in a pound).

If the label says:	The weight in ounces is:
.10	1.6 ounces
.15	2.4 ounces
.20	3.2 ounces
.25 (¼ pound)	4 ounces
.30	4.8 ounces
.33 (⅓ pound)	5.3 ounces
.35	5.6 ounces
.40	6.4 ounces
.45	7.2 ounces
.50 (½ pound)	8 ounces

If the label says:	The weight in ounces is:
.55	8.8 ounces
.60	9.6 ounces
.65	10.4 ounces
.67 (⅔ pound)	10.7 ounces
.70	11.2 ounces
.75 (¾ pound)	12 ounces
.80	12.8 ounces
.85	13.6 ounces
.90	14.4 ounces
.95	15.2 ounces

Finally, you should be aware that any recipe can be adjusted to serve any number. The way to do it is to calculate what the U.S. Navy Cooks' Schools call a working factor. This example will give you an illustration of what to do:

If you need to serve 35 and the recipe is designed to serve 6, divide 35 by 6 and you will get 5.83, which is your working factor for that recipe and those servings. Next multiply the quantity of each ingredient called for by the working factor (e.g., if it calls for 2 cups of something, $2 \times 5.83 = 11.66$ cups, round the number and use 11½ cups; if your recipe is in weights, do the same thing, 1½ lbs. called for times 5.83 equals 8.74 lbs. rounded to 8¾ pounds). This method works to reduce the number of servings for large recipes as well. Seasonings should be adjusted according to taste, however, not simply multiplied or divided.

CHAPTER 4

What Every Cook Needs

What every cook needs are things to cook and things to cooks with—in other words, food and food preparation tools.

Because each cook has individualized preferences in both areas, it is unlikely that an absolutely standard list for either could be developed. There are, however, certain elements of both that are so basic that they can form a kitchen checklist any cook can use.

In this chapter we will look at the various types of equipment that a cook needs ... how the pieces are sized and made, which pieces are essential and which are optional depending on storage space and use, and how to care for your kitchen equipment to make sure it gives maximum useful life. We will also look at the pantry and come up with a shopping list that is a starting point for all kinds of food preparation.

BATTERIE DE CUISINE

The French have a wonderful phrase, *batterie de cuisine,* which strictly speaking means "kitchen equipment" but calls up a far wider range of images than that simple phrase. This doesn't mean that your approach to food preparation need take on the look of a military campaign, but it does imply a certain level of organization and preparedness that, while not strictly necessary, will save you time and energy in the kitchen.

POTS AND PANS FOR STOVE-TOP COOKING

Any kitchenware sales area will display dozens of examples of pots and pans ... different sizes, shapes, and materials. When these individual examples are sorted out, however, you will find that there are only a few basic types represented.

Saucepans have one rigid handle extending out from the wall of the pan.

Saucepots are most commonly found among large-size pots and have two U-shaped handles attached across from each other and near the top.

Skillets may be said to be a cousin of the saucepan since they have a rigid handle on one side only. They have, however, much more shallow sides than the saucepan and usually (although not necessarily) have a greater diameter.

Kettles usually are large containers and have one semicircular carrying handle (or bail) that is fastened through openings on each side of the kettle. This arrangement allows the handle to be extended above the kettle when being carried or to rest on the edge of it when stationary.

For stove-top cooking a kitchen should have at least these:

Double boiler with a lid, which is made up of two saucepans that fit together and can be used either together or separately.

Small skillet, five to seven inches in diameter, a tight-fitting lid not essential but very useful.

Large skillet, nine to twelve inches in diameter with a tight-fitting lid.

Large saucepan, saucepot, or kettle big enough to hold at least four quarts of liquid (for soups, stews, preserve-making), with lid.

Once these essentials are available, the cook can start to branch out and add other items as requirements, storage space, and budget allow. The next level of purchases might include:

Steamer, a three-piece unit similar to the double boiler except that the top pot has holes in its bottom that allow the steam from the water which, boils in the bottom part, to rise and cook the food.

Medium-sized skillet to give the cook a range of skillet sizes from five to seven, eight to ten, and twelve to fourteen inches.

Very large saucepot (twelve to fourteen quarts).

PANS AND CASSEROLES FOR BAKING

The major design difference between utensils used on top of the stove and those used in the oven is the style of handle used. Stove-top utensils have handles that extend well away from the body of the pan (away from the heat of the burner), while pans meant for oven use have handles formed as extensions of the top edge of the body of the utensil.

Square or Rectangular Baking Pan or Dish is used for cakes and other baked goods but can also be used for casseroles. The walls are straight, about 1½ inches high. The design allows square servings to be cut.

Round Baking Pan or Dish is also used for both baked goods and casseroles, but the servings tend to be wedge-shaped for the former and scooped out for the latter. The walls of the pan are straight and about 1½ inches high.

Muffin Pans allow small cakes to be baked. The individual pan usually bakes six or eight muffins or cup cakes. The walls of the individual cups are slightly slanted for easy removal of the cakes.

Tube Pan is a round pan whose product is doughnut-shaped because of the tube that extends from the bottom of the pan to the top. The wall of a tube pan slants very slightly outward so that the bottom is a little wider than the top for easy removal from the pan and a more graceful appearance when served.

Cookie Sheets are large (usually around 12×18 inches, but can be bigger or smaller) rectangular trays with very shallow sides or no sides at all.

Pie Pans are round, usually about nine inches in diameter, and have a slightly sloped wall.

Bread Pans come in a variety of sizes, but one that is about $9 \times 5 \times 3$ inches will produce a "standard" loaf that will weigh about a pound when baked.

For basic baking projects, the kitchen should have at least:

Two eight-inch square cake pans

Two eight-inch round pans

Two muffin pans

One tube pan (thirteen inches in diameter is a good size)

One pie pan

Two bread pans

Your supermarket carries a wide variety of pans made of heavy-gauge aluminum foil. Although they probably will not take the place of standard metal pans, they are certainly usable in certain circumstances ... for baked goods that will be frozen, for instance, or for bakery items that you intend to give to someone else.

Beyond the basic baking equipment, and leaving aside the many size variations for each of the pans that are listed above, there are a vast number of specialty baking pans that beckon the cook:

Cake pans: Bundt pans (with fluted sides and a slightly rounded bottom), springform pans (with a removable bottom, most commonly used for cheesecakes), specially shaped pans (for holidays and special celebrations), tiny pans for baking petit fours and other small cakes in a variety of shapes.

Muffin pans are available in several sizes, not only in the number of cakes that can be baked at one time but also in the size of the cake produced.

Baking sheets can be used not only for cookies but also for making the cake for a jelly roll. These flat sheets are also useful for toasting baked goods under the oven broiler.

Bread pans are available for making individual loaves, cylindrical loaves, round loaves, and fluted loaves, of brioche for instance.

Casseroles can be round, square, or rectangular, with or without a cover, with flared sides or with straight sides that can also be used for soufflés ... virtually any container that is oven-safe can be used for a casserole. Individual servings can be baked in custard cups of various shapes or in any small container that is ovenproof.

The following table will help judge what size pan to use for the volume of the food being baked.

When the recipe calls for a 4-cup baking dish use:
  9-inch pie pan, or
  8 × 1¼-inch round cake pan, or
  7¾ × 3⅝ × 2¼-inch loaf pan.

When the recipe calls for a 6-cup baking dish use:
  9 × 12 rectangular cake pan, or
  10-inch pie pan.

When the recipe calls for an 8-cup baking dish use:
  8 × 8 × 2-inch square cake pan, or
  11 × 7 × 1½-inch rectangular cake pan, or
  9 × 5 × 3-inch loaf pan.

When the recipe calls for a 10-inch baking dish use:
  9 × 9 × 2-inch square cake pan, or
  12 × 7½ × 1-inch baking pan, or
  15 × 10 × 1-inch jelly-roll pan.

When the recipe serves a large group use:
  12½ × 8½ × 2-inch rectangular baking pan (holds 12 cups), or
  13 × 9 × 2-inch baking pan (holds 15 cups), or
  14 × 10½ × 2½-inch baking pan (holds 19 cups).

Specialty baking pans also hold varying volumes:

Tube pans:
  7½ × 3-inch Bundt pan   6 cups
  9 × 3½-inch Bundt pan   9 cups
  10 × 4-inch Bundt pan   12 cups
  9 × 3-inch angel food tube pan   12 cups
  10 × 4-inch angel food tube pan   18 cups

Springform pans:
  8 × 3-inch springform   12 cups
  9 × 3-inch springform   16 cups

Molds:

8½ × 2¼-inch ring mold	4 cups
9¼ × 2¾-inch ring mold	8 cups
7 × 5½ × 4-inch oval "melon" mold	6 cups

Others:

9½ × 3¼-inch brioche pan	8 cups
5 × 10-inch cornbread-stick pan	2 cups

Another "specialty" occurs when you are confronted with metric pan sizes ... below is a conversion table to bring the meters and liters into your cooking vocabulary.

1 inch	2.5 centimeters (cm)
8 inch square	20 cm square
13 × 9 × 1½-inch	33 × 23 × 4 cm
10 × 6 × 2-inch	25 × 15 × 5 cm
12 × 7½ × 1½-inch	30 × 18 × 4 cm
9 × 5 × 3-inch (loaf pan)	23 × 13 × 88 cm
10 inch (skillet)	25 cm
12 inch (skillet)	30 cm
1 quart (baking dish)	1 liter
5-6 cups (ring mold)	1.5 liters

SMALL ELECTRIC APPLIANCES

No cook actually requires small appliances but there is no question that they can make a cook's life much easier. There are new appliances being introduced constantly, but some are such classics that they form a central core of useful additions to your "batterie de cuisine."

Blender. One of those appliances for which there is no real substitute, a blender is usable in many more ways than in whipping up drinks.

Electric Skillet with lid. Available in a variety of sizes, but if you are to have one that will be usable for the greatest variety of dishes it should be about 12 inches across.

Mixer. A small electric hand mixer is extremely useful in the kitchen. It can be your only powered mixer, or it can be used in conjunction with a large counter mixer. Each of them performs a special range of jobs.

Toaster or Toaster Oven. Of the two the latter is the more versatile but also uses more space and duplicates jobs sometimes better handled by the oven in your stove.

Next we come to a category of appliances that are very useful no matter what number you cook for, but the cook has to decide whether their usefulness is enough to warrant the amount of storage space they require when not in use.

Coffee Maker. Even if you are not a coffee drinker yourself, you will need some sort of coffee maker. There is a wide variety of coffee makers around, both electric and those that are used on a stove burner. The kind of coffee you prefer, the amount of coffee you and those you cook for drink, and the space available will be the determinant factors in your choice.

Deep Fryer. These are available in a variety of sizes and do their job extremely well, with much less mess and more safety than an open kettle on top of the stove.

Ice Cream Freezer. Although this is in a list of electric appliances, a ice cream freezer may or may not be electrically powered. The capacity should be in line with the number who will be enjoying the ice cream. There are some miniature, but quite good, freezers that make just a pint at a time.

Microwave Oven. The microwave oven is in a gray area between major and small appliance, but its usefulness is undeniable. Although there are some dishes better prepared by other means, the microwave can do some extraordinary cooking jobs in very little time. There are three considerations regarding a microwave in your kitchen: it will be relatively expensive (will you use it enough to justify the cost?), it will take space (do you have room for it?), and it is most useful if you have at least some of the specialized cooking pieces (both cost and storage space are involved here). If you decide to buy a microwave, spend time learning how to make the best use of all of its potentials as well as its areas of inadequacy.

Popcorn Popper. There is no denying that popcorn poppers are for the most part big, bulky, and hard to store ... but most families are glad to give up storage space for the appliance that produces such a favorite snack. (Hot-air poppers only take up about as much space as a blender, but many people prefer the flavor of conventionally popped corn.)

Pressure Cooker. Pressure cookers are primarily time-savers, in that they can cook food under pressure in only a small portion of the time it would take with normal cooking methods. They allow for better vitamin retention because the food is cooked quickly. They cook less-tender cuts of meat in less time and thereby are energy-efficient. Great care must be used with pressure cookers and manufacturer's directions must be followed exactly. The pressure gauge should be periodically calibrated. For home-canning of non-acid foods, a pressure canner is essential. The pressure cooker can also be used as a simple covered saucepan if the pressure gauge is not used.

Slow Cooker. These are available in a variety of sizes. Slow cookers are especially useful for the cook who is away at a job all day ... there are a surprising number of dinner main dishes that can be prepared in the morning and be nicely ready to serve in the evening.

Waffle Iron. Often you will find a waffle iron that is bifunctional: the grids are reversible and you can use one side to do traditional waffles and the other to grill (open or closed). These double-duty irons are square and produce four square waffle sections. Conventional round waffle irons are usually single purpose.

With the essentials and not-entirely-essentials covered, there is an incredible range of "labor-saving" appliances available for your consideration. *Labor-saving* is in quotes because some of them seem to take more effort to use than a manual tool unless you are preparing meals for a very large group.

Can Openers. If you have the space and open many cans, this appliance might be considered. One advantage is that most of them have a magnet that keeps the lid out of the food when freed from the edge of the can.

Electric Knives and Electric Slicers. If you slice large amounts of food, particularly meat, one of these might be of value.

Food Processor. Useful for a variety of kitchen jobs from grating cheese to kneading bread; however, most of the things it can do can be done more simply and just as well with hand tools in one case or with a heavy-duty counter mixer in the other. There is usually no need to have both a heavy-duty mixer and a food processor, but which you choose is a personal matter.

Ice Crushers. These small appliances can be very useful in the summer or for entertaining but are usually rather messy to use.

Special Cookers. There are a variety of cooking devices that are meant to be used with one particular food ... egg cookers, crepe grills, frankfurter cookers, and rice cookers are some that come to mind. Their value to you depends completely on the amount of use they will get in your particular kitchen.

An interesting development in the past few years has been the availability of appliances that are attached under cabinets and thereby take up no counter space. Obviously appliance designers and manufacturers have heeded the comments from the many cooks who work in small kitchens with counter space that is limited and precious. Appliances as large as microwave ovens and as small as electric can openers are available in this style, and if you are among the many with restricted kitchen space, take a look at these.

HAND TOOLS FOR THE KITCHEN

There are some food-preparation jobs that are simply best done with a hand tool. As with everything else in your "batterie de cuisine," some of these tools are essential, some are optional, and some are frankly frivolous.

Knives are an absolute essential and are so important that they will be described in a separate section following this.

Since most hand tools are used for some limited purpose, the lists of basics will be arranged according to the place and purpose of their use.

Most kitchens have at least a few cabinet drawers available for storing small tools. Insofar as possible, you might consider setting each of the drawers up for a special purpose: a drawer for tools used in stove-top cooking, one for tools used in baking, one for tools that are not used as often as those in the first two categories, and so on.

However you arrange them for your convenience, the tools listed here are the ones you will probably want to start with:

Spatulas: At least two, one with a broad blade (pancake or egg turner) and one with a narrow blade (spreader).

Measuring Spoons: They are so inexpensive it is worth buying two sets, one to measure dry ingredients and another to measure liquid ingredients.

Measuring Cups: Again, it is extremely useful to have one set of four for dry ingredients and either another set for liquid ingredients or a glass one-cup measure (also consider a larger measuring utensil that will hold two, three, or four cups and can double as a small mixing bowl).

Spoons: At least two large metal spoons, one for general mixing and the other slotted to use for draining off liquids. If you use cookware that is Teflon-coated or has some other sensitive surface, you should also have a selection of high-temperature-resistant plastic or wooden spoons to use so that the Teflon surface is not damaged.

Forks: One fork that can be used for turning and holding food when cutting should be sufficient.

Can Opener: Buying the best one you can afford will protect you from a great deal of frustration in the long term.

Mixing Bowls: Usually come in nesting sets of three or four bowls. Plastic, glass, or stainless steel are all available and all suitable.

Cutting Board: Whatever size you can store easily. It is very useful to have more than one, a large one and a small one, perhaps of two different materials. (See the section on wooden and plastic implements later in this chapter.)

Grater: At least one flat grater with a variety of openings is needed. Beyond that there are several different styles depending on your use. The cylindrical grater that turns in a metal container (often called a Mouli grater) is wonderful for cooks who tend to grate their fingers as well as the food.

Rolling Pin: Hard maple makes good rolling pins and they are available either with or without handles. If you buy one with handles, be sure they turn freely. If you do a lot of pastry baking, you might also like a pastry cloth and a knitted cover that fits over the rolling pin to prevent sticking.

Cooling Racks: A cook can manage with just one but two are very useful to have. Use not only for cooling baked goods but also for keeping anything hot from scorching your countertops.

Vegetable Parer: There are two types, one that you can use in one direction only (and usually is combined with a corer) and one that you can use bidirectionally. One of your preference should be sufficient.

Whisks: If you buy just one, get one that has wires about five inches long and can be used for several purposes. Beyond this absolute minimum, one large and one small conventional whisk and one that has a flat bottom would all be useful. Whisks may or may not substitute for an eggbeater, but if you have an electric hand mixer and whisks, you surely can manage nicely without an eggbeater.

Kitchen Shears: Get a sturdy pair that are dishwasher-safe and you will find you use them often.

Storage Containers: As elaborate as a matched set with covers or as simple as former peanut-butter jars, you will need about two with a quart capacity, two with a pint capacity, and three or four to hold small amounts.

Sieves: Two are enough for most purposes—a small one that can be hand-held and a large colander.

Once this basic collection is safely stored in your kitchen drawers and cabinets, it is time to think about optional equipment. Here the individual cook's preference and cooking style

definitely affect what is bought, but once again you will find
listed below some options to consider:

> Pastry blender
> Citrus juice extractor
> Flour sifter
> Serving/utility trays
> Cookie cutters or cookie press
> Vegetable masher
> Teakettle
> Food chopper/grinder (if electric appliance is
>   not used)
> Scales (to weigh by ounce up to at least five
>   pounds)
> Thermometers for oven, freezer, candy, deep
>   fat, and meat
> Funnels (small and large openings)
> Baster
> Corkscrew
> Garlic press
> Ladle
> Meat mallet
> Tongs

Beyond these optionals lies the world of the "not-
necessary-but-great-to-have" ... you have only to visit your
nearest display of kitchen gadgets to find lots that would be
fun (and useful) to have. Only your budget and storage facilities limit the number you can add to your collection.

EXPENDABLE SUPPLIES

There are some kitchen essentials that are not really tools,
nor are they foods. They have a limited purpose and life span,
but no kitchen would be able to function without them.

Wraps: Plastic, foil, and waxed paper; each has its own purpose.

Towels: Paper towels are indispensable. Try to locate the holder between the sink and the stove if possible.

Kitchen Linens: Dishcloths, sponges, dishtowels, pot holders, and work aprons all fall into this category.

Brushes: A sink brush for dishes, one for vegetables, and another narrow one for bottles are essential; lots of other special-purpose brushes are also available.

Storage Bags: Plastic bags, whether saved from shopping trips or those with watertight closures, serve many purposes.

Pot Scrubbers: Both metallic and plastic.

WHAT ARE KITCHEN TOOLS MADE OF . . .

As you purchase and use the implements in your "batterie de cuisine," it is valuable to know something about the materials used in making them. This knowledge will not only make sure you are getting value for your money when you make your purchase, but also will ensure that your kitchen tools last a long time.

STAINLESS STEEL.   Stainless steel and aluminum are probably the materials you will find used most often in manufacturing kitchen utensils. Stainless steel is produced by replacing some of the carbon in steel with chromium and nickel. Steel must be at least 11½ percent chromium in order to qualify as stainless. Most stainless steel is designated 18-8, which means it contains 18 parts chromium and 8 parts nickel.

   Advantages of stainless steel: It does not dent easily. It is corrosion-resistant and does not scratch or pit easily. It is also easy to clean and polish.

Disadvantages of stainless steel: It does not conduct heat quickly or evenly. To overcome this problem, some manufacturers clad the bottom of the pans with copper or aluminum, or make a sandwich with a central portion of a good heat-conducting metal and outer layers of stainless. Unless the other metals are added in significant amounts, however, the conductivity of the stainless is not greatly improved.

Care of stainless steel: Stainless steel is dishwasher-safe. It may be cleaned with detergent and a stiff bristle brush or with a plastic scrubber. Avoid abrasive cleaners or scouring pads because the abrasive material will scratch the polished surface and create dull spots. Special stainless steel polishes are available.

ALUMINUM.   By itself aluminum is a soft metal and so it is normally compounded with another metal (often magnesium or copper) to increase its tensile strength. Aluminum used in kitchen utensils is either cast (making it without seams for "waterless" cooking, pressure cookers, and such) or rolled and drawn. The rolling process tends to compress the aluminum and make its surface harder and less likely to dent. The rolled sheets are then formed into the shape of the desired utensil. Products made from sheet aluminum can be bent and dented but not broken if dropped; products made of cast aluminum can break upon impact.

Advantages of aluminum: Aluminum's greatest asset is its ability to conduct heat quickly and evenly. It is lightweight for its strength, which makes it particularly suitable for pans that will be heavy with ingredients (stockpots, for instance).

Disadvantages of aluminum: Aluminum's greatest asset (excellent heat conductivity) can turn into a liability if the aluminum used in making a pan is too thin, because the high conductivity can lead to scorching and sticking.

Aluminum reacts with chemicals in food and water to cause the surface to pit. The cooking surface of aluminum pans will also darken as a result of contact with certain foods (egg-based sauces, some vegetables). Anodized aluminum will do neither of these things, because the naturally occurring "pores" in the metal are sealed with an electrolytic process.

Care of aluminum: Avoid quick temperature changes, do not add cold water to a hot pan. In general use a moderate cooking temperature because very high temperatures can cause warping, especially in pans made of thin metal. The use of wooden tools will prevent marking on internal surfaces. Dishwashers can cause aluminum to discolor, so it is better to hand-wash aluminum pieces. Clean with detergent and plastic scrubber. If pan has darkened inside, it can be bleached out if you fill it with acidulated water (one part white vinegar to three parts water) and simmer for about fifteen minutes.

CAST-IRON WARE.   One of the very oldest materials used to make cooking implements, cast iron is simply what its name says: iron that is cast into shapes appropriate for cooking implements. If you look at a piece of cast-iron ware under magnification, you can see the rough surface of the manufactured product. It is because of this "jaggedness" that it is necessary to season the pan before using and occasionally later. (A seasoning method is described below.) Cast iron is best when it is used for slow, long-term cooking. It does not lend itself to the preparation of light sauces and other delicate foods.

Advantages of cast iron: Cast iron absorbs heat slowly and distributes it evenly over the surface of the metal. It is particularly good for baking or surface cooking that takes little water and long amounts of time. It will retain heat long after removed from the heat source. Small amounts of iron are absorbed into the food being cooked, which supplements the normal intake of iron (particularly true when acid foods such as tomato-based dishes are cooked slowly in cast iron).

Disadvantages of cast iron: The biggest disadvantage has got to be that it is heavy to handle. It also will rust easily if not stored properly. Cast iron must be cleaned carefully and seasoned properly before the first use and occasionally thereafter.

Seasoning cast iron: Whether the piece is marked "pre-seasoned" or not, it is a wise idea to season the utensil yourself. It is simple to do.

First scour the new piece of cast-iron equipment with a stiff brush and soapy water. Do not use a detergent. Rinse the piece well and dry it thoroughly.

Pour about a tablespoon of vegetable oil into the utensil and spread it carefully over all of the cooking surfaces of the pan. Add enough additional oil to cover the bottom of the pan and put it on a burner set for moderate heat. Heat the oil until it is hot but not smoking. Remove the pan from the burner, pour the oil out, and wipe the pan with a paper towel.

If you do this much you will give your pan a reasonably good preparation for use, but for the final touch you may add a little fresh oil and put the pan in a low temperature oven (no more than 200 degrees F) for about two hours. Remove the pan, let it cool, and wipe all remaining oil from the surface.

The seasoning process prevents rusting and also keeps foods from taking on a metallic taste.

Care of cast iron: The first rule is that you never use detergents or abrasive scouring pads, and you should never wash cast-iron pieces in a dishwasher. Any of these things will remove the seasoning and make the metal vulnerable to rusting again.

You also should never pour cold water into a hot pan, because the temperature differential can cause tiny hairline cracks to form, which will eventually cause the pan to leak.

The best way to care for cast iron is to clean it either with plain warm water and a brush, or with soapy water. Once in a while it is not a bad idea to wipe a warm pan with a piece of waxed paper or a tiny bit of oil on a piece of paper towel. It is also a good idea to put a piece of paper towel between the pans if you store them in a nested stack.

Enameled cast iron: Some manufacturers produce cast-iron ware that is clad in enamel. This added surface does not react with foods, nor does it affect the cooking characteristics of the cast iron. It is, however, sensitive to chipping and cracking and must be handled rather carefully. Only the least abrasive of liquid scrubbing solutions should be used. The interior surface of the pans will usually darken as they are used, but this is an appearance factor only and does not affect their cooking characteristics.

COPPER.   Copper is undoubtedly the most beautiful of the materials used to make cooking utensils. Its mellow gleam turns any kitchen into a warm and wonderful place. It is a superb metal for cooking, as people have known for centuries. Copper pieces can be forged, drawn, stamped, or hammered. Because bare copper reacts adversely with some foods, most copper pieces are lined with a less reactive metal such as tin, nickel, or stainless steel.

Advantages of copper: Among metals most commonly used to make cooking equipment, copper is the most efficient conductor of heat. It evenly distributes heat as soon as it is placed on or in a heat source, and cools just as quickly when it is removed. Because the heat is so evenly distributed, food may be cooked at lower temperatures. (The melting point of tin is 450 degrees F, so if the copper piece is tin-lined, it is especially important to keep cooking temperatures low.) Copper utensils are extremely durable and, because of their sentimental as well as intrinsic value, are often handed down from generation to generation.

Disadvantages of copper: Copper requires special care to keep its beauty. Because copper pieces are expensive it is very important to select carefully both for usefulness and for construction.

Care of copper: You should never heat an empty copper container or allow one to boil dry. It is best to use only wooden or heat-resistant plastic tools when cooking with copper so that the interior is not scratched. You should never use abrasive cleaners on copper or put copper in the dishwasher.

Use a mild detergent and plastic scrubber to clean the interior. The copper itself should be cleaned with a copper cleaner, of which there are a variety available. Be aware, however, that copper polishing powders contain a material that will eventually abrade the surface. It is better, albeit slower, to use a paste polish and a soft cloth, following the directions given with the polish.

Unlined copper. Some utensils are made only of copper, but they are designed for a specific purpose and not for general use.

Copper beating bowls used for beating egg whites are left unlined in order to take advantage of the fact that when a metal whisk is used to beat the egg whites, an electrostatic charge builds up as metal contacts metal. This charge allows more air to be beaten into the whites and can increase their volume by as much as one-third. The copper has a stabilizing effect on the beaten whites, as well, so that it is not usually necessary to add cream of tartar to keep them from falling.

Before each use, an unlined bowl should be washed well with soapy water, rinsed with clear water, and then rinsed again with a strong acidulated-water mixture (vinegar and water, half and half), and finally given another water rinse.

Removing lacquer coating from copperware. Some copper pieces come with a protective lacquer coating that prevents them from tarnishing between time of manufacture and time of sale. This coating must be removed before the piece is used.

To do so, fill a pan (large enough to submerge the piece) with water and add ¼ cup baking soda to each gallon of hot water. Bring the mixture to a boil, then lower the heat till the water just simmers. Very slowly lower the lacquered piece into the water and simmer gently for about twenty minutes. When you remove the piece from the water the coating should either have been dissolved or should easily peel off. Wash and dry the piece carefully and the pan is ready for use.

If you don't have a kettle large enough to submerge the copper piece, you may also use a soft cloth saturated with acetone to dissolve the lacquer. Be aware that acetone is extremely flammable and you must use caution. Keep it and the cleaning cloth completely away from any heat source. Read and follow directions given with the acetone carefully. When the lacquer has been removed, wash and dry the piece carefully before using.

CARBON STEEL. Carbon steel is another metal used for special-purpose utensils, especially those that need to be heated quickly and kept at a high heat, such as woks and omelet pans. The steel is rolled and formed to make the pan and usually the handle is made of steel as well, so care must be used in handling it.

Advantages of carbon steel: Carbon-steel pans heat quickly and evenly and are ideal for very high temperature cooking.

Disadvantages of carbon steel: Carbon-steel pans rust easily and must be initially seasoned and periodically seasoned to keep food from sticking.

Seasoning carbon steel: The seasoning process is similar to that used for cast iron. Clean the pan with soapy water, rinse, and dry thoroughly. Add enough oil to lightly cover the bottom of the pan and heat until the oil almost, but not quite, smokes. Remove the pan from the heat and let it cool slowly. Wipe out oil with a paper towel.

You can prevent your next omelet from sticking if, each time you finish using your omelet pan, you sprinkle a little salt on the pan and rub it around with a paper towel moistened with a little oil. The salt acts as a very gentle abrasive and removes any residue, and the oil reseasons the pan. Be sure that all salt is removed before pan is stored.

Care of carbon steel: Do not use detergents or abrasives to clean carbon steel. It should never be cleaned in the dishwasher. Whenever possible simply wipe out carefully with a paper towel. Do not clean with water any oftener than is really necessary. If stored in nested stacks, put a piece of paper towel between pans.

POTTERY, CERAMIC, AND EARTHENWARE. Clay is the common ingredient in these various types of cookware. The differences between them arise in the way in which the clay is baked and the sorts of surfaces that are applied.

UNGLAZED TERRA-COTTA. The most elemental form of clay cooking equipment is terra-cotta, which in Italian means "baked earth." It is unglazed and has a porous brown surface that absorbs and retains heat. Terra-cotta is not suitable for stove-top cooking or for use in a microwave but slow-bakes to perfection.

Care of Terra-cotta. Terra-cotta ware should not be washed in the dishwasher because its open pores will absorb the strong detergents used and later leach them out into foods being cooked. Instead, simply wash quickly in soapy water or, better still, wash with a brush, using a solution of baking soda and water.

Seasoning Terra-cotta. (Necessary primarily if the clayware was purchased at the factory.) Wash and dry the piece carefully. Fill the pot with water and place it in a very low-temperature oven (about 150-200 degrees Fahrenheit). Leave it in the heated oven for about a half hour, then turn off the heat and let the pan cool naturally until the water returns to room temperature. Pour the water out and it is ready to use. It is sometimes suggested that a bouquet garni be added to the water used to season the pot, but since it may be used for something for which those seasonings are inappropriate, it is probably better to use just plain water.

GLAZED TERRA-COTTA. The glazing is usually quite thin and generally the pieces are not entirely glazed over (bottoms are frequently left unglazed). The glazing tends to cause the heat to be reflected, so its absorbency is not as great as unglazed. The surface is susceptible to cracking, so care should be used when handling it.

Care of Glazed Terra-cotta. May or may not be dish-washer-safe so it is better to hand-wash. The very hot water used in dishwashers can be more than the piece can tolerate, causing it to break at some weak point. The high heat of the drying cycle as well as the strong detergents can also cause damage. If you have a no-heat or air-drying cycle that would be safer.

> **CAUTION: If the piece you have purchased is home-crafted or a souvenir from one of the less-developed countries, you should be aware that some glazes contain lead and can contaminate food cooked or stored in them, especially if that food is slightly acid. If there is any question about the piece, do not use it for culinary purposes. Simply enjoy it as a decoration.**

EARTHENWARE AND POTTERY. Because pottery is fire-glazed at relatively low temperatures, the colors available are deep and bright and very attractive. It is also inexpensive and available in an enormous variety of colors, styles, and designs. Pottery is almost always oven-safe, but you shouldn't put cold pieces directly into a hot oven because the swift temperature change can cause cracking and even breaking. When you remove the pot from the oven, do not put it on a cold surface or pour cold water into it because this can also cause cracks. Just let it cool naturally.

STONEWARE.   Stoneware glaze is fired at a very high temperature and, like porcelain, has a ringing sound when tapped. It is quite durable, crack- and chip-resistant. It is both dishwasher- and oven-safe.

Microwave use of pottery, earthenware, and stoneware. Most pieces made of these materials are microwave-safe, but before using in the microwave it is a wise idea to check to verify that. Microwave instruction manuals will have a specific test designed for the microwave that you use, but short of that here is a general test that works. Put a cup of water in the microwave first to absorb some of the microwave energy. Put your piece in the center of the oven and run the oven on the high setting for fifteen seconds. When the oven turns off, check the dish. The outside should not feel warmer than the inside wall of the oven. If it stays cool it is microwave-safe; if it is warmer than the oven, it is not. Never put pieces with metallic trim or with metallic glazes in your microwave.

GLASS.   There are a variety of heatproof glass utensils available. Before using, it is important to check the instructions to make sure that you understand how it should be used. Most glass products are completely oven-safe (but not necessarily broiler-safe). However, most glass utensils are not safe for use on stove-top burners, so be sure to check manufacturer's instructions. Glass retains heat well although it is not a particularly good conductor of heat. Glass has the advantage of being completely resistant to any ingredient that is cooked in it. It is microwave-safe as long as it does not have metallic trim.

Care of glass products. Glass is dishwasher-safe. Stuck-on particles can be removed with a liquid scouring product and a plastic scouring pad. Soaking in detergent and water will loosen most burned-on bits and make extended scrubbing unnecessary.

Patented glass products. *Pyrex* and *Pyroceram* are patents and trademarks held by the Corning Glass Company. Pyrex is not a simple synonym for glass cooking utensils, it describes a special process that makes glass heatproof. Pyroceram Corningware may be moved from freezer to oven without damage to the utensil. Pyroceram products take special care in cleaning, and manufacturer's directions for care should be followed.

PORCELAIN.   Porcelain is a very special baked-clay product. It is made from a unique white clay, kaolin, and is fired at extremely high temperature, which causes the clay to vitrify, or become glasslike. Fine porcelain is translucent and delicate. It must be handled carefully. While technically dishwasher-safe (unless it has metallic trim), the potential for chipping is much greater in the dishwasher than if you wash by hand. Commercial porcelain, which restaurants use, is much sturdier and not translucent. Porcelain should not be considered heatproof and it should be tested (see test, under "Stoneware") before use in a microwave oven.

WOOD.   Wood utensils have a definite place in your kitchen but must receive appropriate handling. Wood spoons and spatulas are ideal for use on Teflon and other surfaces that are easily damaged. Wood, because it is so porous, will absorb both flavors and color from food, so it is wise to have enough that some can be dedicated to special purposes (the one used to stir spaghetti sauce should probably not be used to stir white sauce). Wood can also scorch if left too near a heat source.

Care of wooden implements. Wood should be kept away from excessive water and from hot-air drying, which means wooden pieces should not be washed in the dish-washer. If you choose utensils made of a fine-grained wood it will last the longest and give the best service. Small wooden implements (such as pepper grinders) should be simply wiped clean with a damp cloth from time to time. Wooden bowls should be hand-washed and wiped dry immediately.

Care of wooden cutting boards. Because wood is porous it not only can absorb flavor and color, it can also give a friendly home to microorganisms that may not be, as they say, beneficial to your health. For that reason, special care should be used in handling your wooden cutting board.

First a cutting board should be made of a fine-grained wood, soft enough not to damage the edge of your knife but still firm and flat. A light coating of a nontoxic mineral oil (special oils are available at most hardware stores) before its first use will go far to seal the wood and preserve it for long use.

If you are going to use wooden cutting boards, you should have more than one because the board that you use for cutting raw meat should not be the same board you use for cutting foods that will be eaten without cooking (salad materials for instance).

Clean wooden cutting boards by washing with soapy water, rinsing quickly, and immediately wiping dry with a towel. The board you use for cutting meat should occasionally have a scouring with a paste made of water and baking soda (rinse and dry as usual). Store the boards vertically.

PLASTIC. The early days of plastic kitchenware brought us products that were definitely not dishwasher-safe, but most kitchenware currently available is made of plastic materials that will withstand the heat of the dishwasher, especially if they are placed in the top section.

Plastic storage containers are probably the most popular plastic kitchenware and can be purchased in an enormous variety of styles and sizes. Plastic utensils such as spoons and spatulas that are suitable for use with Teflon and other sensitive surfaces are available.

There are cutting boards made of specially formulated plastic material that not only have a nonporous surface but can be washed in the dishwasher, which makes them much safer to use than the traditional wooden cutting board.

THE SELECTION, USE, AND CARE OF KITCHEN KNIVES

Your knives are probably your most important single category of kitchen tools. They are used constantly and with proper care can last for generations. Good knives are expensive but worth every cent, so you would be well advised to buy the very best knives your budget will allow.

What makes a good knife? The most important consideration is its ability to achieve and keep a sharp edge. That ability is determined by the metal of which the knife blade is made, so first let's look at what those metals are.

HIGH-CARBON STEEL. If attaining and keeping a sharp edge were the only criterion, then high-carbon steel would be the absolute winner because it not only sharpens to a fine edge easily but also is able to keep its sharpness for a long time. Alas, there is a drawback to high-carbon steel, and that is that the blade stains easily and if not cleaned properly can affect the color and taste of the foods it cuts. Acid foods such as tomatoes and citrus fruits have this effect unless the blade is very carefully cleaned after use.

STAINLESS STEEL. Here we have the other side of the coin ... stainless does not, in fact, stain nor will it affect color or flavor of foods. Unfortunately simple stainless steel blades will not retain a fine sharp edge.

COMBINATION METALS. There are some stainless steel alloys that contain a high portion of carbon, which provides a compromise that delivers both good sharpening characteristics and a nonstaining surface. Vanadium steel is also a high-carbon steel alloy that meets these requirements. Chrome-plated blades require care in removing all acid substances quickly but otherwise take and hold a good edge. Finally there are some blades that contain tungsten steel, which is the hardest of all steel alloys. Tungsten-steel blades are just about impossible to sharpen at home, but with care a professional sharpening can last for a long time.

The construction of knives is as important as the metal from which they are made. Knife blades can be stamped or cut from larger sheets of metal, or can be machine- or hand-forged. Forged knives are best because the forging process allows the metal to develop a fine grain near the edge, which means sharpening will be easier and last longer. Forged and tempered blades are shaped with a taper from the back of the blade to its edge and from the base to the point. This tapering allows the knife to be flexible as well as strong.

Look carefully at the handle of any knife you are considering for purchase. Do not buy knives with painted handles, because the paint will soon chip off. Many knives have handles made of wood that has been impregnated with a plastic material and is very durable. The handle should be moisture- and stain-resistant, and should fit comfortably in your hand when you grip it.

How the handle is attached to the knife is also important. In the best construction, the back end of the knife blade (called the tang) extends through the handle and is completely covered by the handle. The tang is firmly fastened into the handle with two or three rivets. Beware of knives constructed with the blade simply inserted into the handle and fastened with a nail or, worse yet, fastened with a metal collar around the handle. These knives will not last and are not a good value no matter how inexpensive they are.

KNIVES FOR YOUR KITCHEN

As you found when shopping for pans, there is a wide variety of knives to be found in any kitchen specialty shop or the housewares section of any good department or hardware store, but, when analyzed, they fall into only a few basic types.

Paring Knife is the smallest of the standard knives and the one you probably will use the most frequently. They have short blades (2½ to 4 inches), which are pointed. Paring knives are used not only for paring fruits and vegetables but also for dozens of other food preparation jobs, especially if you are cooking for a small family.

French Chef's Knife is bigger than the paring knife, with a blade that runs between eight and twelve inches in length. The distinctive design feature of the French chef's knife is the handle, which is much higher than the edge of the blade so you can use it to mince and chop with plenty of space for your knuckles as you grip the handle. This knife also has extra strengthening in the space between the handle and the blade.

Carving Knife or Butcher's Knife has a blade that is about nine to twelve inches long and extends directly out from the handle; the knife edge is on a line with the lower edge of the handle. These knives are sturdy and suitable for dismembering poultry, cutting large cuts of meat or dense vegetables.

Slicing Knife has a long, narrow blade and is rounded rather than pointed on the end. Slicing knives frequently have a serrated edge.

Cleaver has a large rectangular blade, not pointed. It has a short handle and is used for heavy-duty cutting and also in the preparation of Oriental food.

The basic kitchen collection of knives should include:

> A paring knife
> A French chef's knife, eight-inch blade
> A slicing knife, ten-inch blade

Once these are in your "batterie de cuisine," you should branch out into different lengths as well as other variations on the basic knife types. You will probably find, however, that there are just a few knives that you use all the time no matter how many you ultimately have.

Care of knives: You should use your kitchen knives only for food preparation. Use care never to cut on a hard surface that can damage the edge of the knife. Whether or not you wash your knives in the dishwasher is up to you, but they will be better served if you do not, even if they are indicated to be dishwasher-safe. Do not soak knives in water unnecessarily. If you want the wooden handles to maintain their new look, occasionally rub on a bit of linseed oil or mineral oil.

THE PANTRY

Houses built until about the 1930s often had a small room adjacent to the kitchen where food and food-preparation supplies were kept. It was called the pantry. Modern homes are most often without this luxury, but the concept of a specific area used for food storage is still a valid one, and one that as a cook you should consider. A separate room is not usually possible in modern houses and apartments, but sometimes there is space in the garage, an extra cupboard, or even a closet that can be converted to use this way.

Whatever your physical storage facilities are like, there are certain food items that should be available to you at all times. These are not only the essential ingredients for baked goods and other dishes, but are also the emergency supplies that can allow you to prepare a dinner for unexpected guests or survive several days past your normal shopping day if necessary.

Here is a list of the things most cooks would like to have on hand all of the time:

STAPLE DRY INGREDIENTS

White Flour	Granulated Sugar	Baking Powder
Whole Wheat Flour	Powdered Sugar	Baking Soda
Cornmeal	Brown Sugar	Cornstarch
Rye Flour	Cream of Tartar	Granulated Yeast
Powdered Milk	Unflavored Gelatin	Arrowroot
Cocoa	Coconut	Raisins

STAPLE GRAINS AND PASTAS

Brown Rice	Bulgur	Salad Macaroni
White Rice	Split Peas	Shell Macaroni
Barley	Lentils	Spaghetti
Cereal Grains	Lima Beans	Fettucini Noodles
Garbanzo Beans	Red Beans	Regular Noodles
Rolled Oats	Bread Crumbs	Lasagna Noodles
Popcorn		Couscous

SEASONINGS AND FLAVORINGS

Vanilla Extract	Almond Extract	Lemon Extract
Allspice, ground	Allspice, whole	Alum
Basil	Bay Leaf	Caraway Seed
Cayenne Pepper	Celery Seed	Chili Powder
Cinnamon, ground	Cinnamon, whole stick	Cloves, ground
Cloves, whole	Cumin, ground	Curry Powder
Dill	Dill Seed	Garlic Powder
Garlic Salt	Ginger, ground	Marjoram
Nutmeg, ground	Nutmeg, whole	Onion Bits, dried
Onion Powder	Onion Salt	Oregano
Paprika	Parsley	Pepper, ground
Peppercorns	Rosemary	Sesame Seeds
Tarragon	Thyme	Food Colorings

STAPLE LIQUID INGREDIENTS

Salad Oil	White Vinegar	Soy Sauce
Olive Oil	Cider Vinegar	Pepper Sherry*
Peanut Oil	Wine Vinegar	Catsup
Honey	Tarragon Vinegar*	Prepared Mustards
Flavored Syrups*	Oregano Vinegar*	Tabasco Sauce
	Worcestershire Sauce	

OTHER PANTRY STAPLES

Shortening	Baking Mix*	Flavored Gelatins
Sauce Mixes*	Cake Mixes*	Pudding Mixes*
Bouillon Cubes	Dry Cereal	Tea(s)
Crackers	Cookies	Coffee(s)

CANNED STAPLES

Tuna	Mushrooms	Tomato Sauce
Salmon	Mushroom Soup	Tomato Juice
Clams	Olives, ripe pitted	Tomato Soup
	Olives, ripe sliced	Tomatoes
Canned Fruits	Olives, green stuffed	Cream-Style Corn

REFRIGERATOR STAPLES

Butter/margarine	Mayonnaise	Salad Dressings
Eggs	Cheese(s)	Milk
Mustard(s)	Catsup	Relishes
Jams and Jellies	Peanut Butter	

FREEZER STAPLES

Orange Juice	Vegetables	Nuts
Ice Cream*	Prepared Main Dishes*	Baked Desserts*
Sherbet*	Hamburger Patties	Breads and Rolls*

With these items on hand and a good recipe book or two, you should be able to prepare a wide variety of meals. Keep your pantry stocked with these ingredients all the time, because there is nothing more frustrating than being in the midst of preparing a recipe and discovering that you lack a vital ingredient. Some of these essential ingredients may have a substitution (see Chapter 3), but substitutions are not always possible and never quite the same as the specified ingredient.

*Items that can be either purchased or homemade.

CHAPTER 5

Cook Until Done

"Cook until done" . . . a simple phrase that makes it sound very easy to tell how long a dish should be cooked. The trick is in discovering what "done" means and how you are going to achieve that desirable condition.

The cooking process is accomplished in just one way: by applying heat to the food. And there are just three ways that the heat can be applied: by conduction, by convection, and by radiation. Most cooking processes involve at least two, and quite often all three, of these.

Let's look at each one of the three separately and see how it works.

Conduction occurs when heat is passed directly from one molecule to another. This heat transference takes place in all of the materials involved in the process. For example, when you stir-fry vegetables, first the heat is transferred from the stove burner to the pan. When the pan molecules are hot they begin to transfer heat to the thin layer of oil coating the inside. The oil molecules then transfer heat to the outside of the vegetables. The process continues inside the vegetables until at some point all of the molecules are hot and the vegetables are cooking. It is at this point that physical and chemical changes take place in the food itself, and it is also the point at which the cook assumes control and decides when enough is enough.

Convection uses circulating air or liquid to transfer heat to the food. An example of cooking primarily by convection is the cooking of vegetables in boiling water. The pan containing water is placed on the stove burner, the heat is turned on, and the bottom of the pot becomes hot. The molecules near the bottom heat up, and as they do they begin to rise to the top (following that predictable law of physics that heat rises and cold falls). As they move up, they are replaced by cooler molecules sinking to the bottom. Our initial layer of molecules cools slightly during its upward migration and in its turn moves back again to the bottom to heat even more. The overall temperature of the water continues to increase until the boiling point has been reached. This pattern of rising and falling molecules causes currents of movement that are the key to convection cooking. When the food is added the boiling will usually stop momentarily until the food heats and begins the cooking process. Once again, it is at this moment that you as the cook begin to participate in the process and decide how long it will continue.

Radiation is the third type of heat process. Radiation requires no auxiliary equipment, just the radiation source and the food. Radiation heat sources always produce visible light and involve neither liquid nor air. It is what you do when you broil meat under your broiler or make toast in your toaster. The heat element transfers heat to the food by using electromagnetic particles propelled to the food at the speed of light. The food is heated as it absorbs this radiant energy.

In each of the three examples, more than one of these heat-transferring methods are used: in the broiler both radiant heat and conduction are used; conduction is important when food is boiled; and convection is involved in stir-frying.

So now the food is hot, what do we mean when we say the food is cooked?

First, we mean that the food has been made more digestible. The fibers have been softened and altered so that they are easier to chew and easier to absorb through digestion.

Second, we mean that the food has been enhanced ... it is more attractive, its flavor is improved, its aroma has been emphasized. Those sitting at our table are, in other words, more likely to eat it. This is not just an aesthetic consideration. Our lives and the lives of those for whom we cook depend upon continual intake of food. To encourage enjoyment of this very necessary process, the appeal of the food is very important.

Third, we mean that the food is physically changed in some way. Sometimes we decrease its volume and consequently make it thicker and more flavorful (by reducing the liquid it contains). Sometimes we make it firmer (by causing changes in the protein in meat or gelatin, for instance). Sometimes we change it from a solid to a liquid to make it more appetizing or easier to use (when we melt butter, for example).

Finally, but perhaps most important, we mean that by cooking we have made the food safer to eat by destroying most if not all of the undesirable microorganisms. We have also possibly made it difficult for bacteria, molds, and yeasts to flourish by reducing the amount of liquid available to them. (This aspect of food preservation is more fully discussed in the next chapter, which deals with food storage and preservation.)

COOKING METHODS

There are only a limited number of ways in which food can be cooked and they all fall into two main categories: dry-heat cooking methods and moist-heat cooking methods.

Dry-heat methods are best suited to foods that contain some natural moisture-producing element (either moisture or fat in the food itself), or that are quite delicate, or both (as in the case of many fish fillets, and also baked products such as cake).

The presence of extra integrated fat is the reason you can successfully broil a choice grade of steak but may find a leaner steak more than a bit chewy after broiling.

Dry-heat methods include: broiling, baking, roasting, toasting, sautéing, stir-frying, deep frying, and microwaving.

Moist-heat methods are best suited to use with foods that need the addition of moisture to make them more digestible and palatable. This includes the lean cuts of meat (which often come from older animals), most vegetables, and combination dishes such as soups and stews.

Moist-heat methods include: boiling, stewing, simmering, poaching, braising, steaming, and pressure-cooking.

(A detailed description of each of the cooking techniques mentioned appears in Chapter 1.)

One element that can affect cooking times is the altitude at which you live. Rocky Mountain cooks have an old saying that goes: "Boiling water's not so hot, way up on a mountaintop." There is a sound reason for this. As we go to higher elevations, the atmosphere becomes thinner and the air pressure is less. The effect on cooking is, for instance, that when you boil water in an open pan there is less pressure on the surface of the water, and because of that the molecules can more easily escape into the air. This is the reason that the water will come to a full rapid boil at a lower temperature in Santa Fe (at an elevation of 6,950 feet) than it does in Baltimore (where the altitude is twenty feet above sea level).

The effect of this is that at higher elevations food simply takes longer to cook both on top of the stove and in the oven.

There are one or two other minor matters of atmospheric physics that can affect the time it takes water to boil. On a day when the barometric pressure is low, the temperature at which water boils may be lowered by a degree or two, which means it may require some additional time for food to cook ... not much more, but a little.

It is also worth noting that the tallish pan with a relatively narrow base will cause water to boil at a slightly higher temperature than usual for your altitude. This is because the greater height of the pot means that the water on the bottom is under more pressure than it would be in a wider and shorter pan. This pressure difference means it takes more heat (energy) to bring it to a boil. The effect is that food cooked in a tall, narrow pan will cook a little more quickly.

"COOK UNTIL DONE"

Here is a word of advice to all cooks: never underestimate the importance of good thermometers in your kitchen.

More culinary failures are caused by incorrect cooking temperatures than any other single problem. This is especially true if you rely on the timing instructions in recipes or on boxes of mixes. If your cupcake recipe says to bake for 20 minutes in a 350-degree oven, the cupcakes will turn out right only if your oven really produces 350 degrees and not 325 or 375 degrees.

Invest in at least four cooking thermometers: one for use in your refrigerator and freezer, one for use in your oven, one for meat, and one that can be used for the higher temperatures required for deep-frying and candy making. You'll never regret your purchases.

If you are purchasing a meat thermometer for the first time, or perhaps replacing one you already have had for some reason, look at the newer small-probe "instant" thermometers. These have a number of advantages:

They are somewhat more accurate.

The small hole they make seals quickly so meat juices do not seep out.

Traditional thermometers are left in the meat and can themselves affect the cooking process by conducting heat to the center of the meat.

Internal temperature can be tested at several points during the cooking period, and these small thermometers can be used for a variety of temperature-measuring jobs.

While on the subject of temperature measurement, let's mention the two different temperature measuring systems that you find in cookbooks: the Fahrenheit system, which is the most commonly used in the United States, and the Celsius or centigrade system, which is used most other places.

The Fahrenheit system was developed by Gabriel Daniel Fahrenheit, who lived from 1686 to 1736. He was a physicist particularly interested in inventing and developing the precision instruments of his time, especially measuring devices. Both the alcohol and the mercury thermometers were invented by Fahrenheit. He was also the first to recognize that water boils at different temperatures depending on the atmospheric pressure found at different altitudes.

The Celsius system was originated by Anders Celsius, whose lifetime overlapped that of Fahrenheit slightly (1701–1744). Anders Celsius was a Swedish astronomer. The system he developed was officially designated as the Celsius system in 1948, but the more common name of centigrade system is still in quite common use. Temperatures in this system are based on the metric concept of water freezing at zero degrees and boiling at 100 degrees.

   To convert Celsius temperatures to Fahrenheit, multiply by 9, divide by 5, and add 32. To convert Fahrenheit to Celsius, subtract 32 degrees, multiply by 5, and divide by 9.

   The key temperatures in each system are the temperature at which water boils at sea level and the temperature at which water freezes.

   Water boils at sea level at:
       212 degrees in the Fahrenheit system,
       100 degrees in the Celsius system.

   Water freezes at:
   32 degrees in the Fahrenheit system,
    0 degrees in the Celsius system.

COOKING TEMPERATURE CHART
OF FAHRENHEIT AND CELSIUS (CENTIGRADE)
(Times are appropriate for altitudes up to about 3,000 feet)

	Fahrenheit Scale	Celsius Scale
Candy and Jelly:		
Jelly jells	220	104
Thread stage for icings	230	110
Soft-ball stage for candy	234	112
Firm-ball stage for candy	245	118
Hard-ball stage for candy	250	121
Light-crack stage for candy	265	129
Hard-crack stage for candy	290	143
Baking Temperatures:		
Slow oven (250-325 F)	250	122
	275	135
	300	149
Moderate oven (325-400 F)	325	163
	350	177
	375	191

	Fahrenheit Scale	Celsius Scale
Hot oven (400-450 F)	400	204
	425	218
Very hot oven (450-550 F)	450	232
	500	260
	550	288

If you should find yourself using an oven without thermostatic controls (a wood-burning stove, for instance), or if you are just curious, here is an old-fashioned way to check on oven temperature. Sprinkle about a quarter cup of flour in a pie pan and shake it to distribute it evenly. Place the pan in a heated oven for five minutes. If it turns

delicate brown (tan), the oven is slow (250-325 F);
golden brown, the oven is moderate (325-400 F);
deep dark brown, the oven is hot (400-450 F).

If it takes only three minutes to turn deep dark brown, the oven is very hot (450-550 F).

COOKING MEATS

Meats, poultry, and fish may be cooked by either a dry-heat method or a moist-heat method. Your choice depends upon the meat and what sort of a dish you would like to have as an end product.

In order to broil, bake, roast, barbecue, sauté, or deep-fry meat—all dry-heat methods—the meat product has to be tender before you start. Tenderness, or perceived tenderness, which is almost the same thing, is achieved in one of three ways. Either the meat product has fat interspersed with the muscle tissue (for example, ground beef), or it is taken from an immature animal (such as veal or chicken), or it is in very small pieces (such as individual shrimp).

Here are a few things to keep in mind before using one of these dry-heat methods ...

Always wipe the meat carefully before introducing it to the heat source. If you don't, the moisture that has accumulated on the surface of the meat will turn into steam before it evaporates. If you can avoid this moment of steam the meat will brown quickly and evenly, and the piece will look much better when cooked. This rule applies even to hamburgers. It particularly applies to food that is to be deep-fried, because in that instance you not only have the problem of the layer of steam forming but you also have the additional hazard of the moisture causing the hot fat to spit out of the deep-fryer.

When you roast meat, leave air space all around it by putting the meat up on a rack and by cooking it without a cover. This allows the dry heat to reach all surfaces equally. If the meat is placed directly on the bottom of the pan, it will soon be sitting in the liquid that seeps from the meat as it cooks. This does two things. First, the bottom will cook faster because moist-heat methods tend to be somewhat faster than dry-heat methods, and second, the bottom will not be browned and crisp as a roast should be.

When you barbecue or broil you should judge the distance between the meat and the heat source based on the thickness of the meat. That is, the thicker the meat the farther from the heat source it should be. This is because it takes time for heat to penetrate (via conduction) to the center of a thick piece and by the time it does, the outside surface could be charred by the extremely high temperatures used for broiling and barbecuing. In general, meat should be between three and six inches from the heat source. (Measure from the heat source to the surface of the meat, not from the heat source to the oven rack or broiler-pan surface.)

There is an ongoing argument/discussion between the cooks who insist that meat should be salted before being cooked with a dry-heat method and the cooks who insist with equal vigor that the meat should be salted after cooking. The argument goes like this: The Before-Cooking proponents say that unless salt is added in advance of cooking it cannot adequately penetrate the meat; the After-Cooking school of thought maintains that presalting tends to draw the meat juices to the surface where they evaporate rather than leaving them in the meat where they make it tender. What it really comes down to is a matter of preference, and you should follow yours.

Adding seasonings other than salt is a slightly different matter. Pepper and other seasonings such as herbs should not be presented directly to the heat source because they char and taste bitter. The best time to add them is just after you have turned the piece of meat so that they go on the already cooked side. (One sidelight on using herbs in barbecuing is to soak fresh herbs in water and then place the wet herb branches on the coals or heated rocks. The ensuing smoke will flavor the meat being cooked.)

HOW LONG TO COOK MEAT

The area where cooks have more questions about cooking temperatures and times than any other is when cooking meat. Meat is probably the most expensive general type of ingredient used in meal preparation, and it is important that it is cooked right for the people who will be eating it. The concept of "right" varies greatly from family to family and from person to person in any family. So those variations need to be reckoned with when you decide what "done" means to you.

To accurately determine the doneness of meat, there is no substitute for a good meat thermometer, especially when you are cooking a type of meat that you do not cook on a regular basis.

To use a meat thermometer accurately, insert the point well into the center of the meat, away from bones and fat areas. The reason for this particular placement of the heat probe is that the center of the piece is going to be the last place the heat penetrates and so will be the last to cook. Near a bone may give an incorrectly high temperature reading because bone (being solid) is a better conductor of heat than muscle tissue. On the other hand, fat is a poor conductor of heat, so may show an incorrectly low reading.

COOKING PORK

A special mention about cooking pork is important. Pork (and some meat from wild game, particularly bear) can be infested with a parasite called *Trichinella spiralis.* These tiny worms are encapsulated in cysts that can be found in the raw meat. If the meat is not properly prepared, these live parasites can be taken into the body when the meat is eaten. Once ingested they can take up what amounts to permanent residence. The Center for Disease Control in Atlanta estimates that as many as four percent of Americans carry trichinosis-causing parasites. (Chapter 6 includes more information about trichinosis.) To kill the live *Trichinella,* you must cook the meat to at least 170 F, freeze it to at least 15 F, or process it using an accepted curing process.

SUGGESTED TEMPERATURES AND TIMES
FOR ROASTING MEATS

Cut of Meat	Approx. Weight (lbs.)	Oven Temp. (F)	Cook to Interior Temp. of	Approx. Cooking Time (min./lb.)
BEEF				
Standing rib	4-6	300-325	140 (rare)	26-32
			160 (med.)	34-38
			170 (well)	40-42
	6-8	300-325	140 (rare)	23-25
			160 (med.)	27-30
			170 (well)	32-35
Rolled rib	5-7	300-325	140 (rare)	30-34
			160 (med.)	36-40
			170 (well)	46-50
Rib eye	4-6	350	140 (rare)	18-20
			160 (med.)	20-22
			170 (well)	22-24
Tenderloin, whole	4-6	425	140 (rare)	45-60
Rolled rump	4-6	300-325	150-170	25-30
Sirloin tip	3-4	300-325	150-170	35-40
VEAL				
Leg of veal	5-8	300-325	170	25-35
Loin of veal	4-6	300-325	170	30-35
Rack of ribs	3-5	300-325	170	35-40
Rolled shoulder	4-6	300-325	170	40-45
PORK, FRESH				
Center-cut loin	3-5	325-350	170	30-35
Half loin	5-7	325-350	170	35-40
Sirloin	3-4	325-350	170	40-45
Rolled loin	3-5	325-350	170	30-35
Shoulder				
Picnic style	5-8	325-350	185	30-35
Rolled	3-5	325-350	185	40-45
Cushion style	3-5	325-350	185	35-40

Cut of Meat	Approx. Weight (lbs.)	Oven Temp. (F)	Cook to Interior Temp. of	Approx. Cooking Time (min./lb.)
Boston butt style	3-8	325-350	185	30-35
Leg				
Whole, bone in	10-14	325-350	185	25-30
Whole, no bone	7-10	325-350	185	35-40
Half leg, bone in	5-7	325-350	185	40-45
Crown roast	3-5	325-350	185	30-35

PORK, PROCESSED (SMOKED)
Purchased as Fully Cooked

Ham	5-7	325	130	18-24

Purchased as Uncooked

Whole ham	10-14	300-325	160	18-20
Half ham	5-7	300-325	160	22-25
Shank (butt) ham	3-4	300-325	160	35-40
Shoulder				
Picnic style	5-8	300-325	170	34-36
Roll	2-3	300-325	170	35-40
Canadian bacon	2-4	300-325	160	35-40

LAMB

Leg of lamb	5-8	300-325	175-180	30-35
Shoulder	4-6	300-325	175-180	30-35
Rolled	3-5	300-325	175-180	40-45
Cushion style	3-5	300-325	175-180	30-35
Crown roast	3-4	300-325	175-180	40-45

CHICKEN

Frying chicken	3-4	375	185	18-20
Roasting chicken	5-6	350	185	20-25
Cornish game hen	to 2	400	185	25-35

OTHER POULTRY

Duck	4-5	375	185	20-25

Cut of Meat	Approx. Weight (lbs.)	Oven Temp. (F)	Cook to Interior Temp. of	Approx. Cooking Time (min./lb.)
Goose	8-12	400 for first hour, 325 remainder of time	185	10-12

WILD GAME

Pheasant, dressed		450	185	45-60†
Partridge, dressed		450	185	45-60†
Duck		475	rare	12-15†
		475	med. rare	20-25†
		475	medium	25-30†
Quail		450	185	20-25†
Venison roast	6 lbs.	450	175-180	15-20
Rabbit	2 lbs.	350	175-180	35-45

†Total cooking time, not minutes per pound.

TURKEY (FRESH OR THAWED)
Whole turkey

	Approx. Weight (lbs.)	Oven Temp. (F)	Cook to Interior Temp. of	Approx. Cooking Time (min./lb.)
Not stuffed	6-8	350	185*	22-27
	8-12	350	185*	22-25
	12-16	325	185*	18-20
	16-20	325	185*	16-18
	20-24	325	185*	14-16
	24-28	325	185*	13-15
Stuffed	6-8	325	185*	30-32
	8-12	325	185*	25-30
	12-16	325	185*	22-25
	16-20	325	185*	20-22
	20-24	325	185*	18-20
	24-28	325	185*	18-20
Turkey breast	2-4	325	170	20-25
Turkey thigh	to 2	350	185	25-30

*"Pop-up" timer/thermometers sometimes placed in the turkey by the food processor are not a reliable guide to doneness.

Cut of Meat	Approx. Weight (lbs.)	Oven Temp. (F)	Cook to Interior Temp. of	Approx. Cooking Time (min./lb.)

To Cook a Solidly Frozen Turkey

Cut of Meat	Approx. Weight (lbs.)	Oven Temp. (F)	Cook to Interior Temp. of	Approx. Cooking Time (min./lb.)
Whole turkey				
Not stuffed	12-16	325	185	7½-8½ hours†
	16-20	325	185	8-9½ hours†
	20-24	325	185	9-10 hours†
Half breast	2-4	325	170	4-6 hours†
Turkey pieces	—	325	185	2-2½ hours†

†Total cooking time, not minutes per pound

Always use a meat thermometer and insert it into the thigh between the body and the leg. When your thermometer reads 185 degrees at this location, the turkey is done. Some will feel that the breast is overdone when the thigh is cooked to 185. If that is the case, you can lightly cover the breast with foil during the last fifteen to twenty minutes of cooking (or if turkey is to be sliced before serving, carve off the breast first and while you are slicing the breast pieces return the rest to the oven for another fifteen to twenty minutes to finish cooking.)

SUGGESTED TEMPERATURES AND TIMES
FOR BROILING MEATS

(Cooking times shown are based on the temperature at the surface of the meat being approximately 350 degrees.)

	Weight (lbs.)	Thickness (inches)	Approx. Time (in mins.)*		
			Rare	Med.	Well
BEEF					
Filet mignon (tenderloin)	to ½	1	15	20	25
Rib-steak	1-1½	1	15	20	25
	1½-2	1½	25	30	35
	2-2½	2	35	45	55
Rib-eye steak	½	1	15	20	25
	¾	1½	25	30	35
	1	2	35	45	55
Club (Delmonico)	1-1½	1	15	20	25
	1½-2	1½	25	30	35
	2-2½	2	35	45	55
Sirloin steak	1½-3	1	20	25	30
	2-4	1½	30	35	40
	3-5	2	40	45	50
Porterhouse steak	1-2	1	20	25	30
	2-3	1½	30	35	40
	2½-4	2	40	45	50
T-bone steak	1-2	1½	15	20	25
Strip steak (boneless)	½	1	20	25	30
Ground-beef patties	¼	1	15	20	25

*Thickness is the key factor in determining cooking time: the thicker the piece, the longer it takes.

	Weight (lbs.)	Thickness (inches)	Approx. Time (in mins.)*		
			Rare	Med.	Well

Doneness Scale for Beef
Rare = internal temperature of 140
Medium = internal temperature of 160
Well = internal temperature of 170

PORK, FRESH

	Weight	Thickness	Rare	Med.	Well
Rib chops		1	**	**	20-25
Loin chops		1	**	**	20-25
Shoulder steaks		1	**	**	20-22

PORK, SMOKED (Not Precooked)

	Weight	Thickness	Rare	Med.	Well
Ham, slice	to 1	½	**	**	10-12
	to 2	1	**	**	16-20
Canadian bacon slice		¼	**	**	6-8
		½	**	**	8-10
Bacon slice			**	**	4-5

**Always cook all pork to the well-done stage.

LAMB

	Weight	Thickness	Rare	Med.	Well
Shoulder chops	to ½	1	***	12	***
	to 1	2	***	22	***
Single rib chops	¼	1	***	12	***
Double rib chops	½	2	***	22	***
Loin chops	to ½	1	***	12	***
	to 1	1	***	22	***

***Most people like lamb cooked on the slightly rare side of medium (so the meat is tinged with pink), and that is the basis for these suggested cooking times.

SUGGESTED TEMPERATURES AND TIMES
FOR CHARCOAL-BARBECUED MEATS

Cut of Meat	Size (lbs. or inches)	Covered or Uncovered*	Heat of Coals†	Cook to Interior Temp. of	Approx. Time (min./lb.)
BEEF					
Standing rib roast	4-6 lbs.	Covered	Hot	140 (rare)	25-30
				160 (med.)	30-35
				170 (well)	35-40
	6-8 lbs.	Covered	Hot	140 (rare)	23-25
				160 (med.)	27-30
				170 (well)	32-35
Rolled roast	3-5 lbs.	Covered	Hot	140 (rare)	23-25
				160 (med.)	27-30
				170 (well)	32-35
Steaks	1 inch	Uncovered	Hot	140 (rare)	10-12
				160 (med.)	12-15
				170 (well)	15-20
	1½ inch	Uncovered	Med.	140 (rare)	15-18
				160 (med.)	18-22
				170 (well)	22-26
	2 inch	Uncovered	Med.	140 (rare)	24-30
				160 (med.)	30-35
				170 (well)	35-45
Flank steak	2 lbs.	Uncovered	Hot	Med. rare	10-15
Cubes (kebab)	¾ inch	Uncovered	Hot	Med. rare	5-6
Skewered	1 inch	Uncovered	Hot	Med. rare	8-10
	1½ inch	Uncovered	Hot	Med. rare	10-14
Ground beef	1 inch	Uncovered	Hot	Rare	8-10
				Med.	10-12
				Well	12-15
VEAL					
Leg of veal	5-8 lbs.	Covered	Hot	170	20-22
Loin of veal	4-6 lbs.	Covered	Hot	170	25-30
Chops	¾ inch	Uncovered	Hot	Med.	10-12
	1 inch	Uncovered	Hot	Med.	12-14

Cut of Meat	Size (lbs. or inches)	Covered or Uncovered*	Heat of Coals†	Cook to Interior Temp. of	Approx. Time (min./lb.)
	1½ inch	Uncovered	Hot	Med	15-18
Rolled shoulder	3-4 lbs.	Covered	Hot	170	32-35
PORK					
Center-cut loin	2 lbs.	Covered	Hot	170	20-25
	3-5 lbs	Covered	Hot	170	30-35
Half loin†	5-7 lbs.	Covered	Hot	170	15-18
Shoulder roast†	4-6 lbs.	Covered	Hot	170	24-26
Chops	¾ inch	Uncovered	Med.	Well	8-10
	1 inch	Uncovered	Med.	Well	10-14
	1½ inch	Uncovered	Med.	Well	15-20
Spareribs	2-3 lbs.	Covered	Hot	Well	60-90
LAMB					
Leg of lamb†	5-8	Covered	Hot	150	20-23
Leg, boned, tied	4-5	Covered	Hot	150	26-30
Leg, boned, flat	4-5	Covered	Hot	150	20-23
Shoulder†	5-7	Covered	Hot	150	20-23
Shoulder, boned	4-6	Covered	Hot	150	26-30
Chops	¾ inch	Uncovered	Hot	Med. rare	8-10
	1 inch	Uncovered	Hot	Med. rare	10-12
	1½ inch	Uncovered	Hot	Med. rare	12-14
Cubes (kebab)	¾ inch	Uncovered	Hot	Med.	6-8
skewered	1 inch	Uncovered	Hot	Med.	8-10
	1½ inch	Uncovered	Hot	Med.	10-12

†Bone left in

FISH					
Whole fish	2 lbs.	Covered	Hot	Flakes	10-12
	5 lbs.	Covered	Hot	Flakes	30-35
	7 lbs.	Covered	Hot	Flakes	40-45

Cut of Meat	Size (lbs. or inches)	Covered or Uncovered*	Heat of Coals†	Cook to Interior Temp. of	Approx. Time (min./lb.)
Steaks/fillets	½ inch	Uncovered	Hot	Flakes	5-7
	1 inch	Uncovered	Hot	Flakes	8-10
Cubes (kebab)	1 inch	Uncovered	Hot	Flakes	8-10
Scallops	1 inch	Uncovered	Hot	Firm	5-7
Shrimp	Med. size	Uncovered	Hot	Pink	3-5
Clams in shell	Med. size	Uncovered	Hot	Opens	3-5
Oysters	Med. size	Uncovered	Hot	Opens	4-7
POULTRY					
Chicken,	3-4 lbs.	Covered	Hot	185	60-75
whole	5-7 lbs.	Covered	Hot	185	90-105
Chicken, half	2 lbs.	Uncovered	Med.	185	40-50
Chicken legs	—	Uncovered	Med.	185	30-40
Chicken breast	—	Uncovered	Med.	170	15-20
Cubes	1 inch	Uncovered	Med.	—	10-12
Rock Cornish	2 lbs.	Covered	Hot	185	30-35
Turkey, whole	6-8 lbs.	Covered	Hot	185	16-18
	8-10 lbs.	Covered	Hot	185	14-16
	20 lbs.	Covered	Hot	185	12-14
Rotisserie	6-8 lbs.	Covered	Hot	185	30-32
	8-10 lbs.	Covered	Hot	185	28-30
Turkey, half	8-12 lbs.	Covered	Hot	185	10-12
Turkey leg	1-2 lbs.	Uncovered	Med.	185	30-35
Turkey breast	2-3 lbs.	Covered	Hot	170	30-35
Cubes	1 inch	Uncovered	Med.	—	12-15

*Uncovered means to cook on an open grill. Covered means to use either a barbecue unit with a built-in cover or to in some other way cover the meat to hold the heat in (try making a tent out of heavy-gauge foil, for instance).

†Hot means when you can hold your hand about three inches above the heat source for only two to three seconds, while medium means you can leave your hand there about twice that long. Charcoal is hot when it is glowing orange and just beginning to have the layer of ash appear on the briquettes.

SUGGESTED TEMPERATURES AND TIMES
FOR MOIST-HEAT (BRAISING) MEATS

Cut of Meat	Size or Amount of Meat	Approx. Total Cooking Time
BEEF		
Pot roast	3-5-lb. roast	3-4 hours
Swiss steak	1½-2½ inch	2-3 hours
Corned beef	3-4-lb. piece	4-5 hours
Short ribs	2×2×4	1-2 hours
Chuck steak	½ inch thick	45-60 mins.
Round steak	¾ inch thick	1½ hours
Rump steak	½ inch thick	45-60 mins.
Sirloin tips	½ inch thick	45-60 mins.
Stew-meat pieces	1×1×2 inches	2 hours
Liver, piece	3-4 lbs.	2-2½ hours
Liver, slices	½ inch thick	20-25 mins.
Kidney	whole	1-1½ hours†
Heart	whole	3-4 hours
Heart, slices	to 1 inch	1½-2 hours
Tongue	whole	3-4 hours
Tripe	whole	1-1½ hours
Sweetbreads	whole	20-25 mins.
Brains	whole	15-20 mins.
VEAL		
Stuffed breast	3-4 lbs.	1-2 hours
Rolled breast	2-3 lbs.	1-2 hours
Chops	to ¾ inch	45-60 mins.
Steaks (cutlets)	to ¾ inch	45-60 mins.
Shoulder chops	to ¾ inch	45-60 mins.
Cubed shoulder	1-2-inch cubes	45-60 mins.†
Kidney	whole	45-60 mins.†
Tongue	whole	2-3 hours
Sweetbreads	whole	15-20 mins.
Brains	whole	15-20 mins.

Cut of Meat	Size or Amount of Meat	Approx. Total Cooking Time
PORK		
Chops	to 1½ inch thick	45-60 mins.
Spareribs	2-3 lbs.	1½ hour
Tenderloin, whole	to 1 lb.	45-60 mins.
Tenderloin, steaks	½ inch thick	30 mins.
Shoulder steaks	¾ inch thick	45-60 mins.
Liver, piece	3-3½ lbs.	1½-2 hours
Liver, sliced	½ inch thick	20-25 mins.
Heart	whole	2½-3 hours
Brains	whole	15-20 mins.
LAMB		
Stuffed breast	2-3 lbs.	1½-2 hours
Rolled breast	to 2 lbs.	1½-2 hours
Neck slices	¾ inch	1 hour
Shanks	to 1 lb. each	1-1½ hours
Shoulder chops	to 1 inch thick	45-60 mins.
Kidney	whole	45-60 mins
Heart	whole	2½-3 hours
Sweetbreads	whole	15-20 mins.
Brains	whole	15-20 mins.

†after precooking in simmering water for 45 mins.

POULTRY		
Chicken, fricassee	pieces	3-4 hours
Chicken, simmered	whole 4-5 lbs.	3-4 hours
Turkey, unstuffed		
oven cooking bag	8-12 lbs.	1½-2 hours
	12-16 lbs.	2-3 hours
	16-20 lbs.	2½-3½ hours
	20-24 lbs.	3-4 hours
Turkey, stuffed		
oven cooking bag	8-12 lbs.	2-3 hours
	12-16 lbs.	2½-3½ hours
	16-20 lbs.	3-4 hours
	20-24 lbs.	3½-4½ hours

SUGGESTED COOKING TIMES FOR MICROWAVED MEAT

Meat	Setting	Time (mins.)
BEEF		
Ground beef, crumbled	High	5-6
Ground beef, meatballs	High	6-8
Ground beef, patties (4 ounce)	High	2-3 each
Ground beef, meat loaf (1½ lb.)	High	15-20
Standing rib roast (4-5 lbs.)		
Rare	Med.-High	8-10 per lb.
Med.	Med.-High	10-12 per lb.
Well	Med.-High	12-14 per lb.
Rolled rib roast (3-5 lbs.)		
Rare	Med.-High	8-10 per lb.
Med.	Med.-High	10-12 per lb.
Well	Med.-High	12-14 per lb.
Rib-eye roast (2-4 lbs.)		
Rare	Med.-High	8-10 per lb.
Med.	Med.-High	10-12 per lb.
Well	Med.-High	12-14 per lb.
Tenderloin roast (1-2 lbs.)		
Rare	Med.-High	7-8 per lb.
Med.	Med.-High	8-10 per lb.
Well	Med.-High	10-12 per lb.
Beef cubes (boneless) (1 lb.)	Low	15-20
Beef cube steak	High	1-3
Beef-rib eye steak (1 inch)		
Med.-rare	High	4-5
Beef T-bone steak (1 inch)		
Med.-rare	High	5-6
Beef filet mignon (1 inch)		
Med.-rare	High	4-5
Beef chuck roast (3-5 lbs.)	Med.	19-23 per lb.
Corned beef piece (3 lbs.)	High	25

Meat	Setting	Time (mins.)
VEAL		
Roast	Med.	8-10 per lb.
Chops (to 1 inch), 6 chops	Med.-High	12
PORK		
Chops (to 1 inch thick), 2 chops	Med.	14-18
4 chops	Med.	26-32
6 chops	Med.	35-45
Roast (internal temp. 170 F)	Med.	9-11 per lb.
Ham, precooked		
(internal temp. 115 F)	Med.	12-14 per lb.
Bacon, 2 slices	High	1-2
Sausage, raw, 4 2-oz. patties	High	4-5
Sausage, raw, 4 links	High	2-3
Sausage, prebrowned, 4 patties	High	1-2
Sausage, prebrowned, 4 links	High	1-1½
Franks, 2 in buns	High	1-2
LAMB		
Roast		
Med.	Med.	10-12 per lb.
Well	Med.	14-17 per lb.
Chops (to 2 inch), 4 chops	Med.-High	12
CHICKEN		
Pieces, 2-3 lbs.	High	18-22
Pieces, 1-2 pieces	High	3-6
Whole chicken	Med.-High	9-10 per lb.
TURKEY		
Breast, whole		
(internal temp. 170 F)	Med.-High	9-11 per lb.
Legs and other pieces	Med.-High	11-13 per lb.
OTHER POULTRY		
Rock cornish game hen, whole	High	6-8 per lb.
Duckling, whole	High	7-9 per lb.

Meat	Setting	Time (mins.)
FISH		
Fillets, 1 lb.	High	9-11
Steaks (to 1 inch thick), 1 lb.	High	8-9
Whole trout (to 10 oz.)	High	5-6
SHELLFISH		
Clams, 4-5 oz.	High	3-5
Crab legs, 8 oz., each	High	3-4
Lobster, whole (to 2 lbs.)	High	9-11
Lobster tails, 8 oz., each	High	3-4
Scallops, 1 lb.	High	5-7
Shrimp, peeled, 1 lb.	High	5-6
Shrimp, unpeeled, 1-2 lbs.	High	6-9

MICROWAVE POWER SETTINGS

Because there is yet to be a standardized description for the settings on microwave ovens, setting descriptions can vary from manufacturer to manufacturer. The chart that follows will try to explain what equals what among the various terms used.

Most countertop microwave ovens have a maximum power output of 600 to 700 watts. The so-called lower cooking settings are achieved by turning this maximum power on and off during the cooking time. If you are using a compact microwave, its output will probably be in the range of 400 to 500 watts, and you should add about 30 to 45 seconds to specified cooking times given in recipes.

MICROWAVE SETTING CHART

Output (watts)	Power Level	Number	Power	Description
600-700	High	10	100%	Cook
400-500	Med.-High	7	70%	Bake
300-350	Medium	5	50%	Bake
200-250	Med.-Low	3	30%	Simmer/Defrost
60-100	Low	1	10%	Warm/Defrost

SUGGESTED TEMPERATURES AND TIMES FOR DEEP FAT

Food to be Deep Fried	Temperature F	Time
Fish fillets	370	4 mins.
Shellfish	370	2-3 mins.
Croquettes	390	2-3 mins.
French fried potatoes	370	5-7 mins.
Doughnuts	370	2-5 mins.

Always make sure that the oil has been heated to the right temperature by using a thermometer designed for deep fat. If your oil is not hot enough, the food will be greasy and soggy when it has browned enough to be removed from the oil. If the oil becomes too hot, the outside will be overdone before the interior has adequately cooked.

Incidentally, oil can be reused several times if you strain it through a fine sieve and store it in your refrigerator. Add a bit more each time to compensate for what was absorbed by the food. If you have used it for fish and want to remove the odor, place a few slices of raw potato in the cooled oil and reheat the oil slowly, stirring from time to time. When the potato has browned, discard the slices, and strain and store the oil as usual.

COOKING VEGETABLES

Vegetables may be cooked in a variety of ways: baked, broiled, boiled, stewed, steamed, cooked in a pressure cooker or in a microwave.

In the chart below, the times given are only approximate because the actual cooking time will vary depending on the size of the vegetable, its moisture content, and the way you like vegetables cooked. Use the number as a guide only and test the vegetables from time to time as they cook.

SUGGESTED COOKING TIMES FOR VARIOUS VEGETABLES
in minutes unless otherwise noted
(n/a means that this method is not appropriate
for the particular vegetables)

Vegetable	Bake	Broil	Boil	Steam	Pres-sure†	Micro-wave*
Artichoke	n/a	n/a	30-45	25-30	6-10	14-15
Asparagus, cut	n/a	n/a	2-5	4-5	1-2	9-11
Asparagus spears	n/a	n/a	7-10	8-12	1-2	11-13
Beans, baked	6-8 hr.					
(precook beans for 1 hr., bake at 250)						
Beans, baked	30-40					
(start with canned baked beans, bake at 375)						
Beans, green, French	n/a	n/a	5-8	8-10	2-3	8-10
Beans, green, whole	n/a	n/a	7-12	10-12	3-4	16-18
Beans, green, 1 inch	n/a	n/a	5-8	8-10	2-3	10-14
Beans, Italian ... see *Beans, green*						
Beans, yellow ... see *Beans, green*						
Beet greens	n/a	n/a	5-12	4-8	2-3	7-9
Beets, whole	n/a	n/a	30-45	—	5-10	22-25
Bok choy (sauté 3-4 mins.)		n/a	6-8	3-6	1-2	7-8
Broccoli spears	n/a	n/a	10-15	8-10	1-2	11-13

Vegetable	Bake	Broil	Boil	Steam	Pressure†	Microwave*
Brussels Sprouts	n/a	n/a	10-20	10-15	2-3	7-9
Cabbage, shredded	n/a	n/a	5-8	3-5	1-2	4-5
Cabbage, wedges	n/a	n/a	8-10	5-8	4-6	6-7
Carrots, halves	n/a	n/a	15-25	10-13	3-4	9-11
Carrots, julienne	n/a	n/a	8-10	4-8	2-3	6-8
Carrots, sliced	n/a	n/a	10-20	5-12	2-3	8-10
Carrots, whole	n/a	n/a	20-30	15-18	5-6	11-13
Cauliflower parts	n/a	n/a	5-10	10-15	1-2	8-12
Cauliflower, whole	n/a	n/a	15-25	18-30	3-4	10-15
Celery slices	n/a	n/a	6-8	7-9	2-3	10-12
Collards	n/a	n/a	8-12	7-9	3-5	7-9
Corn on the cob	n/a	n/a	6-8	8-10	4-5	3-4
Cranberry beans, fresh ... see *Fava beans*						
Dandelion greens	n/a	n/a	9-13	5-8	3-4	7-9
Eggplant (sauté slices till tender)			n/a	n/a	n/a	5-6
Fava beans, fresh	n/a	n/a	20-25	n/a	4-6	10-12
Fennel	n/a	n/a	7-10	15-20	1-2	7-9
Garlic (sauté sliced, minced, or whole until golden brown)						
Jerusalem artichoke	n/a	n/a	12-25	10-20	9-12	10-12
Jicama						
(sauté slices 3-4 mins.; julienne 1-2 mins.)					1-2	3-4
Kale	n/a	n/a	8-12	7-9	3-5	7-9
Kohlrabi, whole	n/a	n/a	30-35	n/a	5-7	10-14
Leeks	n/a	n/a	5-10	10-12	3-5	5-7
Lima beans, fresh	n/a	n/a	20-25	n/a	2-5	10-12
Mushrooms (sauté whole 3-4 mins.; slices 2-3 mins.)						
Mustard greens	n/a	n/a	5-8	3-6	1-2	7-9
Okra, sliced	n/a	n/a	5-8	6-10	1-2	5-7
Okra, whole	n/a	n/a	7-10	10-15	2-3	8-10
Onions, dry, sliced	n/a	n/a	8-10	6-8	3-4	8-15
Onions, dry, whole	n/a	n/a	20-25	15-20	5-6	10-12
Parsnips, whole	n/a	n/a	10-15	15-20	7-8	10-12
Pattypan squash	n/a	n/a	10-12	12-15	2-3	8-10
Pea pods	n/a	n/a	n/a	3-5	1-2	6-8
Peas	n/a	n/a	5-8	6-10	1-2	6-8

Vegetable	Bake	Broil	Boil	Steam	Pres-sure†	Micro-wave*
Peppers, green	n/a	n/a	3-5	3-5	1-2	4-5
Potato, quartered	n/a	n/a	15-20	10-15	5-8	2-3
Potato, sliced	10-12	10-12	10-15	5-8	2-3	2-3
Potato, whole	45-60	n/a	30-40	n/a	10-15	4-6
Pumpkin pieces	n/a	n/a	25-30	20-25	10-11	9-14
Rutabaga, whole	n/a	n/a	20-25	25-35	8-12	n/a
Shallots (sauté whole or sliced)			8-10	6-8	3-4	n/a
Spinach	n/a	n/a	2-5	3-6	1-2	7-9
Squash, acorn	n/a	n/a	20-25	15-20	9-11	9-14
Squash, butternut	n/a	n/a	12-15	8-12	10-12	9-14
Squash, Hubbard	n/a	n/a	25-30	20-25	12-13	9-14
Squash, spaghetti	60-75	n/a	20-30	20-30	8-12	10-20
Summer squash, slice	n/a	n/a	3-4	5-7	1-2	5-7
Summer squash, whole	n/a	n/a	8-10	10-12	2-3	9-12
Sunchokes . . . see *Jerusalem artichokes*						
Sweet potato	30-60	n/a	30-35	20-25	10-15	4-6
Swiss chard	n/a	n/a	3-6	5-8	1-2	6-8
Tomatoes, whole	n/a	4-6	10-15	n/a	1-2	n/a
Turnip greens	n/a	n/a	5-8	3-6	1-2	7-9
Turnips, cubes	n/a	n/a	10-15	8-10	3-5	8-10
Turnips, slices	n/a	n/a	5-8	6-10	5-6	10-12
Yam	30-60	n/a	30-35	20-25	10-15	4-5
Zucchini, slices (sauté 3-5 mins.)			3-4	5-7	n/a	5-7
Zucchini, whole	n/a	n/a	5-10	8-12	2-3	9-12

†Notes for Pressure Cooking of Vegetables:

If you are using a four-quart pressure cooker, use ⅓ to ½ cup of water. For a seven-quart cooker, use no less than one cup. Use stock for the liquid if you wish. You should never fill a pressure cooker more than two-thirds full. Start to measure the cooking time when the pressure indicator reaches fifteen pounds. Reduce the pressure as quickly as you can when the time has elapsed. If you add salt, it is best to add it after the vegetables have been cooked.

*Notes for Microwave Cooking of Vegetables:

You should always microwave fresh vegetables at the HIGH setting. The cooking times given in this chart will cook one pound of fresh vegetables to the tender stage. If you like crisper or softer vegetables or if you are cooking a smaller or larger amount, adjust the time accordingly. Always allow vegetables to stand for three to five minutes after microwaving.

SUGGESTED COOKING TIMES FOR DRIED VEGETABLES

Vegetable	Cooking Time (Top-of-Stove)
Black beans	2 hours
Black-eyed peas	30 mins.
Cranberry beans	2 hours
Great Northern beans	1-1½ hours
Kidney beans	2 hours
Lentils	30 mins.
Lima beans	1 hour
Navy beans	1½-2 hours
Pinto beans	2 hours
Soybeans	2½ hours
Split peas	20-30 mins.

SUGGESTED TEMPERATURES AND TIMES
FOR BAKED PRODUCTS

(Times are appropriate for altitudes up to 3,000 feet)*

Product	Pan Size	Temperature (degrees F)	Time (in mins.)
BREAD PRODUCTS			
Biscuits	——	450	12-15
Muffins	——	425	25
Popovers	——	375	50
Yorkshire pudding	——	450	25-30
Cornbread	9 inch	400	35
Spoonbread	1½ qt.	425	50-60
Fruit quick breads	9×5-inch loaf	350	60-65
Yeast breads	9×5-inch loaf	400	50-60
Pizza with toppings	14 inch	450	15-20
CAKES			
Layer	8 inch	350	35-40
Layer	9 inch	350	30-35
Layer	9×13 inch	350	30-35
Sponge/chiffon cake	10-inch tube	350	45-55
Cupcakes	—	350	20-25
Angel food	10-inch tube	350	35-40
Gingerbread	9 inch	350	50-60
Pound cake	9×5-inch loaf	350	65-75
Fruitcake	10-inch tube	300	2 hours
COOKIES			
Bar (baked then cut)		350	25-35
Drop cookies		375	15-20
Ball-shaped cookies		350	12-15
Cut cookies, ⅛ inch thick		400	6
Cut cookies, ¼ inch thick		400	9
Filled cookies		425	8-10
PIES AND OTHER BAKED DESSERTS			
Pastry shell	9 inch	450	12-15
Crumb-crust shell	9 inch	375	8-10

Product	Pan Size	Temperature (degrees F)	Time (in mins.)
Meringue shell	9 inch	275	60-65
Filled pie, 2-crust	9 inch	425	40-50
Filled pie, 1-crust	9 inch	350	50-60
Deep-dish pie	9 inch	450	45-50
Deep-dish pie, indiv.	3-4 inch	425	35-40
Custard pie	9 inch	350	35-45
Meringue topping	9 inch	350	12-15
Custard pudding	cups	300	55-60
Rice pudding	1½ qt.	300	60-90
Bread pudding	1½ qt.	350	60-75
Fruit brown betty	1½ qt.	350	50-60

*As you know, liquids boil at a lower temperature and evaporate faster at higher altitudes. Baked products rise faster because the gases from the leavening agent expand more quickly. If the product rises too fast it will seem a little coarse. If you are baking from scratch you can make the following minor adjustments to ease the situation.

If you live near 5,000 feet: take a scant ¼ teaspoon away from each teaspoon of baking powder called for, also take away about a tablespoon of sugar from each cup called for, and add 2-3 tablespoon of liquid of each cup required.

If you live near 7,000 feet: take a rounded ¼ teaspoon away from each teaspoon of baking powder called for, take away 2-3 tablespoon of sugar from each cup called for, and add 3-4 tablespoon of liquid to each cup required.

SUGGESTED TEMPERATURES
FOR COOKING CANDY AND OTHER CONFECTIONS

Confection	Temperature F and Description	Cold-Water Test
Boiled icings	230-234, thread stage	Syrup forms 2-inch thread from spoon.
Fudge, fondant	234-240, soft ball	Candy can be rolled into a ball in the water but flattens when removed from the water.
Divinity, caramels	244-248, firm ball	Candy can be rolled into a firm (not hard) ball in the water and does not lose its shape out of the water.
Taffy	250-266, hard ball	Candy forms hard but still pliable ball.
Butterscotch	270-290, light crack	Candy forms threads in water that soften when removed from water.
Peanut brittle	300-310, hard crack	Candy forms hard brittle threads that do not soften out of water.
Caramelized	310-320, caramelize	Sugar melts then browns as it cooks.

CHAPTER 6

How to Store (Just About) Everything

Knowing how to store food correctly is important to today's cooks because no matter how efficient you are about shopping, shopping takes time. In most of today's busy households time is a very precious commodity, so the less often you have to shop and the less time you have to spend at it, the better off you are.

Because your time is so valuable, and because most homes either have or can be adapted to have space and facilities for storing foods, it makes sense to have a good understanding of the principles of storage and to use those principles to give you more time, save money, and allow you to prepare more versatile meals.

The amount of food you keep on hand will depend, of course, not only upon the space you have for storage but also the number, sex, and ages of the people you cook for. It's not news that cooking for a family that includes teenagers is quite different from cooking for one or two adults.

Without getting into the details of nutrition, which are covered in the next chapter, here are some very general guidelines regarding daily food consumption for the average person:

Milk products	Adults, 2 cups Children and teenagers under 20, 3 cups
Protein foods	2 servings of at least 4 ounces
Vegetables and Fruits	4 or more servings (1 serving of citrus, 1 serving of a dark green or yellow vegetable at least every other day)
Cereals and Breads	4 or more servings of whole grain or enriched grain products such as bread

These are the "basic four" that nutritionists speak of. In looking at the list you can see that you have a variety of food-storage requirements.

Milk products, with the exception of dried milk, must be stored either by refrigeration or freezing. Evaporated milk may be stored at room temperature until the can is opened; after opening it must be refrigerated.

Protein foods present a variety of storage requirements: fresh meats, fish, and poultry must be refrigerated or frozen; canned products kept at "room temperature" or lower; fresh eggs refrigerated; dried beans, peas, and lentils are the least sensitive to storage deterioration and can be kept for long periods at room temperature.

With fruits and vegetables you again have a range of storage situations, from room temperature to refrigerated to frozen, depending on the product and its manner of preservation.

Cereal and bread products are fairly easy to store on a relatively long-term basis. Boxed foods can be kept at room temperature. Whole grains keep best in glass or metal containers with lids or in sealable plastic bags. Crackers should be kept in an airtight container, especially in humid climates. Bread can be kept in your freezer, refrigerator, or at room temperature, depending on when it will be used.

FOOD-STORAGE PRINCIPLES

There are four things that can cause stored food to become inedible:

1. Temperatures that are too warm, which encourages bacteria, molds, and yeasts to develop.

2. Access to moisture, which all microorganisms need to grow and multiply.

3. Too much light, which can accelerate certain enzyme and other chemical actions.

4. Insects or rodents, whose abilities to get into stored food can be thwarted only by putting the food in glass or metal containers.

Of these four, the most common cause of food spoilage is the temperature at which it is kept. The chart that follows shows what happens over the whole range of temperatures, from the 250 degrees Fahrenheit that can be reached only in a pressure cooker to the minus 32 degrees that can be found in your home freezer.

The microorganisms that cause food contamination love to be warm and moist. In such an environment they multiply like crazy and eat everything in sight. When we speak of microorganisms we are including not only bacteria but also yeasts and molds. All these biological forms can cause problems with food products, and the only way to keep them under control is to keep the food adequately cool or adequately hot.

Fahrenheit Temperature	Centigrade Temperature	
220-250	110-120	Pressure-cooking range (necessary for home-canning low-acid foods such as meats, fish, poultry, and

Fahrenheit Temperature	Centigrade Temperature	
		low-acid vegetables. Bacteria spores are destroyed at these temperatures.
210-220	100	Water boils (range used for home-canning of fruits, some tomatoes, pickles, jams). Bacteria spores destroyed after an extended cooking time at this temperature range.
160-210	70-100	Growing cells of bacteria destroyed; molds and yeasts destroyed.
130-150	55-70	Certain bacteria (thermophilic, or "heat-loving") continue to grow in this temperature range.
100-130	40-55	Growth of most bacteria, yeasts, and mold stops but micro-organisms remain alive.
60-100	15-40	Range of most active growth of bacteria, molds, and yeasts. The range generally termed "room temperature."
40-60	5-15	Certain bacteria (cryophilic, or "cold-loving") continue to grow in this temperature range.
33-40	1-5	Greatly slowed growth rate for bacteria, molds, and yeasts. Refrigerator temperature range.
minus 20-32	minus 20-0	Growth ceases in bacteria molds and yeast but the microorganisms are still alive. Freezer range.

As you can see, the only time you can be sure that all microorganisms have been destroyed is after cooking at high temperatures for an adequate amount of time. Once the food is cooled and made available to the air, the microorganism population starts to build up again. Freezing does not kill bacteria, molds, or spores, it just renders them dormant.

When you are going to cool just-cooked food, do not leave it on the counter before refrigerating, because the food will spend a considerable length of time in the temperature danger zone. Put the food directly into the refrigerator. Ideally it should cool to 40 degrees Fahrenheit within four hours. If you have a large container—soup or chili, for instance—divide it into several smaller dishes so it will cool quickly.

There is one very simple rule to follow: keep it hot or keep it cold.

You may wonder how and why molds can appear on foods stored in your refrigerator. The reason is that molds not only tolerate cool temperatures, but will continue to grow in temperatures down to just above freezing.

What should you do if you find moldy food in your refrigerator?

First, don't smell it ... certain molds are known to cause respiratory problems.

Second, don't try to save it ... wrap the food and throw it out.

Third, clean the refrigerator where the food was kept with soapy water and then wipe the area with a cloth soaked with a vinegar and water solution. You should also take a close look at the food that was stored nearby.

Small spots of mold can be cut off hard cheese (cut an inch away from around the mold spot and an inch into the cheese), but other moldy foods should be discarded without tasting. This means jams and jellies too, for even though the mold may appear only on top, the tendrils can extend throughout the jar.

This information is not meant to alarm, but only to explain why caution, care, and good sense are all important in food preparation and storage.

While thinking about the ramifications of improper storage, let's look for a moment at what some of the real problems can be in terms of health. Food poisoning is no joking matter, as anyone who has suffered through it can attest.

Food poisoning is also not uncommon. It has been estimated that in this country alone and in just one year, there can easily be more than four million cases of salmonella poisoning . . . and that is just one kind of food poisoning.

Here are the six most prevalent types of food poisoning:

STAPHYLOCOCCUS.   It is caused by *Staphylococcus aureus.* The incubation time necessary for the food poisoning to develop is 3 to 12 hours. Symptoms are nausea, vomiting, abdominal cramps, diarrhea, headache, sweating, and low-grade fever. Staph poisoning usually lasts one to two days. Foods commonly involved include meats (especially ham, poultry, and meat sandwiches), cream sauces, custard, and dairy products.

SALMONELLOSIS.   It is caused by various of the *Salmonella* species. The incubation time is 6 to 48 hours. Symptoms are nausea, vomiting, abdominal pain, sudden-onset diarrhea, frequently a fever, sometimes chills and headache. Salmonella food poisoning lasts two to seven days. It is very rarely a cause of death (usually from blood infection). Foods commonly involved include meat and poultry, cracked eggs, and cross-contamination from other foods during food preparation (unclean cutting boards, for example).

VIBRIO PARAHEMOLYTICUS.   It is caused by various of the *Vibrio parahemolyticus* species. The incubation time is 12 to 24 hours. Symptoms are severe stomach pain, nausea, vomiting, and diarrhea, sometimes fever, chills, and headache. Duration is one to two days, and it is rarely a cause of death. Foods commonly involved include marine fish and seafood that are raw or undercooked, or foods cross-contaminated from these foods.

PERFRINGENS.   It is caused by *Clostridium perfringens.* The incubation time is 8 to 22 hours. Symptoms include mild abdominal pain and diarrhea. The duration of the illness is one to two days, and it is rarely a cause of death. Foods commonly involved include cooked meats, gravies, stuffings as prepared or semi-prepared mixtures.

TRICHINOSIS.   It is caused by *Trichinella spiralis,* which is a parasite nematode worm about one millimeter long. The incubation time is 3 to 28 days. During this time the parasites locate themselves in the muscle tissue. A slight infestation may go unnoticed, but as the number ingested increases, symptoms of infection include muscle pains and fever, sometimes with stomach or intestinal symptoms. Because of the life cycle of the parasite, trichinosis poisoning can last as long as months. In severe infestations death may even result if the parasite larvae enter the heart muscles or the brain. The food responsible is undercooked pork; occasionally wild game meat (often bear meat) has also been involved. Cooking the meat to an internal temperature of 170 F will kill the parasite.

BOTULISM.   This is the most serious of all food poisoning illnesses. It is caused by *Clostridium botulinum.* The incubation time can be from a few hours to as much as eight days. The range of symptoms usually starts with stomach and intestinal problems, dizziness, and headache. Dry skin, mouth, and throat, constipation, and weakness form the middle range of symptoms. The final range includes increased muscle weakness or paralysis, double vision, and respiratory failure. The duration of the poisoning is one to twenty days. The death rate is high. The foods commonly involved are home-canned low-acid vegetables and meat products. These foods must always be canned in a pressure cooker for safety, and you should never eat home-canned vegetables or meat products unless you know that they have been prepared in that manner. If you ever suspect you or anyone you know may have been infected with botulism, go to an emergency room immediately for care.

The bottom line is that food poisoning is probably one of the most easily preventable problems that mankind faces. Cleanliness in your kitchen, using proper preservation techniques, and care in storage can prevent it completely.

For more information on preventing food-related diseases, you can call or write the Meat and Poultry Hotline, U.S. Department of Agriculture Safety and Inspection Service, Room 113 South, Washington, D.C. 20250 (800-535-4555), or contact your local county extension service.

FOOD-PRESERVATION TECHNIQUES

Although many fresh food products are easily available year-round, for convenience and variety you will be using preserved foods frequently. Preserving food is an ancient skill developed by earliest societies as a means of surviving through the winter. Some of the techniques, such as drying food, are nearly as old as mankind itself while others, such as freeze-drying and irradiation, are products of the twentieth century.

DRYING

The oldest form of long-term food preservation is drying. Specimens of dried foods have been found in Egyptian tombs, and the Egyptians learned the method from even older civilizations. The Middle East with its brilliant sunlight and dry heat, provided a perfect environment for the development of this technique.

Drying preserves the food by removing up to 98 percent of the moisture and thereby removing the ability of micro-organisms to survive. As with freezing, drying does not kill the microorganisms, it merely causes them to be inactive. As soon as water in any form is available, the bacteria, molds, and yeast start to multiply again. It is therefore essential that dried foods be kept in airtight containers and not stored close to any source of humidity. Near the stove, for instance, steam from food can provide all the moisture that is needed for bacterial growth.

If you live in a hot, sunny location you may be able to sun-dry some products outdoors if you are careful to protect the foods from insects. In less sunny locations or at times of the year other than summer, you will probably use an electric dryer indoors. These dryers use both heat and moving air to desiccate the food. Be sure to follow the manufacturer's directions and test the food carefully to make sure the food is adequately dry before it is put away. There are many home-dried products that can become family favorites ... fruit "leathers," for example, are simple to make from dried fruit puree and make a great low-calorie and healthful snack.

CANNING

Although it is called home-canning, most home-canners do not use metal cans to hold the food but instead use bottles that can be reused year after year. These bottles are sealed with a new flat lid each time they are used. The lid has a soft material around the outside that forms a seal against the edge of the bottle. These flat lids can be used only once. The third part of the package is a metal ring that is screwed onto the bottle and holds the flat lid in place while the processing goes on. This ring should be removed after the bottles have been processed and cooled.

Home-canning is both economical and satisfying ... and can be fun too. Seeing a shelf lined with colorful canned fruits, vegetables, pickles, and preserves can make a cook feel very accomplished.

It is not difficult to can at home, and there are some excellent and inexpensive booklets that give explicit directions for canning a variety of foods. Check with Customer Information, Superintendent of Documents, Government Printing Office, North Capitol and H Streets, Washington, D.C. 20402, for lists of government publications on food preservation. Your county extension service also will have documents and information, and of course there are many commercially published books too.

Without going into detail about canning food at home, here are a few basic, and essential, guidelines.

1. Follow your canning instructions exactly.

2. Always thoroughly wash and scald the bottles before using. Lids should be kept in steaming hot water to soften the sealing ring.

3. Do not overfill the bottles. Food expands when heated and can ooze out and make it impossible for a seal to form. Without the seal, microorganisms can invade and grow in the food.

4. Wipe the edges carefully before putting the flat lid on, to remove anything that may have collected there. Also carefully check for any roughness or cracks on the edge of the bottle, and if you find any do not use the bottle.

5. If you are canning fruits, jams, or pickles (all high-acid foods), a boiling water bath in a stove-top canning

kettle is adequate. If you are canning anything else, you must use a pressure cooker designed for canning. (See following table of high-acid and low-acid foods.)

6. When processing is completed and bottles have cooled, test the seal by pressing down on the middle of the lid. It will not move if the seal is good. If you can cause it to move by pressing, it is not sealed and the food must either be eaten as though it were fresh or else reprocessed with a fresh lid. (Reprocessing will usually cause the food to lose both shape and flavor, however, so it is preferable to get it right the first time.)

7. Store the jars in a cool and dark location.

8. Wipe off the lid before opening and also check the seal to make sure it is still intact. If the seal has been broken, do not eat the food.

ACID LEVELS OF VARIOUS FRUITS AND VEGETABLES
(Listed in descending order of acidity)

High Acid (can be processed in boiling water bath):
plums, gooseberries, dill pickles, apricots, apples, blackberries, sour cherries, peaches, sauerkraut, raspberries, blueberries, sweet cherries, pears, and most varieties of tomatoes.

Low Acid (must be processed in pressure canner):
okra, pumpkin, carrots, turnips, beets, green beans, sweet potatoes, spinach, asparagus, kidney beans, lima beans, peas, corn, hominy, olives, meat and fish, and combinations of meat and vegetables such as soups, chili, or stew.

Commercially canned products generally can be considered safe, but when you buy canned goods check them over and do not buy any that have dents (may mean the seal has been broken) and bulges (may mean that spoilage is already taking place inside the can). Remember, too, that once the container is opened, the food inside is vulnerable to bacterial growth again and should either be used immediately or refrigerated.

FREEZING

Canning and drying require care on the part of the cook but do not require much of an investment in equipment. Freezing, on the other hand, is a very simple process but does require that you have a freezer or true freezer section in your refrigerator in order to store the food at near zero degrees Fahrenheit or lower.

The main requirement for successful freezing is that the food is carefully wrapped so that air cannot penetrate the package. There are a variety of special, heavier-than-normal packaging materials (foil, sealable plastic bags, plastic containers, and so forth) that are suitable for freezing, and they should be used rather than the foils and plastics that you normally use in the kitchen. Again, you should follow directions carefully.

SALTING (CURING)

This is another of the traditional preservation methods. It works because the salt draws moisture away from the food and also makes a chemical environment that is unsuitable for bacterial growth. Salt curing is done in two ways: dry-curing, where the food is covered in salt, and brining, where the food is submerged in a solution of salt and water. It goes without saying that food preserved this way is very salty, and it is not advisable for anyone on a salt-restricted diet to eat such foods.

PICKLING

Microorganisms do not like an acid environment, and that is the basic principle behind this preservation technique. The food is submerged in a solution of water, vinegar, salt, sugar, and spices until it absorbs enough to change its basic chemical character from alkaline to acid. It is important to follow the proportions given in this recipe so that the solution is adequately acid. Use commercial vinegar that has a known acid level, not vinegar that you may have made yourself. Although there was a time when home-pickling meant crocks of cucumbers left open to the air, fortunately that is no longer common. Current knowledge requires that pickles receive a final processing in a boiling water bath to produce a vacuum-sealed bottle.

SOME QUESTIONS AND ANSWERS
ABOUT HOME FOOD PRESERVATION

What causes lids not to seal? If the food in the bottles has not been heated to a high enough temperature, a vacuum may not be formed in the jar and the lid will fail to seal. A seal also will not form if there is any food or other material on the gasket of the lid or on the bottle top. Overfilling the bottles can cause liquid to bubble out during cooking and prevent the seal from forming.

Why can flat lids be used only once? The rubber gasket around the edge of the lid acquires certain indentions and marks after being used, which makes it impossible to seal properly a second time.

Why should metal rings be removed after the bottles have cooled? Moisture can be caught between the bottle and the ring and cause the ring to rust. The ring is no longer necessary after the seal has formed.

Why is liquid sometimes lost during processing? If the bottles are overfilled they will bubble over while in the boiling water bath. Liquid is more likely to escape during pressure canning than during boiling-water-bath canning, because the temperatures reached are much higher. Do not open the jar to add more liquid after food is processed, because you will allow bacteria to enter as soon as the seal is broken.

Why do bottles sometimes break during processing? There are several reasons and all of them are avoidable. Nonstandard bottles (such as mayonnaise bottles) that are made of untempered glass are very likely to break, so you should always use bottles meant for home-canning purposes. Old bottles may have hairline, sometimes almost invisible, cracks that will cause splits. If you put bottles directly on the bottom of the canner rather than in a rack, the bottles can break. Hot food introduced into a cold bottle also can cause a momentary expansion in the glass that cracks the bottle.

Why does food sometimes change color after home-processing? The most common cause of color change is oxidation, which can occur when the food is not covered by liquid but is exposed to air at the top of the bottle. Undercooking as well as overcooking in the canner can also cause color shifts. The pink and bluish colors that sometimes develop in pears, apples, and peaches are a result of chemical changes in the fruits' natural coolants.

What causes mold to form on the top of home-canned foods? Mold can only form if the seal has been broken and air allowed in. Although the mold may be visible only on the surface, tendrils of growth extend completely through the bottle. The food should be discarded without tasting.

Can fruit be canned without sugar? Fruit can be processed in just plain water, a water/honey combination, or the traditional water/sugar mixture. If you use an artificial sweetener, it is best to add it just before serving and not when the fruit is being processed, because heating the artificially sweetened syrup may cause it to develop a bitter taste.

What causes jellies and jams not to set? The chemistry of jelling is precise, so it is essential to follow directions exactly. The fruit will jell only if the relationship between the amount and acid level of the fruit juice, the amount of available pectin, and amount of sugar are exactly right. If any of the three is out of proportion the fruit will not jell. Another common cause for problems with jelly and jam is making too big a batch at one time.

What should you do if your jelly does not jell? The traditional thing to do is use the product as a fruit syrup or topping for desserts. If you want to try one more time, measure ¼ cup sugar, ¼ cup water, and 4 teaspoons of powdered pectin for each quart of jelly. Mix the pectin and water together and bring to a boil, stirring constantly. Add the jelly and sugar, stir well, and bring to a full boil over high heat, stirring constantly. Boil the mixture for 30 seconds, remove from heat, and pour into jars and seal as usual. To remake with liquid pectin measure ¾ cup sugar, 2 tablespoons of lemon juice, and 2 tablespoons liquid pectin for each quart of jelly. Bring jelly to a boil over high heat. Add sugar, lemon juice, and liquid pectin. Bring to a hard boil and boil for one minute. Remove from heat, pour into containers, and seal.

Why is it necessary to blanch foods before freezing? Although freezing slows the enzyme action that causes food to mature, it does not stop it completely. Blanching means to briefly place food in boiling water or steam to stop the enzyme activity. The product is then placed in iced water to cool quickly, and then frozen. By doing this the food will retain its flavor and texture even though frozen on a long-term basis. (At altitudes over 5,000 feet you should blanch foods one minute longer than standard directions state, because your water boils at a lower temperature.)

Why do home-prepared pickles sometimes shrivel up? This can be caused by using too much vinegar, sugar, or salt, by overcooking, or by overprocessing. Follow directions carefully.

What causes pickles to turn dark? Ground spices can cause this, so it is better to use whole spices when pickling. Darkening can also be caused by using iodized table salt, so always use plain salt in making pickles. Some areas have high mineral content (especially iron) in their drinking water, and these chemicals can cause color changes.

If you follow directions carefully, use high quality produce, and store the processed product properly, you will find that home-preserving of foods can be economical, satisfying, and fun.

FREEZE-DRYING

This is a relative newcomer among preservation techniques. It is not possible to freeze-dry food at home because of the equipment required to remove the water from the food. Basically the process involves placing prefrozen food in a vacuum chamber and then subliming the water away. Subliming means to change from a solid (such as ice) to a water vapor without passing through a liquid stage (water), as would normally happen. Foods preserved this way are made edible by rehydrating. They have an extended storage time. But their greatest asset is the entirely new look they have given to camping cuisine. Freeze-dried foods are lightweight and compact, they require no refrigeration, and they are available in an astonishing variety of dishes.

IRRADIATION

This "newest" preservation method is not as new as one might think. As far back as 1908 X-ray treatments were used to kill insects in tobacco, and by 1920 the French were experimenting with using ionized radiation to preserve food.

The technique involves exposing foods to ionizing energy (usually from a radioactive source such as cobalt 60). In low doses it will kill many microorganisms and insects; as the dose is raised it will sterilize food and destroy microorganisms just as exposure to high temperatures will. (Pork is being treated this way in some locations to kill any possible infestation of *Trichinella spiralis* and thereby prevent trichinosis.)

When the food is irradiated most of the radiation energy passes through without being absorbed. The sources of irradiation can be gamma rays, electron beams, or X rays. The amount of radiation energy absorbed by the food depends upon its chemical makeup.

So far about 25 countries have approved the irradiation of about 40 different foods for the purpose of food preservation. In the Netherlands, South Africa, and Japan it is a relatively common method. The World Health Organization, the Food and Agriculture Organization of the United Nations, and the International Atomic Energy Agency have issued general standards for the irradiation of foods for human consumption.

Since evidence indicates that low-dose irradiation does not affect the constituent parts of food adversely, the FDA has made a preliminary conclusion that low-dose irradiation does not affect nutritional values.

Under proper control, food preserved by irradiation is not radioactive nor is there any radioactive residue in the food. At the present time this technology is expensive when compared with the traditional means of preserving foods, and consequently is not widely used.

Having gone through the various ways food is preserved, the next thing is to determine how long individual food types can be kept safe to eat.

FOOD STORAGE: WHAT TEMPERATURES AND HOW LONG

Food	50-70 F / 10-21 C / Dry or Fresh	50-70 F / 10-21 C / Canned	32-50 F / 0-10 C / Refrigerated	0 F / -17.8 C / Frozen
DAIRY PRODUCTS				
Butter	2-4 days		2-3 weeks	1 year
Cheese (natural)	1-2 weeks		2-8 months	1 year
Cheese (processed)	2-3 weeks		6-8 months	1 year
Ice cream				1 month
Milk, fresh			5-7 days	
Milk, evaporated		1 year		
Milk, dry	1 year		2 years	
Eggs, dried	6 weeks		1 year	
Eggs, fresh			1 week	1 year
MEAT PRODUCTS				
Bacon		18 months	1-2 weeks	3 months
Beef			2-7 days	1 year
Beef, ground			2-3 days	2 months
Lamb			2-7 days	1 year
Pork			3-7 days	3 months
Sausage			2-5 days	3 months
Chicken		18 months	2-5 days	3 months
Turkey		18 months	2-5 days	6 months
Fish		1 year	1-3 days	5 months
Ham		18 months	2 weeks	6 months
Jerky	6 months		1 year	
Cold cuts			3-7 days	3 months

Food	50-70 F 10-21 C Dry or Fresh	50-70 F 10-21 C Canned	32-50 F 0-10 C Refrigerated	0 F -17.8 C Frozen
MEAT SUBSTITUTES				
Dry beans/peas	1-3 years			
Peanut butter		6 months	12-18 months	
Nuts, unshelled	1 year			
Nuts, shelled	6 months	1 year	12-18 months	2 years
Tofu			2-4 days	3 months
FATS AND OILS				
Vegetable oils	6 months		1 year	
Shortening	6 months		1 year	
Margarine	6 months		1 year	2 years
Lard	6 months		1 year	
CEREAL PRODUCTS AND GRAINS				
Cornmeal, fresh	2 months			
Cornmeal, degermed	2 years			
Rice	2 years			
Whole grains	2 years			
Flour, white	1 year			
Flour, whole grain	4 months			
Flour, soybean	4 months			
Pasta, uncooked	1 year			
Baking mix	1 year			
Cake mix	1 year			
Baked products	1 week			9 months
SUGARS, JAMS, AND SPREADS				
Sugar, white	indef.			
Sugar, brown	18 months			
Sugar, powdered	24 months			
Sugar substitute	24 months			
Honey, syrups	12 months			
Jams & jellies			1 year	6 months

Food	50-70 F 10-21 C Dry or Fresh	50-70 F 10-21 C Canned	32-50 F 0-10 C Refrigerated	0 F -17.8 C Frozen
FRUITS				
Apples	1 month	1 year	1-6 months	1 year
Apple sauce		1 year	3-7 days	1 year
Apricots	3-5 days	1 year	3-7 days	1 year
Berries	3-5 days	6 months	3-7 days	1 year
Cherries	3-5 days	1 year	3-7 days	1 year
Citrus fruits	3-5 days	6 months	3-5 days	1 year
Cranberries			1 week	1 year
Cranberry sauce		1 year		
Figs	2 weeks	18 months	1 year	
Grapes	2-4 weeks	18 months	2-4 weeks	1 year
Peaches	3-5 days	18 months	7-10 days	1 year
Pears	1-3 days	18 months	4-6 weeks	1 year
Pineapple	3-5 days	18 months	3-7 days	1 year
Plums	2 weeks	18 months	4-6 weeks	1 year
Raisins	12 months			
Dried fruits	12 months			
VEGETABLES				
Beans, green	1-3 days	18 months	3-5 days	1 year
Beets	1-3 days	18 months	3-7 days	1 year
Cabbage	1 month		2-3 months	1 year
Carrots	1 week	18 months	1-3 weeks	1 year
Corn	1 day	18 months	2-3 days	1 year
Onions, yellow	1-6 months			1 year
Peas, green	1 day	18 months	2-3 days	1 year
Potatoes, fresh	1-3 months	18 months		1 year
Potatoes, dried	12-16 months			
French fries				6 months
Spinach		18 months	2-5 days	1 year
Sweet potatoes	8 months	18 months		1 year
Tomatoes		18 months	4-6 days	1 year
Tomato sauce		18 months	2-5 days	1 year
Dried vegs.	1 year			

Food	50-70 F 10-21 C Dry or Fresh	50-70 F 10-21 C Canned	32-50 F 0-10 C Refrigerated	0 F -17.8 C Frozen
MISCELLANEOUS				
Baking powder	1 year			
Baking soda	1 year			
Catsup		12-18 mos	2 months	
Cocoa	2 months		6 months	
Coconut	1 year			
Chocolate	24 months			
Cornstarch	24 months			
Flavorings	24 months			
Gelatin	2 years			
Herbs, dried	6-12 months			
Mayonnaise		2-9 months	1 month	
Mustard		2 years	2 months	
Pudding mixes	1-2 years			
Salad dressings		2-6 months	1 month	
Salt	indef.			
Sauce mixes	6-12 months			
Soup mixes	12-18 months			
Spices, whole	12-24 months			
Spices, ground	6-12 months			
Vinegar	2 years			
Whipped topping	2 years (dry)		1-3 days (prepared)	
Yeast	6-10 months (sealed pkg.)			

GUIDELINES FOR FOOD STORAGE

Most businesses use their inventories on what is called a
F.I.F.O. basis ... First In, First Out. That idea is a good one
for cooks to use as well. In practice it simply means that you
use the oldest products first. By rotating your stored foods this
way you will prevent spoilage, use the foods while they are

still flavorful and have maximum nutrition, and have better control over storage conditions in general.

FROZEN FOODS

It is particularly important that you use your frozen foods on a rotating basis. Because it is easy for things to become "lost" in your freezer, it is not a bad idea to keep a running inventory posted to your freezer door. It need not be elaborate, just a simple list of foods that are in the freezer and an indication of how many packages of each there are. As you use items or put more in, just erase the original number and update it with the change. You will find that most frozen foods are best when used within a year of the time they were frozen.

There are two common problems that develop in frozen foods prepared at home:

The first problem is "freezer burn." This happens when food is not protected from the dehydrating effect of the dry climate that exists in your freezer. The way to avoid it is to make sure each package is carefully wrapped and sealed so that no air can reach the food. You can use self-sealing plastic bags or containers with sealing lids—just be sure that the seals are firm and complete. You can also wrap foods to be frozen in foil. The foil must be heavy-duty and should be folded over several times to make sure the air is kept out. Make a note on the package of the date the food was frozen.

The second problem is particularly common in frozen fruits: when the fruit is thawed it dissolves into mush. This happens because it has taken too long for the food to freeze. The fluid in the cells expands and the cell walls of the fruit are broken. When the fruit thaws, all of the fluid escapes. You can avoid this by freezing small batches so that your freezer can handle the cooling process quickly.

If you don't have a freezer now but are thinking about buying one, here are some things to keep in mind. Freezers are normally sold in sizes indicating their capacity in cubic feet. One cubic foot can hold as much as 35 pounds of packaged frozen food (packed densely and not including lightweight bulky items such as bread). You should allow from three to five cubic feet of freezer storage for each person in your family. Keep in mind, too, that the more often you "turn your inventory," to borrow another phrase from business, the more efficiently you are using your freezer. A good rule of thumb is to use all frozen food within a year of the date it was frozen.

If your freezer ever should lose power, the best thing to do is simply keep the door closed. Food in a fully loaded freezer will remain frozen for one to two days if no outside air is allowed in. Alternatively, you can fill in open spaces in the freezer with dry ice (always wear gloves when handling dry ice) or transfer the stored food to a friend's freezer or a commercial frozen food locker (check your telephone directory Yellow Pages).

As long as ice crystals remain or the temperature of the food has been kept at 40 degrees Fahrenheit or lower, it may be refrozen. This is particularly true of frozen fruits and vegetables and raw meats. Special care should be used with seafood or any foods containing a cream sauce, because they are the most sensitive to bacterial contamination.

Foods that have become completely thawed must be cooked and either eaten within a day or two or canned in the normal home-canning method. Be aware, however, that products that have been frozen, thawed, and then canned are not going to have either the taste or the nutrition they had before being thawed. You have to decide for yourself whether the final canned product will be worth the effort of canning.

DRIED FOODS

Dried foods should of course be stored in airtight containers. Strong plastic bags with self-sealing closures or the kind that are sealed with heat are excellent for this purpose. Glass jars with tight-fitting caps can be used for dried foods you access often. You can also store dried products in your freezer where they will use less room than fresh frozen products but will be protected from normal room humidity.

CANNED FOODS

Canned foods, both commercially canned and home-canned, should be wiped off before opening. Even the cleanest of storage areas accumulates dust, and you do not want to introduce the dust into the food you are going to use. If you buy canned goods in case lots, it is important to note when you bought them and try to use the product within the recommended time period. Commercially canned food products have a very long storage life but eventually, although they may still be perfectly safe to eat, flavor and nutrients are lost.

STAPLE FOODS

If you buy large quantities of such things as rice, dry milk, flour, and sugar, take out what you feel is about the amount you will use in a month and put it in a covered container. The remainder of the bag or box should be tightly closed and kept in a cool, dry place.

It is not necessary to purchase special storage containers. If you wish, you can save the wide-mouth bottles that originally contained such things as peanut butter or applesauce and use them to hold your current supplies of staple products. (If you want to dress them up a bit, you can spray the outside of the lids with paint in some color that goes with your kitchen.)

Spices, herbs, and seasoning mixes should be stored away from the stove in a dark, cool, and dry location. It is usually not a good idea to buy large quantities of ground spices, because once ground the spice begins to lose its flavor. A year is about as long as most ground spices should be kept. Whole spices may be kept longer and really are much better because you grind and use them immediately. The dried leaf herbs should be replaced about once a year too. Although many books advise you to sniff the ground spices and herbs to see if they are still fresh, this is not a particularly good idea because you have no way of knowing how the freshly ground product would smell and also because some ground spices acquire a special sort of fungus contamination that can cause upper respiratory irritation.

FOOD-STORAGE CHECKLIST

From time to time take a quick inspection trip around your kitchen and storage area and check out these points:

1. Is there food stored in cabinets under the sink? Not a good idea for several reasons. The extra humidity can encourage growth of molds, insects have ready access to the food, and household cleaning products can be mistaken for edibles (particularly by children).

2. Are foods frequently left out on open counters for long periods of time? Not a good idea because even food that has been refrigerated comes quickly up to the temperature that encourages bacterial growth. If you prepare your meals several hours in advance, always refrigerate until time to cook and serve.

3. What are you storing near the stove? This is a location that is not only warm but also quite humid because of the steam that rises as food is prepared. Not a good place to store anything that is sensitive to either heat or humidity (this especially includes ground spices and other cooking staples).

4. Check newly purchased food as you put it away. Should it be stored in the refrigerator or in a cupboard? Just because a food product is canned does not necessarily mean it can be stored in your cupboard (canned ham certainly should not be stored anywhere but in the refrigerator, for instance). What about storage after it is opened? Particularly watch out for things that are high in oil (mayonnaise and peanut butter, for example), because they can quickly become rancid and inedible unless stored properly.

5. Invest in an accurate thermometer for your freezer and refrigerator and make sure that food is being held at a low enough temperature to retard growth of microorganisms. Also check the seals on the door to make sure room-temperature air is not leaking in. (A quick way to make this check is to close the door on a dollar bill. If the bill can be removed easily after the door is closed, you need a new gasket.) Periodically move your freezer and refrigerator away from the wall and clean the coil with a soft brush to remove lint and dust. This will help the unit to function more efficiently.

6. Review all the food you have in storage about once a month. Make sure containers are properly sealed. Discard anything that seems even the slightest bit spoiled and do not taste it first.

CHAPTER 7

Nutrition Is Where You Find It

Nutrition is a word used to describe a process. That process is the one that starts as you put food in your mouth and continues until all the value that the food has to offer has been removed, separated into its various components, and put to use in keeping you alive and healthy.

All foods that we eat are composed of protein, carbohydrates, and fats ... sometimes in combination, sometimes in a pure form.

The human body is an astounding chemical factory. It is able to pull nutrients from all sorts of sources ... even those classic junk foods that we love so well. It works best and is able to do a more satisfactory job of keeping itself healthy, however, if it is given a little help.

Much of that help can come from the person doing the cooking, because although many Americans eat in restaurants regularly, most eat at home most of the time.

In 1977 the Senate Select Committee on Nutrition and Human Needs of the United States studied the state of nutrition in this country. In the foreword to the Committee's report, Committee Chairman George McGovern wrote that the purpose of the report was to let people know that the state of nutrition in our country was "as critical a public health concern as any now before us." He went on to say that the recommendations, based on the scientific knowledge available at the time, were made to "provide guidance for making personal decisions about one's diet."

The recommendations of the Committee were revised in 1985 and published by the U.S. Department of Agriculture as "Dietary Guidelines for Americans." As revised, the recommendations were these:

1. Eat a variety of foods.
2. Maintain desirable weight.
3. Avoid too much fat, saturated fat, and cholesterol.
4. Eat foods with adequate starch and fiber.
5. Avoid too much sugar.
6. Avoid too much sodium.
7. If you drink alcohol, do it in moderation.

These are truly modest goals but a good place to start to plan your improved nutrition.

In this chapter we'll look at what we eat and why we need to eat certain things in order to function well. We'll also see what the National Academy of Sciences thinks is an adequate amount of various specific nutrients. You'll be given an overview of what you need to keep in mind during meal-planning sessions and while you are shopping.

First, let's look at the terms used in discussing nutrition and see what they mean.

RECOMMENDED DIETARY ALLOWANCES

The National Research Council and the National Academy of Sciences send representatives to their combined Food and Nutrition Board, whose Committee on Dietary Allowances periodically publishes a list of Recommended Dietary Allowances. These amounts are "intended to provide for individual variations among most normal persons as they live in the United States under usual environmental stresses." In other words, average people in average situations. The only problem is that if you were to individually survey the millions of people in this country, you would probably not find an "average" person among them because each person and each environment is unique.

These Recommended Dietary Allowances (RDAs) should, therefore, be taken only as guidelines, not absolutes. (RDAs noted below are from the ninth edition, published in 1980.)

Your physician is, of course, the person to help you if you have specific problems about food. He may also refer you to a nutrition counselor for additional advice. If you have specific questions about RDAs, drop a note to the Human Nutrition Information Service, U.S. Department of Agriculture, Federal Building Room 325A, Rockville, Maryland 20782. You can also direct inquiries about diet and health to Consumer Inquiries, Food and Drug Administration, 5600 Fishers Lane, Rockville, Maryland 20857.

PROTEIN

Protein is the basic substance of every cell in our bodies. All life-forms require protein in some form to survive. The various proteins are made up of smaller units called amino acids. Most of the 22 amino acids that have been identified to date are manufactured in our bodies. There are eight, however, that we cannot manufacture. They are called "essential amino acids" and must be taken in from food. These essential amino acids are: tryptophan, phenylalanine, leucine, isoleucine, lysine, valine, methionine, and threonine. There is a ninth, histidine, which may be necessary for childhood development.

The amino-acid makeup of a protein determines its nutritive value. Proteins that supply all of the essential amino acids in about the same proportions needed by our bodies rank the highest in value.

Where protein is found. Foods that meet the requirements for supplying adequate amounts of the essential amino acids include meat, fish, poultry, eggs, and dairy products. Protein is also found in vegetable sources, but it is "incomplete" in that it lacks one or more of the essential amino acids. Combining vegetable sources, however, can gather up all of the eight required amino acids in one dish. Frequently, ethnic dishes represent this idea in action ... beans and rice, for example. Soybeans and products made from them are the best nonanimal sources of complete protein.

How protein is used in the body. Protein is used everywhere in your body throughout your life. It makes up your body's building blocks and glue. It makes the hemoglobin that carries oxygen to your cells and carbon dioxide away from them. It makes antibodies to fight infection. Protein can also be used to provide energy for the body, but that is something more easily, more commonly, and more advisedly done by eating carbohydrate sources.

Recommended dietary allowance daily. At least two servings of foods that are complete proteins and contain all of the essential amino acids. Such foods include:

2-3 ounces lean meat, fish, or poultry (weight without bone)
2-3 ounces tofu (soybean curd)
1 egg

In addition, dairy products* should be eaten daily as well in these minimum amounts:

*A sensitivity to the lactose (milk sugar) that is found in milk products is present in a good portion of our population. The intolerance shows up as an inability to digest milk and other dairy products. People with this problem have to make sure they take in adequate protein from nondairy sources.

Children under 9	16-24 fluid ounces of milk†
Children 9-12	24 or more ounces of milk†
Teenagers	32 or more ounces of milk†
Adults	16 or more ounces of milk†
Pregnant women	24 or more ounces of milk†
Nursing mothers	32 or more ounces of milk†

†Or equivalent in other dairy products from table below.

Liquid milk in these amounts can be taken from whole, low-fat, or skim milk, buttermilk, or rehydrated evaporated or dried milk. Cheese and ice cream or ice milk can also be used for part of necessary intake.

1-inch cube cheese	=	approx. ½ cup liquid milk
½ cup cottage cheese	=	approx. ⅓ cup liquid milk
2 tbsp. cream cheese	=	approx. 1 tbsp. liquid milk
½ cup ice cream	=	approx. ⅓ cup liquid milk

Taken in grams of "pure protein" these are the daily Recommended Dietary Allowances by the National Academy of Sciences:

Children 1-3 years	23 grams
Children 4-6 years	30 grams
Children 7-10 years	34 grams
Females 11-18 years	46 grams
Females 19 or more years	44 grams
Pregnant women	Age + 30 grams
Nursing mothers	Age + 20 grams
Males 11-14 years	45 grams
Males 15 or more years	56 grams

Deficiency Symptoms

Too little protein can result in poorly formed muscles, organs, and brain tissue, and poor hair, teeth, and bone structure. Extreme shortage of protein in the body can ultimately result in anemia, malnutrition, and inability of the blood to clot.

Excessive-Intake Symptoms

People who eat protein in extremely excessive amounts can cause themselves difficulties that may ultimately cause kidney disease and the loss of calcium from the body. (This latter problem is something that older women should be particularly careful about because of the potential to speed up the onset of osteoporosis.)

CARBOHYDRATES

Carbohydrates are compounds of carbon, hydrogen, and water and are of vegetable origin. They enter our diets in three forms: starches, sugars, and fibers (cellulose). Carbohydrates are also spoken of as being either simple or complex. Simple carbohydrates are sugars that the body can absorb very quickly. Complex carbohydrates are most commonly found in whole grains, which combine fiber with the starch, take longer to digest, and provide more nutrients than simple carbohydrates.

Where carbohydrates are found. All plant products are composed of carbohydrates ... everything from lettuce to corn to sugar beets to wheat. It is possible to exist, and some people do exist, on just carbohydrates. Carbohydrates are almost always the backbone of any national diet. In Africa and Asia carbohydrate sources provide the great majority of calories taken in. Good sources of starch are grains and products made from grains, potatoes, dry beans, and dry peas. Natural sources of sugars are cane and beet sugars, honey, molasses, and fruits. Fiber is found in all vegetables in varying amounts; the highest fiber content is found in wheat bran.

How carbohydrates are used in the body. As electricity is to a light bulb, so carbohydrates are to us. They keep us going. Through our metabolic processes, starches and sugars are changed into glucose (blood sugar), which is the body's staple to supply energy for body processes and to support growth. Cellulose provides fiber and bulk for better digestion, and possibly aids in the prevention of certain diseases.

Recommended dietary allowances daily. At least five servings of grain-based foods (bread, pasta, cereal, rice, or other grain). Typical servings would be: one slice of bread, one ounce dry cereal, ⅔ cup cooked cereal or grain product (such as rice), or ¾ cup cooked pasta.

In addition, four or more servings should be eaten daily of fruits and vegetables. These servings should include some source of vitamin C and also a regular source of vitamin A (see the listings below for good sources). A typical serving of vegetable or fruit is about ½ cup if it can be measured that way, or a medium-size whole fruit (such as banana, apple, orange, and so forth).

The ideal daily intake of carbohydrates is closely tied to the recommended calories for each person's age, height, and optimum weight.

Deficiency Symptoms

Eating inadequate amounts of carbohydrates can ultimately cause the body to use its own muscle and organ structure (composed of protein) to provide energy for survival. This process causes physical deterioration and ultimate starvation.

FATS

Fats are concentrated sources of energy. Weight for weight they provide twice the number of calories as protein or carbohydrates.

While fats are a necessary portion of the nutritional triad (proteins-carbohydrates-fat), this is an area where you can definitely have too much of a good thing. According to most nutritionists, Americans have far too much of a good thing, and not only their bathroom scales but also their overall health shows it. It has been estimated that "average" Americans take in 40 percent or more of their daily calories in the form of fats. Most nutritionists would like to see fat consumption cut to no more than 30 to 35 percent of the daily calories.

Cutting too far back on fat intake is not a good idea however. According to the U.S. Department of Agriculture, even people on a severely fat-restricted diet should get about 25 percent of their calories from fats. Fats move slowly through the digestive system and keep hunger from recurring too soon.

There are several kinds of fat. Discussions and controversies in recent years about their benefits and problems have made their names familiar to us.

The **saturated fats** are the ones with the worst reputation because of their association with cholesterol. The cholesterol question has not been completely resolved and new information is appearing all the time, but there seems to be some positive link between cholesterol in the blood and problems in the circulatory system. Consequently, we have been advised by the medical research establishment to limit our intake of foods containing cholesterol and saturated fats.

Cholesterol is a waxy material produced in the liver and in some of the body's cells. It has a number of beneficial uses in our bodies' chemical processes, but too much of it in the blood seems to contribute to the development of hardening of the arteries, the condition that is the basis for many heart attacks and strokes.

Saturated fats can be identified easily because they are normally solid at room temperature.

Monounsaturated fats are found in some vegetable oils. Current research in human nutrition indicates that, like polyunsaturated oils, monounsaturated fats may help to lower cholesterol levels in the blood, which decreases chances for heart disease or strokes.

Polyunsaturated fats all come from vegetables. Many polyunsaturates also contain linoleic acid, which is not manufactured by our bodies, but is essential to nutrition. Unsaturated fats are normally in a liquid form at room temperature.

Where various kinds of fat are found. Saturated fat is found in animal products, meats, dairy products, eggs, some fish, and in products that contain these foods or are cooked in animal fat. Monounsaturated fats are found in olive, canola, and peanut oil, almonds, avocados, peanuts, and some other seeds and fruits. Polyunsaturated fats are found in vegetable oils: corn oil, cottonseed oil, safflower oil, sesame oil, soybean oil, and wheat germ oil to name a few.

The following chart will give you some idea of the fat content of some common meats and meat products:

Meat or Fish	% of Fat
Bacon, before cooking	60% fat
Sirloin steak, broiled	45% fat
Prime rib, roasted	34% fat
Pork roast, baked	28% fat
Ham (regular), baked	24% fat
Hamburger, regular	30% fat
Hamburger, lean	18% fat
Hamburger, extralean	14% fat
Chicken with skin, baked	20% fat
Chicken without skin, baked	5% fat
Codfish, baked	15% fat
Red snapper, baked	5% fat

How fats are used in the body. In addition to providing energy sources for the body's requirements, fats also make up part of the structure of cells, form a protective cushion around vital organs, and carry fat-soluble vitamins around the body.

Recommended dietary allowance daily. Nutritionists generally recommend that fat intake not exceed 35 percent of the total calories taken in during any day.

Deficiency Symptoms

Too little fat in your diet can result in an inadequate supply of the fat-soluble vitamins A, D, E, and K being available for good nutrition. A deficiency of fat is not common in this country . . . quite the reverse!

THE VITAMINS

Vitamins are organic chemical compounds that make it possible for our bodies to use the food they take in. Although all vitamins are composed of the same elements—carbon, hydrogen, oxygen, and sometimes nitrogen—each compound arranges these elements in a slightly different way and the result is that each does a slightly different job.

Vitamins were first identified in the early 1900s, when it was finally recognized that the lack of "something" caused people to have such diseases as scurvy, beriberi, and pellagra. When the "somethings" were analyzed, they were determined to belong to a class of chemical compounds called amines. Since they had to do with life, the Latin word for life (vita) was used as a prefix and thus was invented the word "vitamines." The final "e" was dropped and we were left with the word we know today.

At first, no one knew exactly what they were, from a chemical standpoint, so they were simply assigned letter designations: A, B, C, and so forth. As research continued, human requirements for the compounds were clarified, and understanding of the workings of the compounds modified. The letter or letter-plus-number designations in many cases have been replaced with the names of the chemical compounds involved. Now we have both single letter designations and chemical names in common use. In our discussion, both will be given wherever appropriate.

Vitamins are required in only tiny amounts to do their work. Usually recommended amounts are given in milligrams (1/1,000th of a gram) or micrograms (1/1,000th of a milligram). Some vitamins are measured in International Units (IUs).

VITAMIN A (RETINOL)

What is vitamin A? Vitamin A is an oil-soluble vitamin and is stored in your liver. Because of this, it can be accumulated in your body over long periods of time. This long-term storage capability is the reason behind the warnings about excessive intake of vitamin A.

Where is vitamin A found? In its elemental form, beta-carotene, it is found in yellow and dark-green vegetables (the beta-carotene is part of the pigment that colors the vegetables). When you eat it in this form, it is converted into vitamin A as part of the digestive process. When the beta-carotene is eaten and processed by animals, we find ready-to-use vitamin A in such things as eggs, dairy products, and liver.

How is vitamin A used in the body? Vitamin A is necessary for new cell growth, for healthy tissues, and is essential for good vision.

Recommended Dietary Allowance Daily
of Retinol*

Infants to 1 year	420 milligrams
Children 1-3 years	400 milligrams
Children 4-6 years	500 milligrams
Children 7-10 years	700 milligrams

Females 11 or more years   800 milligrams
Pregnant women   1,000 milligrams
Nursing mothers   1,200 milligrams
Males 11 or more years   1,000 milligrams

*1 milligram of retinol = 6 milligrams of beta-carotene

Deficiency Symptoms

Reduced ability to see in low-light situations, high sensitivity to light, and other eye problems. Vitamin A deficiency may also cause dry rough skin that can become susceptible to infection.

Excessive-Intake Symptoms

Although vitamin A as it naturally occurs in plants (as beta-carotene) is virtually nontoxic, pure retinol in large doses can cause various problems including swelling of feet and ankles, fatigue, weight loss, thinning of hair. Children are especially sensitive to overdoses of vitamin A.

VITAMIN B-1 (THIAMINE)

This is, as all B-complex vitamins are, a water-soluble vitamin. This means that it is not stored in the body and therefore must be taken in on a regular basis. Amounts in excess of the amounts required for immediate use are eliminated.

Where is thiamine found? Thiamine is found in a variety of places: in pork, soybeans, peas, nuts, beans, and wheat products. It is also in brewer's yeast and blackstrap molasses.

How is thiamine used in the body? This vitamin is required for good digestion, for growth, fertility, for good functioning of the nervous system, and for carbohydrate metabolism.

Recommended Dietary Allowance Daily

Infants to 6 months	0.3 milligram
Infants 6 months to 1 year	0.5 milligram
Children 1-3 years	0.7 milligram
Children 4-6 years	0.9 milligram
Children 7-10 years	1.2 milligrams
Females 11-22 years	1.1 milligrams
Females 23 years or more	1.0 milligram
Pregnant women	Age + 0.4 milligram
Nursing mothers	Age + 0.5 milligram
Males 11-14 years	1.4 milligrams
Males 15 years or more	1.2 milligrams

Deficiency Symptoms

Poor appetite, irritability, swelling, improper functioning of the nervous system, involuntary contractions of muscles throughout the body. Ultimately an inadequate intake can result in beriberi.

VITAMIN B-2 (RIBOFLAVIN)

Riboflavin is another of the water-soluble B-complex family.

Where is riboflavin found? B-2 is to be found abundantly in green leafy vegetables, whole grain products, liver, dairy products, eggs, lean meats, blackstrap molasses, and some nuts.

How is riboflavin used in the body? Riboflavin's primary function is in digestion, where it is essential for the efficient metabolism of both carbohydrates and proteins. It is also important to cell growth and in the production of antibodies.

Recommended Dietary Allowance Daily

Infants to 6 months	0.4 milligram
Infants 6 months to 1 year	0.6 milligram
Children 1-3 years	0.8 milligram
Children 4-6 years	1.0 milligram
Children 7-10 years	1.4 milligrams
Females 11-22 years	1.3 milligrams
Females 23 years or more	1.2 milligrams
Pregnant women	Age + 0.3 milligram
Nursing mothers	Age + 0.5 milligram
Males 11-14 years	1.6 milligrams
Males 15-22 years	1.7 milligrams
Males 23-50 years	1.6 milligrams
Males 51 years or more	1.4 milligrams

Deficiency Symptoms

Signs of deficiency of intake of riboflavin include lip sores and cracks as well as diminution of vision. Sometimes a bright red tongue is an indication of deficiency. Riboflavin deficiency may also be involved in formation of cataracts and in retardation of growth.

VITAMIN B-3 (NIACIN)

Also in the B-complex family, niacin is another water-soluble vitamin. It is a very stable vitamin and easy to obtain.

Where is niacin found? There are many inexpensive sources of niacin. Among the sources are liver, meats, peas, beans, whole grain cereal products, and fish.

How is niacin used in the body? Niacin's primary function is in maintaining healthy condition of all tissue cells.

Recommended Dietary Allowance Daily

Infants to 6 months	6 milligrams
Infants 6 months to 1 year	8 milligrams
Children 1-3 years	9 milligrams
Children 4-6 years	11 milligrams
Children 7-10 years	16 milligrams
Females 11-14 years	15 milligrams
Females 15-22 years	14 milligrams
Females 23 or more years	13 milligrams
Pregnant women	Age + 2 milligrams
Nursing mothers	Age + 5 milligrams
Males 11-18 years	18 milligrams
Males 19-22 years	19 milligrams
Males 23-50 years	18 milligrams
Males 51 years or more	16 milligrams

Deficiency Symptoms

Extremely inadequate intake of niacin is the cause of pellagra, which was once, next to rickets, the most common deficiency disease in the United States. Pellagra is characterized by a swollen bright red tongue, rough skin, mouth sores, diarrhea, and mental disorders. Serious deficiencies can result in such symptoms as headaches, insomnia, and muscular weakness.

PYRIDOXINE-PYRIDOXAL-PYRIDOXAMINE (VITAMIN B-6)

Vitamin B-6 has three forms, but all are used by the body in the same way. B-6 is also water-soluble and not stored by the body.

Where is vitamin B-6 found? The various forms of this vitamin are easy to obtain and are found abundantly in liver, whole grain cereals and grains, potatoes, lean meats, green vegetables, and corn.

How is vitamin B-6 used in your body? Like all B-complex vitamins, B-6 is essential for proper growth and maintenance of body functions. It is particularly involved in the metabolism of protein and also aids in maintaining the proper balance between sodium and potassium in the body.

Recommended Dietary Allowance Daily

Infants to 6 months	0.3 milligram
Infants 6 months to 1 year	0.6 milligram
Children 1-3 years	0.9 milligram
Children 4-6 years	1.3 milligrams
Children 7-10 years	1.6 milligrams
Females 11-14 years	1.8 milligrams
Females 15 or more years	2.0 milligrams
Pregnant women	Age + 0.6 milligram
Nursing mothers	Age + 0.5 milligram
Males 11-14 years	1.8 milligrams
Males 15-18 years	2.0 milligrams
Males 19 or more years	2.2 milligrams

Deficiency Symptoms

Deficiencies of pyridoxine include mouth soreness, dizziness, nausea, and weight loss.

FOLIC ACID (FOLACIN)

Yet another member of the B-complex family, folic acid is needed only in minuscule amounts for good health.

Where is folic acid found? The best natural sources for folic acid are liver, navy beans, and dark-green leafy vegetables. Other good sources are nuts, fresh oranges, whole wheat products, and brewer's yeast.

How is folic acid used in the body? Folic acid's primary job is related to metabolism, the conversion of food into energy. It is also important in the manufacture of red blood cells. Like the other B-complex vitamins it is also involved in growth.

Recommended Dietary Allowance Daily

Infants to 6 months	30 micrograms
Infants 6 months to 1 year	45 micrograms
Children 1-3 years	100 micrograms
Children 4-6 years	200 micrograms
Children 7-10 years	300 micrograms
Females 11 or more years	400 micrograms
Pregnant women	800 micrograms
Nursing mothers	500 micrograms
Males 11 or more years	400 micrograms

Deficiency Symptoms

Deficiency in folic acid can result in a type of anemia. It is also possibly involved in the graying of hair and in some digestive disturbances.

CYANOCOBALAMIN (VITAMIN B-12)

Another vitamin that we require in the most minute amounts in order to function adequately is this sixth member of the B-complex group.

Where is B-12 found? The most accessible sources of B-12 are organ meats, lean red meats, milk, eggs, and shellfish. B-12 is not present to any measurable degree in plants, which means the strict vegetarians ("vegans," those who eat no animal products at all) should supplement their diets with this vitamin.

How is B-12 used in the body? B-12's primary responsibility is the proper functioning of all cells but particularly those in the bone marrow, nervous system, and intestines. It is also involved in the normal development of the red blood cells.

Recommended Dietary Allowance Daily

Infants to 1 year	Consult your baby's doctor
Children 1-3 years	2 micrograms
Children 4-6 years	2.5 micrograms
Children 7-10 years	3 micrograms
Females 11 years or more	3 micrograms
Pregnant women	4 micrograms
Nursing mothers	4 micrograms
Males 11 years or more	3 micrograms

Deficiency Symptoms

A deficiency in vitamin B-12 can cause pernicious anemia, and if the deficiency is prolonged a degeneration of the spinal cord can occur.

OTHER MEMBERS OF THE B-COMPLEX FAMILY

PANTOTHENIC ACID. Pantothenic acid is needed to support a variety of body functions including proper growth and maintenance. It is involved in digestion and also in the production of adrenal hormones. It can be readily found in liver, eggs, potatoes, peas, whole grains, and peanuts. An inadequate intake of pantothenic acid can cause headaches, fatigue, poor muscle coordination, nausea, and cramps.

BIOTIN. At one time biotin was called vitamin H, but it was later realized that it belonged in the B-complex group and that name was dropped. It is essential in metabolizing food from all three food types—carbohydrates, proteins, and fat. Biotin is found in good amounts in eggs, milk, and meats. One idiosyncrasy of biotin, however, is that there is a compound present in raw egg whites that can destroy it. (You might keep this in mind if you feed your cat or dog raw whole eggs.) This is a vitamin that we produce in our own intestinal tracts, so deficiencies are quite rare.

PARA-AMINOBENZOIC ACID (PABA). This interesting member of the B-complex group has taken on a high visibility in recent years because it has been found that when a diluted amount is rubbed on the skin, sunburn can be prevented. It is, therefore, an important ingredient in most sunscreens, which have been recommended to aid in the prevention of skin cancers. Internally it is involved in protein metabolism and blood cell formation. Natural sources of PABA include blackstrap molasses, brewer's yeast, organ meats, and wheat germ. An inadequate intake most commonly presents itself in the form of digestive complaints.

CHOLINE. Choline is involved in the proper functioning of the liver, thymus gland, and kidneys. It is found in brewer's yeast, beans and peas, organ meats, fish, soybeans, and wheat germ.

INOSITOL. The final member of the B-complex group that we will discuss is inositol. It is involved in the functioning of several organs including your heart, liver, and kidneys, and also in the operation of the nervous system. Research seems to indicate that deficiencies of inositol can be involved in excessive cholesterol, some digestive problems, and hair loss.

ASCORBIC ACID (VITAMIN C)

Ascorbic acid is absolutely essential to health. Although almost all other mammals synthesize their own ascorbic acid internally, humans have to take in their vitamin C from food sources.

There is probably more controversy about vitamin C intake than that of any other vitamin, and if you are interested there are a number of books that vehemently take each side of the argument.

Vitamin C is the least stable of the vitamins and is susceptible to destruction by both heat and oxidation. This is why cooking and storage can leave a food product that would seem like a good source of vitamin C with only minimal amounts of it.

Where is ascorbic acid found? It is most abundant in citrus fruits, tomatoes, green peppers, broccoli, greens (turnip, mustard, etc.), strawberries, and other vegetables.

How is ascorbic acid used in the body? Vitamin C is essential for tissue growth and repair. It aids in tooth and bone formation. Research also seems to indicate that it plays a role in your body's efforts to protect itself from infection.

Recommended Dietary Allowance Daily

Infants to 1 year	35 milligrams
Children 1-10 years	45 milligrams
Females 11-14 years	50 milligrams
Females 15 years or more	60 milligrams
Pregnant women	80 milligrams
Nursing mothers	100 milligrams
Males 11-14 years	50 milligrams
Males 15 years or more	60 milligrams

Deficiency Symptoms

Scurvy, one of the oldest of mankind's identified diseases, is the result of severe deficiency in the intake of ascorbic acid. It was the bane of sailors on long voyages until it was recognized that lime or lemon juice could prevent this terrible debilitating disease (hence the nickname for the British sailor, "limey"). Early signs of deficiency include bleeding gums, easy bruising, weakness, lassitude, irritability, and loss of weight.

Excessive-Intake Symptoms

Too much vitamin C can result in nausea, diarrhea, headaches, and in some people the development of kidney stones.

CALCIFEROL (VITAMIN D)

The second fat-soluble vitamin to look at is vitamin D. Daily requirements of this vitamin are very small and it is probably the most inexpensive of all because it can be manufactured by your skin, using the ultraviolet rays the sun provides.

Where is vitamin D found? In addition to sunshine, vitamin D is also easily available in fish, fortified milk, and egg yolks.

How is vitamin D used in the body? Vitamin D's main job is to aid in the absorption of calcium and phosphorus necessary for bone formation.

Recommended Dietary Allowance Daily

Infants to one year	10 micrograms
Children to ten years	10 micrograms
Females 11-18 years	10 micrograms
Females 19-22 years	7.5 micrograms

Females 23 years or more	5 micrograms
Pregnant women	15 micrograms
Nursing mothers	15 micrograms
Males 11-14 years	8 micrograms
Males 15 years or more	10 micrograms

Deficiency Symptoms

Vitamin D deficiency causes rickets, bone deformation, potbelly appearance, and sometimes stunted growth.

Excessive-Intake Symptoms

Because it is oil soluble and because such minute amounts are needed for good health, it is possible to take in too much vitamin D. Signs of excessive intake include nausea, weight loss, weakness, and excessive urination.

THE TOCOPHEROLS (VITAMIN E)

Along with vitamin C, vitamin E is a very controversial food substance because of the varied, and extravagant, claims that have been made about its value. Clearly research will ultimately prove or disprove the various claims, and in the meantime we have to make our own judgments based on the best information we can gather. It is an oil-soluble vitamin and therefore can be accumulated in the body.

Where is vitamin E found? It is easily available in vegetable oils, beans, eggs, the germ of grains (particularly wheat germ), liver, fruits, and vegetables.

How is vitamin E used in the body? The primary function of vitamin E in your body is to act as an antioxidant, which is something that prevents oxygen from destroying other substances.

Recommended Dietary Allowance Daily

Infants to 6 months	3 International Units
Infants 6 months to 1 year	4 International Units
Children 1-3 years	5 International Units
Children 4-6 years	6 International Units
Children 7-10 years	7 International Units
Females 11 or more years	8 International Units
Pregnant women	10 International Units
Nursing mothers	11 International Units
Males 11-14 years	8 International Units
Males 15 or more years	10 International Units

Deficiency Symptoms

No specific diseases have been directly associated with an inadequate intake of vitamin E, with the possible exception of one form of infant anemia that seems to improve when vitamin E is added to the diet. The research on this vitamin will be interesting to watch.

Excessive-Intake Symptoms

Too much vitamin E can result in headaches, nausea, light-headedness, blurred vision, and can lead to a deficiency in vitamin K.

VITAMIN K

Vitamin K is necessary for the manufacture of prothrombin in the liver, and this substance is involved in the coagulation of blood. There are three forms of vitamin K. One form is found naturally in such vegetables as spinach, lettuce, kale, cabbage, and cauliflower, and also in liver and egg yolks. The second form is manufactured in our own bodies by certain microorganisms in the intestines. The third form (called menadione) is made synthetically and is more potent than the first two forms.

Too little vitamin K in your diet can result in excessive bleeding from cuts and abrasions and possibly even liver injury. No specific RDA is made for this vitamin.

THE MINERALS

Minerals are inorganic chemical elements needed by the body for growth and maintenance. Minerals are also an essential part of the digestive juices and of the fluids of the body cells.

CALCIUM

Calcium is the most abundant mineral element in the body. In combination with phosphorus it is largely responsible for the hardness of bones and teeth. Almost all of the calcium in our bodies is found in these two places.

Where is calcium found? Milk and other dairy products are by far the most outstanding source of nutritional calcium; however, calcium is also present in some dark-green leafy vegetables (because of the plant's ability to absorb the mineral from the soil) and in bones found in some canned fish (particularly salmon and sardines). Calcium is such an important nutrient, especially for postmenopausal women, that if for some reason dairy products cannot be eaten, calcium supplements should be seriously considered. (As was noted in the section on protein sources, an inability to digest milk and other dairy products is not uncommon among adults.)

Some Good Sources of Calcium

Dairy Products	Milligrams of Calcium
	per cup
Whole milk	291
2% low-fat milk	297
1% low-fat milk	300
Skim milk	302
Reconstituted dry milk	279
Evaporated milk	594
Evaporated skim milk	736
Buttermilk	285
Chocolate milk	285
Cheeses	per ounce
American processed	174
Blue	150
Cheddar	204
Cottage (2% low-fat, ½ cup)	77
Edam	207
Monterey Jack	212
Mozzarella (part skim milk)	183
Muenster	203
Ricotta (part skim, ½ cup)	337
Swiss	272
Yogurt (low-fat)	per cup
Plain	415
Flavored	389
Fruit	345
Desserts	per ½ cup
Baked custard	148
Ice cream, hard	88
Ice cream, soft	137
Pudding made with milk	125

Other Sources of Calcium

Canned salmon with bones, 3 oz.	167
Canned sardines with bones, 3 oz.	372
Canned shrimp, 3 oz.	99
Tofu (processed with calcium sulfate), 4 oz.	145
Collards, ½ cup cooked	179
Turnip greens, ½ cup cooked	126
Bok choy, ½ cup cooked	126
Kale, ½ cup cooked	103
Spinach, ½ cup cooked	84
Orange, 1 medium	54
Almonds, 1 oz.	66
Macaroni and cheese, ½ cup	175

How is calcium used in the body? As we have already noted, calcium's main job is to provide hardness and density to bones and teeth. In minute amounts, however, it is involved in the functioning of the heart and circulation system, in the clotting of blood, and in healthy muscles and nerves.

Recommended Dietary Allowance Daily

Infants to 6 months	360 milligrams
Infants 6 months to 1 year	540 milligrams
Children 1-10 years	800 milligrams
Females 11-18 years	1,200 milligrams
Females 19-50 years	800 milligrams
Females 51 years or more	1,000 milligrams*
Pregnant women	1,200 milligrams
Nursing mothers	1,200 milligrams
Males 11-18 years	1,200 milligrams
Males 19 years or more	800 milligrams

*The 1980 RDA lists 800 mg as the recommended amount for women over 51, but in 1985 a revised recommendation raised the recommended minimum to 1,000 milligrams daily.

Deficiency Symptoms

The most notorious deficiency disease associated with an inadequate intake of calcium is osteoporosis, which is most common among people in their later years. Although men can suffer from this problem, it is far more common among older women. During menopause the secretion of estrogen decreases significantly, and this decrease has an effect on the body's ability to use calcium efficiently. Osteoporosis is the result of calcium leaving the bone structure. This process causes the bones to soften and break easily, the loss of height, and poor posture. Deficiencies in other age groups include tooth decay, muscle cramps, and insomnia.

PHOSPHORUS

Where is phosphorus found? Phosphorus is commonly available in eggs, fish, whole grains, organ meat, poultry, and some cheeses.

How is phosphorus used in the body? Phosphorus is primarily used together with calcium to form strong bones, but also functions as a factor in overall metabolism (particularly in metabolism of calcium and sugar), heart muscle contraction, and kidney function.

Recommended Dietary Allowance Daily

Infants to 6 months	240 milligrams
Infants 6 months to 1 year	360 milligrams
Children 1-7 years	800 milligrams
Females 11-18	1,200 milligrams
Females 19 years or more	800 milligrams
Pregnant women	1,200 milligrams
Nursing mothers	1,200 milligrams
Males 11-18 years	1,200 milligrams
Males 19 years or more	800 milligrams

Deficiency Symptoms

Loss of appetite, fatigue, and some nervous disorders.

Excessive-Intake Symptoms

Excessive amounts of phosphorus can result in a calcium imbalance in the body and calcium deficiency.

MAGNESIUM

Where is magnesium found? Magnesium is found in good amounts in nuts, whole grains, dry beans and peas, and dark-green vegetables.

How is magnesium used in the body? Magnesium is required for the activity of several enzymes, it affects the functioning of nerves and muscles, and is involved in bone maintenance.

Recommended Dietary Allowance Daily

Infants to 6 months	50 milligrams
Infants 6 months to 1 year	70 milligrams
Children 1-3 years	150 milligrams
Children 4-6 years	200 milligrams
Children 7-10 years	250 milligrams
Females 11 years or more	300 milligrams
Pregnant women	450 milligrams
Nursing mothers	450 milligrams
Males 11-14 years	350 milligrams
Males 15-18 years	400 milligrams
Males 19 years or more	350 milligrams

Deficiency Symptoms

Serious deficiency in magnesium can lead to disturbances in the central nervous system, insomnia, muscle cramps, and irregular heartbeat.

Excessive-Intake Symptoms

Excessive amounts of magnesium can result in calcium imbalance.

IRON

Where is iron found? Only a few foods contain much iron ... liver is probably the best single source. Other foods that contain good amounts include other organ meats, red meat in general, shellfish, dry beans and peas, egg yolk, dried fruits, and blackstrap molasses.

How is iron used in the body? Only small amounts of iron are required, but these minimal amounts are necessary in order for the body to produce hemoglobin, the red substance in blood that carries oxygen from the lungs to the cells and carbon dioxide from the cells back to the lungs in exchange.

Recommended Dietary Allowance Daily

Infants to 6 months	10 milligrams
Infants 6 months to 1 year	15 milligrams
Children 1-3 years	15 milligrams
Children 4-10 years	10 milligrams
Females 11-50 years	18 milligrams
Females 51 years or more	10 milligrams

Pregnant women and nursing mothers:
> *The increased iron requirement during pregnancy requires more iron than is normally*

present in average American diets. It is best
to follow a doctor's advice regarding iron
supplements during these periods.
Males 11-18 years   18 milligrams
Males 19 years or more   10 milligrams

Deficiency Symptoms

The most common problem associated with iron deficiency is iron-deficiency anemia, which shows up as increased fatigue and pale skin. Some other signs of possible deficiency include brittle nails and constipation.

ZINC

Where is zinc found? Zinc is found in red meats, yeast, eggs, pumpkin, sunflower seeds, and in grains grown in zinc-rich soil.

How is zinc used in the body? Small amounts of zinc are found to be important in a variety of bodily functions, including the ability of the immune system to respond to infections, in our senses of taste and smell, in tissue repair, and in the detoxification of certain elements.

Recommended Dietary Allowance Daily

Infants to 6 months   3 milligrams
Infants 6 months to 1 year   5 milligrams
Children 1-10 years   10 milligrams
Females 11 years or more   15 milligrams
Pregnant women   20 milligrams
Nursing mothers   25 milligrams
Males 11 years or more   15 milligrams

Deficiency Symptoms

Zinc deficiency has been related to such things as slow healing of cuts and abrasions, loss of sense of smell and taste, increased frequency of infectious illness, and loss of muscle tone.

IODINE

Where is iodine found? The most common dietary source for iodine is iodized salt. Iodine is found in seafoods or other products from the ocean such as kelp.

How is iodine used in the body? Iodine is important to the proper functioning of the thyroid gland. This gland is one of the body's regulators and is involved in metabolism of fat and in energy production. Iodine availability also affects hair, nails, and skin.

Recommended Dietary Allowance Daily

Infants to 6 months	40 micrograms
Infants 6 months to 1 year	50 micrograms
Children 1-3 years	70 micrograms
Children 4-6 years	90 micrograms
Children 7-10 years	120 micrograms
Females 11 years or more	150 micrograms
Pregnant women	175 micrograms
Nursing mothers	200 micrograms
Males 11 years or more	150 micrograms

Deficiency Symptoms

Before the common availability of iodized salt, it was not uncommon to see people with goiters, a swelling-out of the thyroid gland, which is located at the base of the neck. Such a sight is a rarity in this country now. Other signs of iodine deficiency, and perhaps an impairment of the functioning of the thyroid, include cold hands and feet, dry hair, and in some instances obesity.

OTHER MINERALS THAT WE ALL REQUIRE DAILY

CHROMIUM.   Chromium is found in whole grains, corn oil, brewer's yeast, and clams. It is used in the production of energy, in regulating blood sugar (glucose), and also in regulating insulin production. An inadequate supply of chromium can be involved in some aspects of diabetes and hypoglycemia.

COPPER.   Copper is found in legumes (dried lentils, peas, and beans), nuts, organ meats, seafood, raisins, and molasses. It is involved in bone formation, hair and skin color, and in the production of hemoglobin. An inadequate supply of copper can result in general weakness and skin sores.

MANGANESE.   Manganese is found in bananas, bran, celery, egg yolks, dark-green leafy vegetables, legumes, pineapples, and whole grains. It is involved in the activities of enzymes, growth, reproduction, and in utilization of vitamins B-1 and E. An inadequate supply of manganese can cause dizziness, loss of hearing and ringing in the ears, and loss of muscle coordination.

POTASSIUM.   Potassium is found in bananas, dates, figs, peaches, tomatoes, citrus fruits, peanuts, blackstrap molasses, seafoods, and raisins. It is involved in growth and muscle and nerve functioning. An inadequate supply of potassium can result in constant thirst, dry skin, general weakness, insomnia, and weak reflexes. People who take diuretics for any reason should be aware that significant potassium can be lost through the urine, and they should talk to their doctor about possible additional intake of potassium to compensate for this loss.

SELENIUM. Selenium can be found in whole grains, fruit, nuts, and some vegetables. Only very minute amounts are required and excessive amounts can be very toxic. Its use by the body is as an antioxidant, and it seems to be involved in the aging process.

SODIUM. Sodium is all too available in our diets. Although the controversy regarding what constitutes excessive amounts and the effect of an excess of sodium on the body still is unsettled, it would be difficult for any twentieth-century person to have an insufficient intake. Sodium is used to regulate the amount of fluids in cells throughout the body and is also involved in proper muscle contraction. (A section on sodium in the diet is included in this chapter.)

SULPHUR. Sulphur is found in bran, cheese, clams, eggs, nuts, fish, and wheat germ. It is used in body tissue formation, particularly in the formation of collagen. There are no known effects of an inadequate supply at this time.

WATER

Before leaving specific nutrients, a word about water is in order. Water is essential for life. You can live for days, even weeks, without food, but only a few days without water.

About one-half to two-thirds of the body is made up of water. It is the medium of body fluids, secretions, and excretions.

Water carries essential nutrients from one part of the body to another. It is necessary during digestion because it holds all the nutrients in solution and permits them to pass through the intestinal walls into the bloodstream. It is required to regulate body temperature through evaporation through the skin and lungs. Last but not to be forgotten, water carries the waste products out of the body.

It takes a regular and generous intake of water to perform these functions. In general six to eight cups of liquid a day will meet dietary needs. This intake can be in the form of water, milk, juices, soft drinks, coffee, tea, and so forth. Solid foods also provide a surprising amount of water. Fruits and vegetables are particularly good sources.

SODIUM AND YOUR DIET

The Nutrition Board of the National Academy of Sciences has determined that an adult's nutritional needs for sodium can be met with between 1,100 and 3,300 milligrams of salt per day. One teaspoonful of salt contains 1,938 milligrams, so you can see that for many people, between one and two teaspoons of salt more than meets their body's requirements.

For many of us, even this much is too much. Many people must restrict their salt intake because of medical reasons, particularly high blood pressure.

One of the greatest problems in restricting sodium intake is that salt is found not only in your table salt shaker, but also in just about everything you eat. For that reason, this listing of the sodium (salt) content of some common foods will give you some idea of just how much sodium you take in during your normal eating of meals and snacks.

It is very important that people on sodium-restricted diets read labels and be aware of some of the salt compounds found in processed foods: monosodium glutamate (MSG), sodium phosphates, sodium citrate, sodium caseinate, sodium benzoate, and sodium nitrite are some that are commonly used.

As you will see from this list, the best foods for salt-restricted diets are fresh fruits and vegetables, simple grains, and baked or broiled meats. In general the highest salt content will be found in processed and convenience foods.

The information on this list is taken from a report prepared by the Science and Education Administration of the U.S. Department of Agriculture (issued in 1980). It should be taken to be representative examples of sodium content, not absolute measurements, since many of the amounts are for a "medium" or some other nonexact size. In prepared foods, different manufacturers use different recipes, so the amount of sodium in any type of food may vary from brand to brand.

If you are on a sodium-controlled diet, you should work with your doctor to determine exactly how much salt you can safely tolerate and how that salt should be obtained.

Food Item	Portion Size	Milligrams of Salt
BEVERAGES AND JUICES		
Carbonated drinks		
Cola, regular	8 fluid oz.	16
Cola, low-calorie	8 fluid oz.	21
Ginger ale	8 fluid oz.	13
Root beer	8 fluid oz.	24
Cocoa		
Mix with water added	8 fluid oz.	232
Cocoa powder with milk	8 fluid oz.	138
Coffee	8 fluid oz.	2
Fruit juices		
Apple cider or juice	8 fluid oz.	5
Grapefruit juice, canned	8 fluid oz.	4
Orange juice, diluted frozen	8 fluid oz.	5
Pineapple juice, canned	8 fluid oz.	5
Prune juice, canned	8 fluid oz.	5
Lemonade, reconstituted	8 fluid oz.	50
Milk and milk drinks		
Milk, whole or low-fat	8 fluid oz.	122
Buttermilk	8 fluid oz.	257
Chocolate milk	8 fluid oz.	149
Tea	8 fluid oz.	1

Food Item	Portion Size	Milligrams of Salt
Tomato juice, canned, regular	8 fluid oz.	878
Tomato juice, canned, low-salt	8 fluid oz.	9
Vegetable juice mixture	8 fluid oz.	887

CEREALS AND GRAINS

Barley, cooked	1 cup	6
Cereals		
Cornflakes, regular	1 cup	256
Cornflakes, low-salt	1 cup	10
Puffed rice	1 cup	2
Rice Krispies	1 cup	340
Shredded wheat	1 biscuit	3
Wheaties	1 cup	355
Rice, brown, cooked	1 cup	10

CHEESE, EGGS, FISH, MEAT, AND POULTRY

Cheese		
Cheddar, regular	1 oz.	176
Cheddar, low-sodium	1 oz.	6
Cottage cheese, regular	4 oz.	457
Cream cheese	1 oz.	84
Parmesan	1 oz.	528
Swiss	1 oz.	74
Eggs, whole	1 egg	59
Fish		
Cod, broiled with butter	3 oz.	93
Halibut, broiled with butter	3 oz.	114
Ocean perch, fried	3 oz.	128
Salmon, broiled with butter	3 oz.	99
Salmon, canned, pink	3 oz.	443
Tuna, oil-pack canned	3 oz.	303
Tuna, water-pack canned	3 oz.	288
Meat		
Beef, cooked lean	3 oz.	55
Corned beef, cooked	3 oz.	802

Food Item	Portion Size	Milligrams of Salt
Dried (chipped) beef	1 oz.	1,219
Lamb, cooked lean	3 oz.	58
Pork, fresh lean, cooked	3 oz.	59
Pork, bacon, cooked	2 slices	274
Pork, ham, cooked	3 oz.	1,114
Organ meat		
Calf liver, fried	1 oz.	33
Chicken liver, simmered	1 oz.	16
Sausages and prepared meats		
Frankfurter	1 frankfurter	639
Salami, beef and pork	1 slice	234
Sausage, pork, cooked	1 link	168
Poultry		
Chicken breast with skin	½ breast	69
Chicken leg with skin	1 leg	47
Turkey breast with skin	3 oz.	182
Turkey leg with skin	1 leg	195
FRUITS		
Apples	1 apple	2
Apple sauce (sweetened or not)	1 cup	8
Apricots, raw	3 apricots	1
Apricots, canned, unpeeled	1 cup	10
Avocado	1 avocado	22
Banana	1 banana	2
Berries		
Raspberries, raw	1 cup	1
Raspberries, frozen	1 package	3
Strawberries, raw	1 cup	2
Strawberries, frozen	1 cup	6
Cherries, raw	1 cup	1
Cherries, canned	1 cup	10
Dates, dried	10 dates	1
Figs, dried	1 fig	2
Fruit cocktail, canned	1 cup	15

Food Item	Portion Size	Milligrams of Salt
Grapefruit	½ fruit	1
Grapes, Thompson seedless	10 grapes	1
Melons		
Cantaloupe	½ melon	24
Honeydew	⅛ melon	28
Watermelon	¹⁄₁₆ melon	8
Nectarines, raw	1 nectarine	1
Orange	1 orange	1
Peaches, raw	1 peach	1
Peaches, canned	1 cup	10
Pears, raw	1 pear	1
Pears, canned	1 cup	15
Pineapple, canned	1 cup	7
Plums, raw	1 plum	1
Plums, canned	1 cup	7
Prunes, cooked	1 cup	8
Prunes, dried	5 prunes	2
Raisins, seedless	1 cup	17

VEGETABLES

Food Item	Portion Size	Milligrams of Salt
Asparagus, fresh cooked	1 spear	1
Beans, lima, fresh cooked	1 cup	2
Beans, lima, frozen cooked	1 cup	128

(Lima beans are presorted before freezing by being put in a salt-water bath; imperfect beans rise to the top but all beans so treated absorb some of the salt.)

Food Item	Portion Size	Milligrams of Salt
Beans, snap, fresh, cooked	1 cup	5
Beans, snap, frozen, cooked	1 cup	3
Beans, snap, canned, regular	1 cup	326
Beans, snap, canned, low-sodium	1 cup	3
Beets, fresh, cooked	1 cup	73
Beets, canned, regular	1 cup	479
Beets, canned, low-sodium	1 cup	110
Broccoli, fresh, cooked	1 stalk	23
Broccoli, frozen, cooked	1 cup	35

Food Item	Portion Size	Milligrams of Salt
Cabbage, fresh, cooked	1 cup	16
Cabbage salad (cole slaw)	½ cup	68
Carrots, fresh, cooked	1 carrot	34
Carrots, canned, regular	1 cup	386
Carrots, canned, low-sodium	1 cup	58
Cauliflower, fresh, cooked	1 cup	13
Celery	1 stalk	25
Corn, fresh, cooked	1 ear	1
Corn, canned, cream style	1 cup	671
Corn, canned, kernel regular	1 cup	384
Corn, canned, kernel low-sodium	1 cup	2
Eggplant, fresh, cooked	1 cup	1
Onion, yellow or white	1 medium	10
Onion, green (scallion)	1 medium	2
Peas, fresh, cooked	1 cup	2
Peas, frozen, cooked	½ cup	80
Peas, canned, regular	1 cup	493
Peas, canned, low-sodium	1 cup	8
Peppers, green	1 medium	9
Potatoes, baked or boiled	1 medium	5
Potatoes, instant, mashed	1 cup	485
Potatoes au gratin	1 cup	1,095
Potato salad	½ cup	625
Radish	4 small	2
Sauerkraut, canned	1 cup	1,554
Spinach, fresh, raw	1 cup	49
Spinach, frozen, cooked	1 cup	65
Squash, summer, fresh, cooked	1 cup	5
Squash, winter, baked, mashed	1 cup	2
Sweet potatoes, baked	1 medium	20
Tomato, fresh, raw	1 medium	14
Tomatoes, canned whole	1 cup	390
Tomatoes, canned, low-sodium	1 cup	16
Vegetables, mixed, frozen, cooked	½ cup	45

Food Item	Portion Size	Milligrams of Salt
CONDIMENTS, SAUCES AND DRESSINGS		
Pickles		
Dill	1 medium	928
Sweet	1 medium	128
Sauces		
A.1. Sauce	1 tbsp.	275
Catsup	1 tbsp.	156
Soy sauce	1 tbsp.	1,029
Tartar sauce	1 tbsp.	182
Worcestershire sauce	1 tbsp.	206
Dressings		
Blue cheese	1 tbsp.	153
French, bottled, regular	1 tbsp.	214
French, bottled, low-sodium	1 tbsp.	3
Italian, bottled	1 tbsp.	116
Mayonnaise	1 tbsp.	133
Thousand island	1 tbsp.	109
BREADS AND CRACKERS		
Breads		
French	1 slice	116
Rye	1 slice	139
White, regular	1 slice	114
White, low-sodium	1 slice	7
Whole wheat	1 slice	132
English muffin, white	1 medium	239
Crackers		
Graham	1 cracker	48
Rye	1 cracker	70
Saltine	1 cracker	70
SWEETS AND DESSERTS		
Cake, angel food	1/12 cake	134
Cake, devil's food	1/12 cake	402
Cake, yellow or white	1/12 cake	240

Food Item	Portion Size	Milligrams of Salt
Pound cake	1/12 cake	171
Cookies, chocolate chip	2 cookies	69
Cookies, oatmeal with raisins	2 cookies	55
Ice cream, regular, vanilla	1 cup	105
Pie, apple	1/8 pie	208
Pie, cherry	1/8 pie	169
Pie, lemon cream	1/8 pie	92
Pie, pumpkin	1/8 pie	169

CONVENIENCE FOODS
Prepared main dishes

Chili con carne with beans	1 cup	194
Beef dinners, frozen		
Beef slices	1 dinner	998
Meat loaf	1 dinner	1,304
Swiss steak	1 dinner	682
Chicken dinners, frozen		
Chicken chow mein	1 cup	718
Chicken pot pie	1 pie	907
Fried chicken dinner	1 dinner	1,153
Enchiladas	1 pkg	725
Fish dinner	1 dinner	1,212
Hash, corned beef, canned	1 cup	1,520
Ravioli, canned	1 cup	1,065
Spaghetti and meatballs, canned	1 cup	1,054
Tuna pot pie, frozen	1 pie	715
Turkey dinner, frozen	1 dinner	1,228
Turkey pot pie	1 pie	1,018

FAST FOODS FROM RESTAURANTS

Cheeseburger	1 burger	709
Chicken dinner	1 portion	2,243
Fish sandwich	1 sandwich	882
Frankfurter	1 frankfurter	728
French fries	3 ounces	200

Food Item	Portion Size	Milligrams of Salt
Hamburger	1 burger	990
Milk shake	1 milk shake	226
Taco	1 taco	401

SNACKS

Corn chips	1 ounce	231
Popcorn with oil and salt	1 cup	175
Popcorn, plain	1 cup	1
Potato chips	10 chips	200
Pretzels, regular, twist	1 pretzel	100
Peanuts, dry-roasted with salt	1 cup	986
Peanuts, regular with salt	1 cup	601
Peanuts, unsalted	1 cup	8
Pecans, unsalted	1 cup	1
Walnuts, unsalted	1 cup	3

LABELS—A GOOD SOURCE FOR INFORMATION ABOUT NUTRIENTS IN FOODS

One of the most reliable sources of information regarding prepared food products is the product label on the container. Since 1973 the U.S. Food and Drug Administration has required certain basic information to appear on the container. This basic information includes the name of the product, the net contents or net weight (on canned food the net weight includes the liquid in which the food is packed), and the name and place of business of the food processor.

In many instances manufacturers provide much more information but are required to give nutritional data only if protein or vitamins are added or if some nutritional claim is given on the container (such as "now contains fewer calories" or "fortified with vitamin C," for example).

Almost all containers you see in markets today have a nutritional label. Consumers have demanded to know something about the food they are eating, and the manufacturers have responded. Included in this short table of information (and almost always found in this order) are the typical serving size, number of typical servings per container, number of calories, and amounts of protein, carbohydrates, fat, and sodium per serving. Some food processors also list cholesterol, fatty acid, and potassium content. Finally the percentages of the Recommended Dietary Allowances (RDAs) are given.

Since mid-1986 the FDA has required the inclusion of sodium information, although many food manufacturers have been including it for some time. The sodium requirements permit processors to use the following terms to describe their products: "sodium free" when the product has less than five milligrams of sodium per serving; "very low sodium," 35 milligrams or less; "low sodium," 140 milligrams or less per serving; and "reduced sodium," where the usual level of sodium has been reduced by at least 75 percent.

One thing to be aware of in this new sodium labeling is that a phrase like "unsalted" or "no salt added" or something similar can be seen on foods once processed with salt but now produced without it. A food so labeled, however, may in fact contain some sodium. Sometimes the salt is just no longer sprinkled on top (for example in the case of low-salt crackers), but the cracker itself is still made with salt.

Here is a typical nutritional label you might see in a supermarket:

Nutritional Information Per Serving
Serving size = ½ cup
Servings per container = 9

Calories	190
Protein	2 grams
Carbohydrate	24 grams
Fat	9 grams
Sodium	55 milligrams

Percentage of U.S. Recommended Daily
Allowance:

Protein	4
Thiamine	10
Niacin	2

Contains less than 2 percent of the U.S.
RDA of vitamin A, vitamin C, riboflavin,
calcium, and iron.

It is not hard to achieve nutrition adequate to prevent
deficiency diseases. The amount and variety of nutrients that
are necessary to proceed beyond adequate to optimum differs
from individual to individual. Cooks are the control point to
make sure that the people for whom they cook are getting as
close to optimum nutrition as possible.

In many cases good nutrition can best be achieved through
using fresh produce and meat sources. This can take more
time, to be sure, but the result from both a nutritional and a
gustatory viewpoint is well worth the small additional effort.

By the same token, the cook should be aware that produce that is frozen straight from the field may retain more of
its nutrients than supposedly fresh produce that has lan-
guished for several days from field to wholesaler to retailer to
your kitchen.

There are many food faddists who insist they have discovered the miracle food/nutrient/additive of the century. Be
cautious. Such "miracles" must be investigated very carefully.

Read all you can about nutrition so that you can make good decisions. There are many excellent books on family nutrition and frequent magazine articles as well.

Nutrition is where you find it. The more knowledge about nutrition you as a cook can bring to food preparation, the more valuable your food will be from a nutrition standpoint. Cooking and eating nutritious food is not impossible; with the abundance of food we have available it is not even difficult. But it must be consciously done.

Food Additives

Food additives have received a lot of attention in the past twenty years or so. This is in part because of the increased use of preprocessed foods in meal preparation. While additives play a necessary role in these very convenient items, their use also raises questions about long- and short-term safety to consumers. In order that you, as a cook, can have some idea about what the additives are, what kinds of foods contain them, and why they are put into foods, this Appendix lists the additives that are most commonly used.

Food additives of various sorts have been used for thousands of years. Their original purpose was to preserve food that was caught or harvested in the summer and fall for use in the winter and early spring.

Prehistoric cooks discovered early on that drying would allow them to keep grain and wild fruits in baskets in their winter shelters. Roots were buried in the soil nearby, and meat and fish were either dried or salt-cured if ample salt was available. For groups living in the northern latitudes, rudimentary freeze storage was also used—a small niche carved into the hillside in a remote part of their living quarters that stayed cold throughout the winter.

Later generations found that causing the fruit to absorb large amounts of sugar would help to preserve it, and that soaking some vegetables such as cabbage and cucumbers in a vinegar brine would extend their usability. And so were born the early preserves and pickles whose myriad descendants we enjoy today. Incidentally, the most commonly used food additives today are still salt and sugar ... perhaps things haven't changed as much as it would seem!

The Federal Food and Drug Act of 1938 defines the term *food additive* as any substance that "results, or may be reasonably expected to result, directly or indirectly, in its becoming a component ... of any food." This definition has been interpreted to include materials used not only in production and processing but also in treating, packaging, transporting, or storing food.

The history of consumer protection in the arena of food processing is an interesting one. Until the 1900s there was no protection, and processors were free to add whatever they chose to food, medicines, and cosmetics. At the turn of the century Dr. Harvey W. Wiley, now considered to be the father of the consumer-protection movement, pioneered against chemical preservatives such as boric acid, formaldehyde, and salicylic acid being added to food products. As a result of his efforts, the first Federal Food and Drug Act was passed in 1906. He continued as the Chief Chemist at the U.S. Department of Agriculture until 1912.

In 1938 the Federal Food, Drug, and Cosmetic Act was passed. The simple purpose of this bill was to ensure that foods were honestly labeled and packaged.

It was not until the 1950s, however, that the Food and Drug Administration that had been created by the 1906 law was able to push for the ability to require testing of additives. The landmark legislation called the Food Additives Amendment was passed in September 1958. It required FDA approval of any new food additive before it could be marketed, and placed on the manufacturer the responsibility for testing to prove the material's safety. These tests also had to be reviewed and approved by the FDA.

The amendment divided additives into three major classifications:

1. Substances generally regarded as safe for human consumption;
2. Substances for which additional information was needed;
3. Substances that are prohibited.

The initial approved list of additives ("Generally Regarded as Safe for Human Consumption") has come to be known as the GRAS (Generally Regarded as Safe) list. The initial list was composed of substances that had been in use over a long period and were considered by qualified scientists to be safe for human use. The substances on the initial list were exempted from the preuse testing requirement of the law.

The second group of substances were additives for which there was considered to be not enough information to make a valid decision regarding their overall safety, and for which additional testing was required.

The third group of substances were considered to be unsafe for human consumption and were prohibited from use in food products because of their toxicity.

The 1960 Color Additive Amendments brought all colors, both natural and synthetic, under the Food, Drug, and Cosmetic Act. These amendments also included what has become known as the Delaney Clause, which prohibits the use of any additive "if it is found, after tests which are appropriate ... to induce cancer in (people or animals)."

The next phase of the program developed during the early 1980s when the Select Committee on GRAS Substances (SCOGS) was formed. This committee's job is to review and evaluate reports of research regarding food additives, and to make decisions regarding their use. The committee has developed five classes into which the research is divided:

Class I. The substance retains GRAS status with no limitations other than good manufacturing practice.

Class II. The substance retains GRAS status with limitations regarding the amount that can be added to foods.

Class III. The substance retains GRAS status but additional tests must be conducted within a specified period. GRAS status is retained until the tests are conducted and reevaluated.

Class IV. The substance must have safer usage standards adopted in order to continue to retain GRAS status. Without these changes the substance will be removed from the GRAS list.

Class V. The test data on the substance is insufficient to make a valid evaluation.

Additives are never given permanent approval. Their safety is continually under review.

With this as background what follows is a list of the additives you are most likely to come across. When the additive is on the GRAS list as of April 1, 1986, that information is listed. When the GRAS classification is not listed, however, it does not mean that the additive is not safe, it just means that it does not have full GRAS status at this time.

The list is arranged alphabetically. This is not a definitive list by any means because new additives are being developed and put into use all the time and occasionally additives formerly regarded as safe are removed from the approved list also. (Cyclamates, for instance, were removed in 1969.)

When initials are the most common way the additive is noted, that is the way it is listed here with the complete name spelled out as well. When there is more than one way the additive is listed, you will find references back to the complete entry.

FOOD ADDITIVES

What They Are . . . What They Do . . . Where They Are Found

ACACIA, ACACIA GUM . . . see *Gum Arabic.*

ACETAL. Used in the production of artificial flavors such as apple, banana, peach, and whiskey. Found in bakery goods, ice cream, candy, and beverages.

ACETALDEHYDE. In its natural form found in apples, broccoli, cheese, coffee, grapefruit and other citrus fruits, and berries. In its artificial form used to produce berry, butter, chocolate, apple, apricot, banana, grape, peach, black walnut, rum, and wine flavors in bakery goods, gelatins, chewing gum, candy, ice cream, and beverages. Also used in the production of perfumes, dyes, plastics, and drugs. GRAS.

ACETATES (found as Calcium, Potassium, or Sodium Acetate). Are used as a buffer (smoothing) ingredient in such things as syrups, breakfast cereals, candies, beverages, and ice cream. GRAS.

ACETIC ACID (Ethyl Acetate, Methyl Acetate). Acetic acid is one of the earliest commonly used food additives. In its natural form it is found in apples, bananas, grapes, some berries, and pineapple. Vinegar is a common source for acetic acid and is normally in the range of four to six percent acetic acid. In its artificial form used to produce lemon, butter, berry, grape, banana, apple, cherry, peach, pineapple, brandy, rum, mint, whiskey, almond, and cream soda flavors in bakery goods, ice cream, gelatins, puddings, chewing gum, and liquor. It is also used to balance acid/alkaline levels in foods. GRAS.

ACETOIN (Acetylmethylcarbinol.) Occurs naturally in broccoli, grapes, pears, and some meats. Used in the artificial flavors included in bakery goods, beverages, ice cream, candy, margarine, and shortening. GRAS.

ACETYLMETHYLCARBINOL ... see *Acetoin.*

ACETYLATED MONOGLYCERIDES. These are fat-derived products, very flexible when warm but waxlike at room temperatures. Used in such confections as chocolate-covered ice cream bars and jelly beans.

ACID CALCIUM PHOSPHATE ... see *Calcium Phosphate.*

ACONITIC ACID (Citridic Acid). In its natural form found in cane and beet sugars. In its natural and synthetic form it is used in the fruit and liquor flavors used in beverages, ice cream, bakery goods, candy, liquor, and chewing gum. It is also used in the manufacture of plastics. GRAS.

ADIPIC ACID. In its natural form found in beets. Used to control acid/alkaline levels, to prevent oils from turning rancid, and to give a tartness to beverages and gelatin desserts. GRAS.

AGAR. Is made from red algae found off the coasts of southern California, Japan, and Spain. The plant is collected and then boiled to produce a gelatinous substance. It is used as a thickener and stabilizer in such things as bakery products, ice cream, low-sugar preserves and jellies, and in candies. GRAS.

ALDEHYDE ... see *Decanal.*

ALGINATES (found as Ammonium Alginate, Calcium Alginate, and Potassium Alginate, Brown and Red Algae). Like agar, alginates are produced from seaweeds. In food processing they have a variety of uses: as a stabilizer in whipped cream packed in pressure cans; as a clarifier in cheeses, dressings, and wines; as stabilizers and water retainers in bakery products, ice creams, and other confections. GRAS.

ALLYL CYCLOHEXENE ACETATE, ALLYL CYCLOHEXENE PROPIONATE, ALLYL HEXANOATE, ALLYL MERCAPTAN, ALLYL NONANOATE, ALLYL OCTANOATE, ALLYL PHENYL-ACETATE, ALLYL SORBATE, ALLYL SULFIDE, and ALLYL ISOTHIOCYANATE. All of these are used in the manufacture of artificial flavors used in beverages, ice cream, bakery goods, candy, gelatin desserts, and chewing gum. Allyl isothiocyanate is also used in condiments, processed meat products, and pickles. No known toxicity.

ALUMINUM CALCIUM SILICATE. Anticaking agent. GRAS.

ALUMINUM SULFATE (Cake Alum, Patent Alum, Aluminum Ammonium Sulfate, Aluminum Potassium Sulfate, Aluminum Sodium Sulfate). Used as a firming agent in such things as sweet and dill pickles. It is also used in making antiperspirants, agricultural pesticides, antiseptics, and detergents. GRAS.

AMMONIATED GLYCYRRHIZIN. One of the sweetest substances known and used in making root beer, wintergreen flavoring and licorice flavoring. GRAS.

AMMONIUM ALGINATE ... see *Alginates*.

AMMONIUM BICARBONATE. Used as a leavening agent in some baked foods. GRAS.

AMMONIUM CARBONATE. GRAS.

AMMONIUM CASEINATE ... see *Casein*.

AMMONIUM CHLORIDE. Used in baked goods that use yeast as a leavening agent, as food for the yeast and a general dough conditioner. GRAS.

AMMONIUM HYDROXIDE. GRAS.

AMMONIUM PHOSPHATE (Monobasic and Dibasic). Used by bakers to improve bread and bread-type products by regulating the acid/alkaline balance. GRAS.

AMMONIUM SULFATE. Used by bakers, brewers, and vintners as a buffer and leavening agent. GRAS.

AMYL BUTYRATE. Used as an artificial flavor in beverages, ice cream, candy, baked goods, gelatin desserts, and chewing gum. No known toxicity.

ANETHOLE. Found naturally in anise, fennel, and star anise. Used as an artificial flavor in beverages, ice cream, candy, chewing gum, liquors, and bakery products. GRAS.

ANISOLE. A synthetic agent with a pleasant odor, used in artificial flavors such as licorice, root beer, and wintergreen, in beverages, frozen desserts, candy, and baked goods. No known toxicity.

ANNATTO. An extract from a tropical tree that is used to add a yellow to orange color to such dairy products as butter, cheese, cottage cheese, buttermilk, and margarine. It is also used in beverages, ice cream, bakery goods, cake mixes, cereals, and color-processed meats such as bologna and frankfurters. No known toxicity.

ARABINOGALACTAN. Used as a stabilizer, thickener, and texturizer to give body and improved texture. On FDA priority list of additives to be studied for possible toxic effects.

ARTIFICIAL COLORS. Over 90 percent of all coloring products used in foods are synthetic. Most are made from coal tar (which is produced when coal is heated in a vacuum). Artificial colors are found most commonly in bakery goods, ice cream, candies, powdered desserts, beverages, and processed-meat products. (See the entry for *FD and C Colors*.)

ARTIFICIAL FLAVORS. Over 2,000 flavorings are used by food processors. Under the Food, Drug, and Cosmetic Act of 1938 specific flavors do not have to be listed on the label, the overall term *artificial flavors* may be used. About 500 of the flavors commonly used are natural in origin, the remainder are synthetic. Some flavors are available in both natural and synthetic forms, usually under slightly different names (natural vanilla and synthetic vanillin, for example). Flavor formulas are among the most closely guarded manufacturing secrets for food processors.

ASCORBIC ACID (Sodium Ascorbate, Calcium Ascorbate). More familiarly known as vitamin C, it is used primarily as a preservative and antioxidant in foods to prevent early spoilage. It is commonly found in frozen fruit, dry milk, beer, beverages, candy, processed-meat products, and low-sugar preserves. GRAS.

ASCORBYL PALMITATE. Preservative agent. GRAS.

ASPARTAME. Developed in the 1970s both as a substitute for sugar (it is about 180 times sweeter than sucrose) and as a safe artificial sweetener, since cyclamates had been removed from the market and use of saccharin had been questioned. FDA gave approval for its general use in 1981.

ATTAR OF ROSES ... see *Rose Bulgarian.*

AZODICARBONAMIDE. Used in bakery goods as a flour bleaching agent, dough conditioner, and to generally improve the quality and texture of baked goods. On FDA list for further study regarding possible toxic effects of short- and long-term use.

BEET SUGAR ... see *Sucrose.*

BENTONITE. GRAS.

BENZALDEHYDE. In its natural form is found in cherries, some berries, and almonds. Used as an artificial flavor to simulate almond taste in beverages, ice cream, bakery goods, gelatin desserts, chewing gum, liquors, and candy. Although a central nervous system depressant in large doses, it is on the GRAS list in approved amounts.

BENZOATE OF SODA ... see *Benzoic Acid.*

BENZOIC ACID. Found in its natural form in cherry tree bark, raspberries, tea, anise, and cassia bark. Has been in use since the seventeenth century (first described in 1608). It is used as a preservative and antifungal agent. It is also used as a flavoring to simulate lemon, chocolate, orange, and other fruit flavors in beverages, candy, bakery goods, and chewing gum. Also used in margarine. GRAS but FDA is requesting further study.

BENZOIC ALDEHYDE ... see *Benzaldehyde.*

BENZOIN (Gum Benzoin, Gum Benjamin). Refers to several tree gums that contain benzoic acid. Used in chocolate, cherry, rum, spice, and vanilla flavorings in beverages, ice cream, candy, bakery goods, gelatin desserts, and chewing gum. Nontoxic.

BENZOYL PEROXIDE. Used as a bleaching agent for flours and some cheese (blue and Gorgonzola, for instance). On GRAS list at this time but under further study by FDA.

BENZYL ACETATE, BENZYL ALCOHOL, BENZYL BUTYRATE, BENZYL CINNAMATE, and BENZYL PROPIONATE. These are all artificial flavoring agents used primarily in beverages, ice cream, candy, baked goods, gelatin desserts, and chewing gum.

BERGAMON ... see *Linalyl Acetate.*

BETA-CAROTENE. This natural form of vitamin A is found in many fruits and vegetables and in animal fat. It is used as a coloring agent in such foods as margarine, nondairy creamers, cake mixes, and dairy products to produce a yellow color. GRAS.

BHA (Butylated Hydroxyanisole). Used as an antioxidant and preservative in many foods that contain fat or oil. These foods range from potato chips to ice cream to dry mixes to shortenings. Although on the GRAS list, the FDA's research into possible long-term effects of BHA in human diet continues. Now considered safe when total content is not over 0.02 percent of fat and oil content.

BHT (Butylated Hydroxytoluene). Chemically similar to BHA, BHT is used as both an antioxidant and emulsion stabilizer in many products that contain oil or fat. BHT is prohibited as a food additive in England. Although still on the FDA's GRAS list, BHT is currently under further study in this country as well.

BICARBONATE OF SODA ... see *Sodium Bicarbonate.*

BIOTIN. Dietary supplement additive related to the B-complex family of vitamins. GRAS.

BORNYL ACETATE. Used as an artificial flavor in beverages, ice cream, bakery goods, candy, syrups, chewing gum, and gelatin desserts to simulate pineapple flavor.

BRITISH GUM ... see *Dextrin.*

BROMATES (calcium bromate, potassium bromate). Used as dough conditioners in yeast breads. Research has indicated toxicity when used in large amounts.

BROMINATED VEGETABLE OILS ... see *BVO.*

BURNT LIME ... see *Calcium Oxide.*

BUTANE, ISOBUTANE.   GRAS.

BUTYL ACETATE, BUTYL BUTYRATE, BUTYL CINNAMATE, BUTYL PHENYLACETATE.   All are used as artificial flavoring in beverages, ice cream, candy, bakery goods, gelatin desserts, and chewing gum.

BUTYL LACTATE ... see *Lactic Acid.*

BUTYL PARABEN.   Used as a preservative to extend shelf life and prevent spoilage.

BUTYLATED HYDROXYANISOLE, BUTYLATED HYDROXY-TOLUENE . . . see *BHA* and *BHT.*

BUTYRIC ACID.   Found naturally in butter acids, apples, strawberries, and grapes. Used in its synthetic form as a flavor for butter, butterscotch, caramel, and fruit in beverages, ice cream, candy, gelatin desserts, bakery goods, chewing gum, and margarine. GRAS.

BVO (Brominated Vegetable Oil).   A BVO is manufactured when a vegetable oil (such as olive, sesame, corn, or cottonseed) is combined with bromine (a nonmetallic liquid element) to form a high density oil. BVOs are used in beverages, ice cream, and bakery products. The FDA has serious concerns about this substance, and in 1970 the FDA removed BVOs from the GRAS list, although it is still considered safe up to levels of 300 parts per million in foods. If used at all now, it is found almost exclusively in snack-type foods.

CAFFEINE.   Is found in its natural form in cocoa, coffee, cola nuts, and tea. It is also obtained as a byproduct of the decaffeinating of coffee and tea. It is used as a flavoring in cola and many other soft drinks. The FDA has advised that pregnant women should avoid caffeine as it is able to pass through the placental barrier. It also has taken under further study the effects of caffeine consumption in children. It is a nervous system stimulant, dilates the blood vessels, and causes the release of insulin. It can cause nervousness and insomnia in some people. GRAS when used in cola-type beverages in accordance with good manufacturing practices.

CAKE ALUM ... see *Aluminum Sulfate*.

CALCIFEROL (Vitamin D-2). Used as a nutritional supplement in cereals, milk, margarine, infant formulas, and grain products. Currently on GRAS list, but FDA has requested further studies.

CALCIUM ACETATE ... see *Acetates*.

CALCIUM ACID PHOSPHATE ... see *Calcium Phosphate*.

CALCIUM ALGINATE ... see *Alginates*.

CALCIUM ASCORBATE ... see *Ascorbic Acid*.

CALCIUM BROMATE ... see *Bromates*.

CALCIUM CARBONATE. Dietary supplement, one of the more accessible forms of dietary calcium. GRAS.

CALCIUM CASEINATE ... see *Casein*.

CALCIUM CHLORIDE. Used as a firming agent in processed fruit, canned tomatoes, some cheeses, and jellies. GRAS.

CALCIUM CITRATE. In its natural form found in citrus fruits. Used to regulate the acid/alkaline balance in food products. GRAS.

CALCIUM CYCLAMATE ... see *Cyclamates*.

CALCIUM DIACETATE ... see *Calcium Salts*.

CALCIUM DISODIUM (EDTA).　Used as a chelating agent for removing minute metallic bits that are an inevitable result of current manufacturing technology. These metallic bits are not only unacceptable by their own nature but also because they cause changes in color, taste, and smell of food products. It is also used to prevent browning in processed fruits and vegetables and to preserve the vitamin C available in fruit juices. It is currently on a priority list for further FDA study into its possible toxicity.

CALCIUM GLUCONATE ... see *Calcium Salts*.

CALCIUM GLYCEROPHOSPHATE.　Dietary supplement. GRAS.

CALCIUM HEXAMETAPHOSPHATE.　An emulsifier and texturizer used in breakfast cereals, angel food cake, flaked canned fish (to prevent crystal formation), ice cream, beer, puddings, and processed cheeses. GRAS.

CALCIUM LACTATE ... see *Lactic Acid*.

CALCIUM OXIDE (Quicklime, Burnt Lime).　Used as a dough conditioner and yeast food in bread products and also as an alkaline/acid balancer. GRAS.

CALCIUM PANTOTHENATE.　Dietary supplement. GRAS.

CALCIUM PEROXIDE.　Used as a dough conditioner and oxidizing agent for yeast bread products. On GRAS list at this time but under further study by FDA.

CALCIUM PHOSPHATE (Calcium Acid Phosphate).　Found in three forms: tricalcium (tribasic calcium) phosphate, dicalcium (dibasic calcium) phosphate, and monocalcium (monobasic calcium) phosphate. Tricalcium phosphate is used as an anticaking agent in table salt, granulated sugar, and other such products. Dicalcium phosphate is used as a dough conditioner in yeast bread products, as a carrier for bleaching agents, and as a mineral supplement in cereals. In addition to these functions, monocalcium phosphate is used a firming agent for low-sugar preserves, canned potatoes, and tomatoes. GRAS.

CALCIUM PROPIONATE. A preservative used particularly in baked goods to prevent molding and growth of bacteria. It is also found in chocolate products, bakery goods, and processed cheese. It occurs naturally in many foods (Swiss cheese for example). We form it ourselves as a byproduct of fat and amino acid metabolism. Currently on GRAS list but FDA is conducting further studies.

CALCIUM PYROPHOSPHATE. Dietary supplement. GRAS.

CALCIUM SALTS (term used to cover such additives as Calcium Acetate, Calcium Chloride, Calcium Citrate, Calcium Diacetate, Calcium Gluconate, Calcium Hydroxide, Calcium Iodate, Calcium Sulfate). Calcium salts are used as firming agents in bread and canned tomatoes and potatoes. They are used as emulsifying agents in frozen desserts and evaporated milk. GRAS.

CALCIUM SILICATE. An anticaking agent found in baking powder and table salt. GRAS when used at levels not to exceed five percent in baking powder and two percent in table salt according to good manufacturing practices.

CALCIUM SORBATE ... see *Sorbic Acid.*

CALCIUM STEARATE. Used as a dough conditioner and as an emulsifier and whipping agent in bakery products and in dried and frozen egg whites. GRAS but on FDA list of substances requiring further study.

CALCIUM SULFATE (Plaster of Paris). Used by bakers as a firming agent, yeast food, and dough conditioner. Also added to flours, aged cheeses, artificially sweetened fruit, canned potatoes, and tomatoes. It is also used as an alkali ingredient in cottage cheese and as a carrier for bleaching agents in yeast bread products. GRAS.

CANE SUGAR . . . see *Sucrose.*

CAPRALDEHYDE, CAPRIC ALDEHYDE, CAPRINALDEHYDE . . . see *Decanal.*

CAPRYLIC ACID. A fatty acid that occurs in milk of cows and goats and in palm and coconut oil. It is used as a preservative and in artificial flavorings. GRAS.

CAPSICUM. Naturally found in dried pepper-like plant from Africa. Used as a spice in soft drinks (particularly ginger ale) and in candies and confections. Also used in sausages and other processed meats and in condiments (cayenne pepper and Tabasco sauce). On the FDA GRAS list but can irritate mucous membranes or cause digestive distress in some people.

CARAMEL. Very commonly found additive used to produce creamy to brown color in many foods. Produced by cooking sugar and water until dark brown in color. GRAS but listed for further study.

CARBON DIOXIDE. GRAS.

CARBONATE. In its natural form found in coral, marble, and limestone. Used as a white dye in foods and also to balance the acid/alkaline levels in foods. The primary ingredient in baking powder, it is also used in candy making, emulsification, and as a carrier for other agents. GRAS.

CARMINE (Cochineal). A red food color made from an insect *(Coccus cacti)* found in Mexico that feeds upon various types of cactus. The coloring is used in applesauce, confections, bakery products, and processed meats.

CAROB BEAN GUM (Locust Bean Gum). Used as a thickener and texturizer in such products as chocolate milk and other chocolate-flavored beverages, whipped cream in pressure dispensers, and other dairy products. This a natural product from the carob plant. GRAS but on list of additives for further study by FDA.

CAROTENE ... see *Beta-Carotene.*

CARRAGEENAN (Carrageenan Chondrus Extract). Found naturally in Irish moss, a seaweedlike plant that grows along North Atlantic coastlines. It is used primarily as an emulsifier in any food products in pressure-can dispensers, in chocolate products, syrups, cheese spreads, frozen desserts, salad dressings, and low-sugar jams and jellies. It is also used by brewers to stabilize the foaming action of beer. GRAS.

CARVACROL. Naturally occurs in such herbs as oregano, lovage, marjoram, and savory. As an artificial flavoring it is used in beverages, frozen desserts, candy, bakery goods, and condiments to simulate fruit, mint, and spice flavors. Excessive amounts can be very toxic.

CARVEOL. Found naturally in caraway and grapefruit. A synthetic version is used as a citrus and spice flavor in beverages, ice cream, candy, and bakery goods. No known toxicity.

CARVOL ... see *Carvone.*

CARVONE (Carvol). In its natural form is found as an essential oil in caraway and dill seeds as well as spearmint. As an artificial flavor it is used in beverages, frozen desserts, candy, bakery goods, and liquors. Also used in perfumes and soaps. GRAS.

CASEIN (Ammonium Caseinate, Calcium Caseinate, Potassium Caseinate, Sodium Caseinate). The principal protein of cow's milk, it is tasteless and odorless. It is used as a texturizer for frozen desserts and also in the manufacture of plastics, adhesives, and paints. GRAS.

CAUSTIC SODA ... see *Sodium Hydroxide.*

CELLULOSE GUM ... see *Sodium Carboxymethyl Cellulose.*

CHOLINE BITARTRATE, CHOLINE CHLORIDE.   Dietary supplements from the B-complex family of vitamins. GRAS.

CHONDRUS EXTRACT.   Stabilizing agent. GRAS.

CINCHONA ... see *Quinine.*

CINNAMALDEHYDE (Cinnamic Aldehyde).   An artificial flavoring used to produce a cinnamon taste in candies, beverages, chewing gum, condiments, and processed meats. Also used in perfume manufacture. GRAS.

CINNAMIC ALDEHYDE ... see *Cinnamaldehyde.*

CINNAMYL ALCOHOL, CINNAMYL ANTHRANILATE, CINNAMYL ISOVALERATE, CINNAMYL PROPIONATE.   All of these are artificial flavors used to simulate cinnamon in beverages, confections, chewing gum, and bakery goods. No known toxicity.

CITRAL.   An artificial strong lemon flavor used in candies, bakery goods, frozen desserts, and chewing gum. Used in manufacture of strawberry, citrus, apple, cherry, grape, spice, ginger, and vanilla flavorings for beverages, ice cream, candy, bakery goods, gelatin desserts, and chewing gum. GRAS.

CITRATE SALTS ... see *Calcium Citrate, Potassium Citrate, and Sodium Citrate.*

CITRIC ACID.   One of the oldest additives, it occurs naturally in citrus fruits, coffee, and peaches. It is used as a fruit flavoring in sweets. It is also used as an agent in maintaining acid/alkaline balance in many products. It is used in the curing of meats, and to make canned peppers, tomatoes, potatoes, and lima beans firm. It is also used as an antioxidant and preservative in a number of products. GRAS.

CITRIDIC ACID ... see *Aconitic Acid.*

CITRONELLAL, CITRONELLOL, CITRONELLYL ACETATE, CITRONELLYL FORMATE, CITRONELLYL ISOBUTYRATE. All of these are artificial flavorings used in the manufacture of beverages, frozen desserts, candy, bakery goods, gelatin desserts, and chewing gum.

CMC ... see *Sodium Carboxymethyl Cellulose.*

COCHINEAL ... see *Carmine.*

COCOA BUTTER (Theobroma Oil). A naturally occurring fat used as a base for some chocolate products. It is creamy in color and has a slight chocolate taste. It is also used in ointments, creams, and soaps.

COLOROSE ... see *Invert Sugar.*

COPPER GLUCONATE, COPPER SULPHATE. Dietary supplements. GRAS.

CORN SUGAR, CORN SYRUP ... see *Dextrose.*

CREAM OF TARTAR ... see *Potassium Bitartrate.*

CUPROUS IODIDE. GRAS.

CYCLAMATES (Sodium Cyclamate and Calcium Cyclamate). Artificial sweeteners about 30 times sweeter than refined sugar. Widely used in low calorie foods, particularly soft drinks, until 1969 when they were removed from all foods for human consumption because they were found to cause bladder cancer in rats. Not GRAS.

DECANAL (Aldehyde, Capraldehyde, Caprin Aldehyde, Capric Aldehyde, Decylaldehyde).   Occurs naturally in some citrus fruits. It is used to produce a slightly floral taste in confections and also in berry, citrus, and honey flavorings. GRAS.

DECYLALDEHYDE ... see *Decanal.*

DEXTRIN (British Gum, Starch Gum).   This is manufactured by treating starch with acid, alkali, or enzymes. It is used to prevent the crystallizing of sugar in candy, to stabilize foam in beer, and as a thickening agent in various foods. GRAS.

DEXTROSE (Corn Sugar, Corn Syrup).   Dextrose is the most commonly found sugar form. The natural sweetness of fruits and honey is brought about by the presence of dextrose. In food products it is found in everything from the obvious (such as candies and bakery products) to the unlikely (such as catsup, processed meats, and peanut butter). GRAS.

DIACETYL (Diethyl Tartaric Acid).   As a natural substance it is found in cheese, cocoa, coffee, pears, and some berries. As an artificial flavoring it is found in many popular flavors of confections, beverages, chewing gum, and some shortening products. GRAS.

DIAURYL THIODIPROPIONATE.   Preservative agent. GRAS when total content is not over 0.02 percent of fat or oil content.

DIBASIC AMMONIUM PHOSPHATE ... see *Ammonium Phosphate.*

DIBASIC CALCIUM PHOSPHATE ... see *Calcium Phosphate.*

DIBASIC POTASSIUM PHOSPHATE ... see *Potassium Phosphate.*

DICALCIUM PHOSPHATE ... see *Calcium Phosphate.*

DIETHYL PYROCARBONATE (DEP). Used as a fermentation inhibitor in bottled still wines, beer, and orange juice. FDA does not require the listing of DEP on beverage labels.

DIGLYCERIDES ... see *Glycerides.*

DILAURYL THIODIPROPIONATE. A common additive used as an antioxidant and preservative. GRAS but listed for further study.

DIMETHYL POLYSILOXANE. Used to prevent foaming in beverages, melted fats, syrups, and other products. No known toxicity.

DIOCTYL SODIUM SULFOSUCCINATE (DSS). Primarily used as an agent to encourage the dissolving of powdered foods in water. Used in powdered beverage mixes and other foods containing hard-to-dissolve materials.

DIPOTASSIUM PHOSPHATE. Used as a buffering agent in such things as nondairy creamers, it also makes powders easier to dissolve in water. GRAS.

DISODIUM ACID PYROPHOSPHATE . . . see *Sodium Acid Pyrophosphate.*

DISODIUM 5 INOSINATE (IMP). Found naturally in meats and fish, it is used as a flavor enhancer in that it has no particular flavor of its own but brings out the flavor in foods that contain it. It is commonly found in such things as soup mixes, sauces, condiments, and canned vegetables. It is similar to monosodium glutamate in effect but more potent and also more expensive. GRAS but should probably be avoided by those who must avoid caffeine or uric acid, or who have gout.

DISODIUM GUANYLATE (GMP). A product similar to monosodium glutamate and disodium 5 inosinate in that it has little flavor of its own but enhances the flavors of foods that contain it. It is found naturally in some mushrooms and some fish. It is found in soup mixes, sauces, condiments, and canned vegetables. GRAS with the recommendations as noted above for disodium 5 inosinate.

DISODIUM PHOSPHATE. Used variously as an emulsifier (in cheeses), in processed meats to retain juices, as an acid/alkaline balancer in chocolate products, beverages, and sauces. GRAS.

DODECANOIC ACID ... see *Lauric Acid.*

EDTA (Ethylene diamine tetra acetic acid) ... see *Calcium Disodium.*

ERYTHORBIC ACID (Isoascorbic Acid). Used in conjunction with coloring agents in beverages, bakery goods, and processed meats. It has about one-twentieth the potency of the vitamin C in ascorbic acid. Commonly used in the brine in which pickling takes place. GRAS.

ETHANAL ... see *Acetaldehyde.*

ETHYL ACETATE ... see *Acetic Acid.*

ETHYL ALCOHOL. GRAS.

ETHYL ANTHRANILATE, ETHYL BENZOATE, ETHYL CINNAMATE, ETHYL FORMATE, ETHYL HEPTANOATE, ETHYL HEXANOATE, ETHYL LACTATE, ETHYL LAURATE. These are all artificial flavorings used primarily in beverages, bakery goods, candies, chewing gum, and frozen desserts. They have no known toxicity.

ETHYL BUTYRATE. Artificial flavoring. GRAS.

ETHYL FORMATE.   GRAS.

ETHYL LACTATE ... see *Lactic Acid.*

ETHYL MALTOL.   This compound is produced naturally during the baking/roasting process used in bread making, coffee roasting, and in the heating of milk with cellulose and starch. It is used as a flavor enhancer in chocolate-flavored foods and can also be found in gelatin desserts, beverages, and ice cream. It is also used to mask the bitter aftertaste in foods sweetened with saccharin. Currently on GRAS list but under further study by FDA.

ETHYL METHYL PHENYLGLYCIDATE, ETHYL PROPIONATE, ETHYL SALICYLATE, ETHYL VALERATE.   Again, these are artificial flavorings used in the manufacture of sweets and confections. No known toxicity (except possible allergic reactions to ethyl salicylate).

ETHYL VANILLIN.   Artificial vanilla flavoring used primarily in bakery goods, ice cream, and candies. GRAS.

FARNESOL.   This is a fairly common compound that occurs naturally in such things as anise and oils of citronella, lemon grass, balsam, and rose. It is used in the manufacture of such artificial flavors as apricot, banana, cherry, melon, peach, citrus, and berry. No known toxicity.

FATTY ACIDS.   Can be one or more of the following liquid and solid acids: capric, caprylic, lauric, myristic, oleic, palmitic, and stearic. Used as emulsifiers and lubricants in the food-processing industry. No known toxicity.

FD and C Colors (Food, Drug, and Cosmetic Colors).   When the first legislative control over colors added to foods occurred in 1906, there were seven colors authorized after testing for possible harmful effects to humans. The first seven were orange, erythrosin, ponceau 3R, amaranth, indigotin, naphthol yellow, and light green.

In 1938 new legislation superseded the 1906 law. Colors were assigned numbers rather than names and each was required to be certified before use. At that time fifteen colors were in use.

In 1950, after it was determined that certain dyes used in some candies were causing problems, Orange No. 1, Orange No. 2, and Red No. 32 were removed from the list of accepted colors. After later research, Red 1, Yellows 1, 2, 3, and 4, Carbon Black, and Violet 1 have also been removed from the acceptable list. Red 2 was authorized for the coloring of orange peel only (supposedly no more than two parts per million of the color additive calculated on the weight of the whole fruit). Red 4 was authorized for the coloring of maraschino cherries only.

The FDA permanent list of acceptable color additives includes Orange B (used for sausage casings), Citrus Red 2 (with restriction as noted above), Blue 1, Red 3 and 40, and Yellow 5. The other food coloring agents are still on what is considered to be a temporary list. Food coloring agents found to be completely acceptable by the World Health Organization are the following: Red 2, Yellow 5 and 6, Blue 1, and Green 3.

FERRIC PHOSPHATE (Iron Phosphate), FERRIC PYROPHOSPHATE, FERRIC SODIUM PYROPHOSPHATE, FERROUS FUMARATE, FERROUS LACTATE, and FERROUS SULFATE. All are dietary supplements to add iron to commonly eaten foods such as cereals, flours, and bakery products. GRAS.

FERROUS GLUCONATE. Used by olive processors to obtain the black color of ripe olives. If used in excess can cause the olives to soften. GRAS.

FICIN. Naturally found as a product of some tropical trees, this material is used primarily as a meat tenderizer (ten to twenty times more potent than papain tenderizers). It is also used by brewers and as a substitute for rennet in the cheese-making process.

FLAVORINGS ... see "List of GRAS Spices and Other Natural Seasonings and Flavorings," which follows this list.

FORMIC ACID.   Naturally occurs in apples, peaches, some berries, and valerian root. It is used as a fruit flavoring for beverages, confections, and bakery goods. GRAS.

FRUCTOSE.   This sugar is found naturally in honey and many fruits. It is used in ice cream to prevent graininess and in many health-food products. It is, however, sugar, no matter how "natural" its source may be.

FUMARIC ACID.   Fumaric acid is found in all living things, both animals and plants. In food processing it is used to provide tartness and acidity to desserts, beverages, and candy. It is also sometimes used as an antioxidant in bakery products.

FURCELLERAN.   Used as a jelling agent in low-sugar products, and as an emulsifier and thickener. It is made from a red seaweed found in the waters of the North Atlantic. On the current list for further FDA study.

GERANIAL ... see *Citral.*

GERANIOL (Geranyl Acetate, Geraniol Acetate).   Occurs naturally in apples, bay leaves, tea, citrus fruits, and coriander. It is used in the simulation of apple, berry, lemon, cherry, peach, honey and spice flavors in beverages, ice cream, bakery goods, candy, chewing gum, gelatin desserts, and toppings. GRAS.

GLUCONO-DELTA-LACTONE.   Used in the manufacture of jelling and soft-drink powders, and in dairies and breweries. Meat processors use to decrease the time needed to smoke meat and as a color-fixing agent. No specific data on its toxicity is currently available.

GLUCOSE. A simple sugar, sweeter than sucrose, used to flavor processed meats and sometimes as an extender in syrups. No known toxicity.

GLUTAMIC ACID, GLUTAMIC ACID HYDROCHLORIDE. Sometimes used as a salt substitute. GRAS but both are on FDA list of additives requiring further study.

GLYCERIDES (Monoglycerides and Diglycerides). These very commonly used additives are found in such things as margarine, bakery goods, bread products, ice cream, shortening, and chewing gum, where they are used as emulsifying and defoaming agents. GRAS but FDA has diglycerides on the list of additives for further study.

GLYCERIN (Glycerol). This substance is a byproduct of the manufacture of soaps and is used as a humectant to prevent drying-out in marshmallows and other jelled candies. Also used as a texturizer and plasticizer. Found in beverages, bakery goods, gelatin desserts, and processed meat products. GRAS.

GLYCERYL ABIETATE. Used in alcoholic and nonalcoholic drinks as a density adjuster for citrus oil. Also is used as a plasticizing agent in chewing gum. No known toxicity.

GLYCERYL MONOSTEARATE. Multipurpose additive. GRAS.

GUAR (Guar Gum). Found naturally in the guar plant, which is grown in India and Pakistan as cattle feed. The gum has five to eight times the thickening ability of starch and is used as a stabilizer in frozen fruits, icings, and beverages. It also is used as a binder for meats, bakery goods, dairy products, and salad dressings. GRAS if used within recognized acceptable amounts but scheduled for further study regarding toxicity.

GUM ARABIC (Gum Senegal, Acacia). Taken from the acacia tree, this substance has been in use for thousands of years (the Egyptians used it as an ingredient in their paint products). As a food additive it prevents sugar from crystallizing, and acts as a thickener for confections and a foam reducer for beer and soft drinks. GRAS.

GUM BENJAMIN ... see *Benzoin.*

GUM BENZOIN ... see *Benzoin.*

GUM GHATTI. GRAS.

GUM SENEGAL ... see *Gum Arabic.*

GUM TRAGACANTH. Made from the gummy resin of the roots of the tragacanth plants found in the Middle East. This additive has been in use since pre-Christian times. It has been listed in the U.S. Pharmacopoeia since 1820. It is a thickening agent particularly useful in acid-based foods. GRAS.

HELIOTROPIN ... see *Piperonal.*

HELIUM. GRAS.

HEPTANAL (Heptyl Aldehyde). Distilled from castor oil, this synthetic flavoring is used in citrus, apple, melon, liquor, and almond flavorings in beverages, ice cream, candy, bakery goods, and liquors. No known toxicity.

HEXANAL (Hexaldehyde, Hexoic Aldehyde). Occurs naturally in apples, coffee, cooked chicken, strawberries, and tea. Used to simulate butter, fruit, honey, and rum flavors for beverages, ice cream, candy, bakery goods, gelatin deserts, and chewing gum. No known toxicity.

HEXYL ALCOHOL. A synthetic flavoring agent occurring naturally in apples, strawberries, and tea. Used to simulate berry, coconut, and other fruit flavorings for beverages, ice cream, candy, bakery goods, and gelatin desserts. GRAS.

HVP ... see *Hydrolyzed Vegetable Protein*.

HYDROCHLORIC ACID. Used as a modifier of food starch and in the manufacture of gelatin. Also used as an acid/alkaline balancer in breweries. GRAS.

HYDROGEN PEROXIDE. Found as a bleach and oxidizing agent, and also as a bactericide in dairy products. On GRAS list at this time when used as a bleach in accordance with good manufacturing practice, but under further study by the FDA.

HYDROLYZED VEGETABLE PROTEIN (HVP). Made usually from soybean protein, this is used as a flavor enhancer in canned beef stew and chili, and in mixes for gravy, sauces, and soups. Contains MSG. GRAS for adults but further study has been recommended regarding the safety for children.

IMP ... see *Disodium 5 Inosinate*.

INDIAN TRAGACANTH ... see *Karaya Gum*.

INDOLE. Occurs naturally in jasmine oil, coal tar, and in orange flowers. Used in simulating raspberry, strawberry, chocolate, orange, coffee, and cheese flavorings for beverages, ice cream, candy, bakery goods, and gelatin desserts.

INOSITOL. Dietary supplement from the B-complex vitamin family. GRAS.

INVERT SUGAR (Invert Syrup, Inversol, Nulomoline, Colorose). A combination of half glucose and half fructose to produce a sugar sweeter than sucrose. It is also more soluble in water than sucrose and less likely to crystallize. It also is useful in preventing foods from drying out. Used medically in intravenous solutions. GRAS.

IRON PHOSPHATE ... see *Ferric Phosphate*.

**ISOAMYL ACETATE, ISOAMYL BENZOATE, ISOAMYL CIN-
NAMATE, ISOAMYL ISOVALERATE, ISOAMYL LAURATE,
ISOAMYL PHENYLACETATE.**   All are synthetic flavorings used
primarily in sweet foods. No known toxicity.

ISOASCORBIC ACID ... see *Erythorbic Acid.*

ISOPROPYL CITRATE, MONOISOPROPYL CITRATE. A
product that is manufactured by combining citric acid with
isopropyl alcohol. It has the antioxidant capacity of citric
acid and the additional ability to penetrate fats and oils, which
citric acid alone cannot do. Used in vegetable oils, margarines,
and other foods containing a lot of fat. GRAS.

KAOLIN.   GRAS.

KADAYA ... see *Karaya Gum.*

**KARAYA GUM (Kadaya, Katilo, Kullo, Kuterra, Sterculia,
Indian Tragacanth, Mucara).**   This is manufactured from
the gum of the sterculia tree, which grows only in India. It is
used as a thickening and stabilizing agent (primarily in phar-
maceuticals and cosmetics). In food products it is found in
such things as gelatins, gumdrop candies, and ice cream.
GRAS.

KATILO ... see *Karaya Gum.*

KULLO ... see *Karaya Gum.*

KUTERRA ... see *Karaya Gum.*

LACTASE ENZYME.   GRAS.

**LACTIC ACID (Butyl Lactate, Ethyl Lactate, Calcium
Lactate).**   Found as a liquid in virtually all organisms. It is
produced commercially in the fermentation of whey, corn-
starch, potatoes, and molasses. It is used as an acidulant in

beverages, candy, olives, dried egg whites, cottage cheese, bread products, and other bakery goods. Calcium lactate is a nonacidic salt of lactic acid, which serves to inhibit discoloration in fruits and vegetables. Used to simulate such flavors as butter, butterscotch, lime, nuts, chocolate, and spices. GRÅS.

LACTOSE (Milk Sugar). Lactose is found naturally in the milk of mammals. Commercial lactose is produced from whey. It is used most often in food products as a humectant to prevent drying. It is one-sixteenth as sweet as sucrose and it is used to sweeten some foods such as cereals and whipped toppings. GRAS.

LACTYLIC STEARATE. Used by bakeries as a preservative and to add bulk to bread.

LAURIC ACID (Dodecanoic Acid). Found in vegetable oils, particularly coconut and laurel oils. It is used in the manufacture of flavors used in beverages, ice cream, candy, bakery goods, and powdered desserts. Also used to make soap, cosmetics, and detergents.

LECITHIN. GRAS.

LIMESTONE, GROUND. GRAS.

LIMONENE. Artificial flavoring. GRAS.

LINALOOL. Naturally occurs in basil, citrus fruits, peaches, tea, ginger, laurel, and other essential oils. Used in the simulation of such flavors as chocolate, citrus, grape, cola, peach, and some spices in beverages, ice cream, candy, bakery goods, processed meats, and chewing gum. GRAS.

LINALYL ACETATE, LINALYL ANTHRANILATE, LINALYL BENZOATE, LINALYL BUTYRATE, LINALYL CINNAMATE, LINALYL HEXANOATE, LINALYL PROPIONATE. All are synthetic flavorings used to simulate such flavors as citrus, apple, pineapple, apricot, and other fruit flavors. GRAS.

LINOLEIC ACID.   Dietary supplement that is one of the essential fatty acids. GRAS.

LOCUST BEAN GUM ... see *Carob Bean Gum.*

LOW METHOXYL PECTIN ... see *Pectin.*

MAGNESIUM CARBONATE. Used as an alkali in some dairy products, ice cream, and canned peas. GRAS.

MAGNESIUM CHLORIDE. Used to enhance color retention and as a firming agent. GRAS.

MAGNESIUM CYCLAMATE. Used as an artificial sweetener until 1969 when it was banned. Not GRAS.

MAGNESIUM HYDROXIDE. Used as an alkali in canned peas and as a drying agent and color-retention agent in the manufacture of cheese. GRAS.

MAGNESIUM OXIDE. An alkali used as a neutralizer in frozen dairy products, cocoa, and canned peas. GRAS.

MAGNESIUM PHOSPHATE. Dietary supplement. GRAS.

MAGNESIUM SILICATE. Used as an anticaking ingredient in table salts, granulated sugar, and other similar products. GRAS.

MAGNESIUM STEARATE. GRAS.

MAGNESIUM SULFATE. Dietary supplement. GRAS.

MALIC ACID. Found naturally in all living cells, malic acid is found abundantly in such fruits as apples, cherries, and peaches as well as tomatoes, coffee, and rhubarb. It is used in food processing as an acidulant and fruit-flavoring agent. It is also used in the process of aging some wines. GRAS.

MALTO-DEXTRIN. Maltol and dextrin are combined to form this substance, which is used as a flavor and texture enhancer in some candies, particularly chocolate candy. GRAS.

MALTOL. Found in the bark of the larch tree, pine needles, and in roasted malt, this adds a "fresh-baked" aroma to bakery goods. It is also used as an ingredient in synthetic chocolate, coffee, fruit, maple, nut, and vanilla flavorings for beverages, ice cream, candy, bakery goods, gelatin desserts, and chewing gum. No known toxicity.

MANGANESE CHLORIDE, MANGANESE CITRATE, MANGANESE GLUCONATE, MANGANESE GLYCEROPHOSPHATE, MANGANESE OXIDE, MANGANESE SULFATE. All are dietary supplements. GRAS.

MANNITOL. This is a widely used additive with about two-thirds the sweetness of sucrose. It is manufactured from a variety of plants, including some seaweeds. It is one of the sweeteners used in sugar-free products and also used as an anticaking agent. Currently GRAS but under further study.

MENTHYL ACETATE. Occurs naturally in peppermint oil and is used as a natural flavoring agent in confections and bakery goods. GRAS.

METHIONINE. An essential amino acid that is used in food processing to give deep-fry cooking oil an extended fresh taste when cooking things such as potato chips or other foods. GRAS but scheduled for further study.

METHYL ACETATE ... see *Acetic Acid.*

METHYL ACRYLATE. An odorless, transparent, and elastic substance used in packaging, particularly in coating paper and in making plastic film. GRAS for packaging only.

METHYL ANTHRANILATE. Artificial flavoring. GRAS.

METHYL BENZOATE, METHYL ANISATE, METHYL BUTY-RATE, METHYL CINNAMATE, METHYL DISULFIDE, METHYL HEPTANOATE, METHYL HEXANOATE, METHYL ISOBUTY-RATE, METHYL LAURATE, METHYL NONANOATE, METHYL OCTANOATE, METHYL SULFIDE, METHYL VALERATE. All are used in synthetic flavorings primarily to produce fruit flavors of various kinds.

METHYLCELLULOSE. A synthetic thickening agent and stabilizer made from wood pulp or cotton. It is used in a variety of low-calorie products as well as serving as a carrier for flavorings, an edible film on food products, and a clarifier for some liquid products (such as vinegar). GRAS.

MILK SERUM ... see *Whey.*

MILK SUGAR ... see *Lactose.*

MODIFIED STARCH. Carbohydrate substances that have been chemically modified to enhance the properties of thickening and/or jelling. Also has been used in some baby foods on the premise that it is easier for babies to digest. Because of the chemical alteration, questions have been raised regarding its safety for infant use and it is on a priority list for further FDA study.

MONOAMMONIUM GLUTAMATE, MONOPOTASSIUM GLU-TAMATE. Multipurpose additives. GRAS.

MONOBASIC CALCIUM PHOSPHATE ... see *Calcium Phosphates.*

MONOCALCIUM PHOSPHATE ... see *Calcium Phosphates.*

MONOSODIUM GLUTAMATE (MSG). This substance occurs naturally in some seaweeds, in soybeans, and sugar beets. Used to intensify flavors in condiments, meats, soups, candy, and bakery goods. Used extensively in Oriental cuisine. Has been removed from baby foods. Currently GRAS but scheduled for further FDA study.

MONOSODIUM PHOSPHATE.   Derived from animal fat. Used as an emulsifier and buffer and in processed meat products to prevent loss of fluids from the meat. GRAS.

MSG ... see *Monosodium Glutamate.*

MUCARA ... see *Karaya Gum.*

NERAL ... see *Citral.*

NIACIN, NIACINAMIDE.   Dietary supplements from the B-complex family of vitamins. GRAS.

NICKEL.   GRAS.

NITRATE (Potassium and Sodium).   Used as a preservative and color enhancer particularly in meat products, the two nitrates are the center of concern and no little controversy because of their potential roles as cancer-causing agents. In the stomach the nitrates combine with secondary amines to cause nitrosamines, which have been concluded to be cancer-related. Baby-food manufacturers have removed nitrates from their products. The FDA and the food-processing industry are under great pressure to resolve the question of nitrate safety. Until resolved it is wise to eat only conservative amounts of products that contain this substance.

NITRITE (Potassium and Sodium).   The same precautions apply to the nitrites as to the nitrates. They are potential cancer-causing agents used primarily as preservatives, particularly to prevent the growth of the botulism bacteria (*Clostridium botulinum*) and secondarily as a colorant. The FDA has high priority on this research. If the role of nitrates and nitrites as preservatives is not as essential as has been believed and if in fact the agents are primarily colorants, many feel that they should be banned. There are strong feelings on each side of the situation. Until the issue is settled, caution is the best position for cooks.

NITROGEN. GRAS.

NITROUS OXIDE. Commonly known as laughing gas. In foods it is used as a whipping agent and propellant in pressure containers of whipped dairy and nondairy toppings. GRAS.

NONYL ALCOHOL (Nonalol). A synthetic flavoring used in butter, citrus, peach, and pineapple flavorings for beverages, ice cream, candy, bakery goods, and chewing gum.

NULOMOLINE . . . see *Invert Sugar.*

OAT GUM. A plant extract used as an antioxidant in butter, cream, and candy and as a stabilizer and thickener in cheese and cheese spreads. No known toxicity.

OCTADECANOIC ACID . . . see *Stearic Acid.*

OCTYL BUTYRATE . . . see *Butyric Acid.*

OLEIC ACID. Substance obtained from plant and animal fats and oils. Used as a defoaming agent, as a synthetic flavor for butter, cheese, and spice, and as a lubricant and binder.

OLEORESIN TURMERIC. A natural substance from the turmeric plant used to flavor and color pickles and other condiments and some processed meats. GRAS.

OZONE. GRAS.

PALMITIC ACID. Naturally occurs in some spices, coffee, tea, and many plant and animal oils. Used to produce butter or cheese flavorings in seasoning preparations. No known toxicity.

PANTOTHENIC ACID ... see *Sodium Pantothenate.*

PAPAIN. An extract from the papaya fruit used as a meat tenderizer because of its protein-digesting capabilities. It is used just before the meat is to be cooked and is deactivated by cooking (if not deactivated, it would eventually completely dissolve the meat). GRAS.

PATENT ALUM ... see *Aluminum Sulfate.*

PECTIN (Low Methoxyl Pectin and Sodium Pectinate). In its natural form it is found in all parts of plants and is used by them as a strengthening and cementing agent. In its role as a food additive it is found most abundantly in orange and lemon rind and is used as a stabilizer, thickener, and bodying agent for beverages, ice cream, confections, salad dressings, and preserves. No known toxicity.

PEPTONES. GRAS.

PEROXIDES ... see *Benzoyl Peroxide, Calcium Peroxide and Hydrogen Peroxide.*

PHOSPHORIC ACID. Used in soft drinks as an acidulant and flavoring and also found in ice cream, cheeses, candies, jellies, and bakery goods. It is also used in the rendering of animal fats. GRAS.

PIPERONAL. Artificial flavoring. GRAS.

POLYSORBATE 60. **(Polyoxyethylene 20 Sorbitan Mono-stearate, Polysorbate 65).** Used as flavor carriers and emulsifiers in many food products, particularly desserts. There has been some controversy about them, but the substances have been determined to be safe for human consumption by the UN Food and Agriculture Organization/World Health Organization combined Committee on Food Additives. FDA is conducting further studies.

POLYSORBATE 80 (Sorbitan Monooleate). Used as a plasticizer in chewing gum, and a defoaming agent. It is found in beverages, candy, frozen desserts, bakery products, nondairy creamers. Like polysorbate 60 it has been the center of some controversy in the past but is currently determined to be safe by the FAO/WHO Committee on Food Additives.

POTASSIUM ACETATE ... see *Acetates*.

POTASSIUM ALGINATE ... see *Alginates*.

POTASSIUM BICARBONATE. GRAS.

POTASSIUM BISULFITE, POTASSIUM METABISULFITE. Preservative agents. GRAS.

POTASSIUM BITARTRATE (Cream of Tartar, Sodium Potassium Tartrate, Tartaric Acid, Tartrate). A naturally occurring crystal used in baking powder, as a buffering ingredient in candies and preserves, and as a stabilizer in some baked goods.

POTASSIUM BROMATE ... see *Bromates*.

POTASSIUM BROMIDE. Used when washing fruits and vegetables as a preservative. Can cause allergic reactions in some people.

POTASSIUM CASEINATE ... see *Casein*.

POTASSIUM CHLORIDE. Primarily used as a substitute for common table salt (sodium chloride) for people on salt-restricted diets. Also used in the brewing industry to improve fermentation. GRAS.

POTASSIUM CITRATE. Used as a buffer in preserves, low-sugar jellies, and in other confections. GRAS.

POTASSIUM GLYCEROPHOSPHATE. Dietary supplement. GRAS.

POTASSIUM HYDROXIDE. GRAS.

POTASSIUM IODATE, POTASSIUM IODIDE. Added to common table salt (sodium chloride) as a source of iodine. Table salt can contain no more than 01. percent potassium iodide. GRAS in specified amounts and in accordance with good manufacturing practices.

POTASSIUM NITRATE and NITRITE . . . see *Nitrate and Nitrite.*

POTASSIUM PHOSPHATE. Found in monobasic and dibasic forms. Used as a yeast food in winemaking. No known toxicity.

POTASSIUM SORBATE. Used as a preservative, a mold and yeast inhibitor, and a fungus preventant in a wide variety of foods. Used by cheese makers to retard the growth of mold while allowing the necessary growth of bacteria. GRAS.

POTASSIUM SULFATE. GRAS.

POTASSIUM SULFITE . . . see *Sodium Sulfite.*

PROMANE. GRAS.

PROPIONIC ACID. Occurs naturally in dairy products, in apples, strawberries, and tea and from wood pulp. Used as a synthetic flavoring in beverages, ice cream, candy, bakery goods, and cheese. Also used as a preservative. GRAS.

PROPYL GALLATE. Used as an antioxidant and also in synthetic fruit flavorings of beverages, ice cream, candy, bakery goods, and gelatin desserts. Often found used in combination with BHA and BHT. Currently on GRAS list but scheduled for further FDA study.

PROPYLENE GLYCOL.   Used as a humectant in making such things as candy, bakery goods, beverages, and shredded coconut. Sometimes used in processed meats to prevent discoloration. GRAS.

PROPYLPARABEN.   A preservative that will inhibit growth of molds and bacteria in almost all foods. GRAS.

PYRODIXINE HYDROCHLORIDE.   Dietary supplement from the B-complex vitamin family. Occurs naturally in coffee. Used to produce coffee and rum flavors in beverages, confections, and bakery goods. No known toxicity. GRAS.

PYROPHOSPHATE.   Used to enhance the action of antioxidants in shortening and lard. GRAS.

QUICKLIME . . . see *Calcium Oxide.*

QUININE (Quinine Extract, Quinine Bisulfate, Quinine Hydrochloride, Quinine Sulfate).   All are related to the substance taken from the cinchona tree. A traditional treatment for malaria, also used to add a bitter flavor to beverages. No known toxicity but scheduled for further testing.

RENNET (Rennin).   Found naturally in the inner lining of the stomach of calves. Used in making cheese. GRAS.

RIBOFLAVIN.   Dietary supplement from the B-complex family of vitamins. GRAS.

ROSE BULGARIAN (Attar of Roses, True Otto Oil).   An extract obtained from rose blossoms that have just opened, and used in a variety of berry and fruit flavorings found in beverages, ice cream, bakery goods, gelatin desserts, and chewing gum. GRAS except for certain individual allergic reactions.

SACCHARIN (Sodium Saccharin).   Because it is 300 to 500 times sweeter than sucrose, it has been used since the late

1800s as a sugar substitute for people on sugar- or calorie-restricted diets. From a taste standpoint its primary drawback is that it leaves a bitter aftertaste. From a health standpoint, saccharin has been determined to cause cancer in laboratory animals and so all products that contain it must now carry a printed warning to that effect. The FDA suggests restricting intake to fifteen milligrams per day for each kilogram of body weight, or one gram a day for a 150-pound person. Since the labels on foods are required to list the amount of saccharin contained in the product, it is possible to monitor intake.

SACCHAROSE ... see *Sucrose.*

SAINT-JOHN'S-BREAD ... see *Carob Bean Gum.*

SALT ... see *Sodium Chloride.*

SALTPETER (Potassium Nitrate) ... see *Nitrate.*

SAP ... see *Sodium Acid Phosphate.*

SERUM LACTIS ... see *Whey.*

SILICA AEROGEL. Multipurpose additive used particularly as an antifoaming agent. GRAS.

SILICON DIOXIDE. Naturally occurring in rocks of various sorts and used primarily as an anticaking agent in powdery food substances. No known toxicity.

SODA LYE ... see *Sodium Hydroxide.*

SODIUM ACETATE ... see *Acetates.*

SODIUM ACID CARBONATE ... see *Sodium Bicarbonate.*

SODIUM ACID PHOSPHATE (SAP, Sodium Acid Pyrophosphate, Disodium Acid Pyrophosphate). Used as an acid/

alkali balancer in products containing flour. Also used in canned tuna. GRAS.

SODIUM ACID SULFITE . . . see *Sodium Bisulfite.*

SODIUM ALUMINOSILICATE. Anticaking agent. GRAS for use at a level not to exceed two percent of the content and in accordance with good manufacturing practice.

SODIUM ALUMINUM PHOSPHATE. Used as an acid/alkaline balancer in cheese and self-rising flours. GRAS.

SODIUM ALUMINUM SULFATE. Used as a bleaching agent for flours. GRAS.

SODIUM ASCORBATE . . . see *Ascorbic Acid.*

SODIUM BENZOATE . . . see *Benzoic Acid.*

SODIUM BICARBONATE (Bicarbonate of Sodium, Sodium Acid Carbonate). Used to leaven a variety of baked products and also to balance acid/alkali level, in such things as tomato soup and frozen desserts. GRAS.

SODIUM BISULFITE (Sodium Metabisulfite, Sodium Acid Sulfite, Sodium Hydrogen Sulfite). Used to prevent discoloration and bacterial growth in ale, wine, beer, soft drinks, grape products, sliced fruits and vegetables, dehydrated potatoes, and soup mixes. Considered GRAS in current use patterns but additional studies have been recommended to study effects of higher intake levels. GRAS.

SODIUM CALCIUM ALUMINOSILICATE HYDRATED. Anticaking agent. GRAS at levels not to exceed two percent of content and in accordance with good manufacturing practices.

SODIUM CARBONATE. Synthetic additive used to neutralize some acids found in dairy products, and also in the processing of olives and cocoa products. GRAS.

SODIUM CARBOXYMETHYLCELLULOSE (Cellulose Gum, CMC). Widely used cellulose derivative. Often referred to as CMC, it is used as a stabilizer in many foods that are packed in pressure containers, in beverages and bakery goods. It is used in canned pie fillings and preserves to keep fruit distributed and in beer to control foaming.

SODIUM CASEINATE ... see *Casein.*

SODIUM CHLORIDE (Salt). Used as an almost universal seasoning agent and as a preservative for meats, vegetables, and butter. GRAS except for people on salt-restricted diets.

SODIUM CITRATE (Trisodium Citrate). Used in dairy products as an emulsifier, to regulate acid/alkali balance, and to retain carbonation in soft drinks. GRAS.

SODIUM CYCLAMATE ... see *Cyclamates.*

SODIUM ERYTHROBATE (Sodium Isoascorbate). Used in processed meat to enhance color. Also used as an antioxidant in a variety of foods. No known toxicity.

SODIUM GLUCONATE. Used as a sequestering agent. GRAS.

SODIUM HEXAMETAPHOSPHATE. Used as an emulsifier, sequestering agent, and texturizer in breakfast cereals, angel food cake, flaked fish, frozen desserts, puddings, and artificially sweetened jellies. Because it is able to keep calcium, magnesium, and iron salts in solution, it is often used as a water conditioner.

SODIUM HYDROGEN SULFITE ... see *Sodium Bisulfite.*

SODIUM HYDROSULFITE. Used as a preservative (bacterial inhibitor) and to prevent fermentation when processing sugars and syrups. No known toxicity.

SODIUM HYDROXIDE (Caustic Soda, Soda Lye). Varied uses in food processing: a modifier for food starch, a glazing agent for pretzels, a peeling agent for roots and fruits, in refining oils and fats, in sour cream, butter, and cocoa products, and as a neutralizer in canned peas. GRAS.

SODIUM HYPOPHOSPHITE. GRAS.

SODIUM ISOASCORBATE . . . see *Sodium Erythorbate.*

SODIUM METABISULFITE. Used as a bacterial inhibitor in wine and beer, and as an antifermenting agent in sugars and syrups. It is also used as a preservative for fruit and vegetable juices and an antidiscoloration agent in fruits and fruit products. GRAS.

SODIUM METAPHOSPHATE. Sequestering agent. GRAS.

SODIUM METASILICATE. GRAS.

SODIUM NITRATE and SODIUM NITRITE . . . see *Nitrate* and *Nitrite.*

SODIUM PANTOTHENATE. Dietary supplement from B-complex family of vitamins. GRAS.

SODIUM PECTINATE. Used as a stabilizer and thickener for liquids in frozen products, frozen desserts, salad dressings, and preserves. No known toxicity. GRAS in normal quantities.

SODIUM PHOSPHATE. Multipurpose additive. GRAS.

SODIUM POTASSIUM TARTRATE . . . see *Potassium Bitartrate.*

SODIUM PROPIONATE. Preservative used to prevent mold and fungus growth in foods. GRAS.

SODIUM PYROPHOSPHATE (Tetra Sodium Phosphate).
Used as an emulsifier and texturizer in processed cheeses and
"instant" puddings. GRAS.

SODIUM SACCHARIN . . . see *Saccharin.*

SODIUM SEQUICARBONATE.   GRAS.

SODIUM SILICATE.   Used in dry food packaging. GRAS.

SODIUM SORBATE . . . see *Sorbic Acid.*

SODIUM SULFATE.   GRAS.

SODIUM SULFITE.   Primary use in food processing is to prevent discoloration in cut fruits and vegetables. It is also used as
a bacterial inhibitor by vintners, brewers, and distillers and as
a general preservative for juices, meats, and egg yolks. GRAS.

SODIUM TARTRATE.   GRAS.

SODIUM TRIPOLYPHOSPHATE (STPP).   USDA approved as
an additive for canned meats to prevent fluid loss. Also used
as a texturizer in other foods. GRAS.

SORBIC ACID (Calcium Sorbate, Sodium Sorbate).   Made
from the berries of the mountain ash tree and also manufactured synthetically. Used as a mold and yeast inhibitor in
beverages, bakery goods, chocolate, and other beverage syrups, fresh fruit cocktail, salads, cheesecake, pie fillings, and
artificially sweetened jellies and preserves. It is chemically
similar to fat and is metabolized by the body as though it were
a food substance. GRAS.

SORBITAN MONOOLEATE . . . see *Polysorbate 80.*

SORBITOL.   Found naturally in berries and other fruits, algae and other seaweeds, sorbitol is used as a sugar substitute

(particularly for use by diabetics). It is also used as a thickening agent, and a stabilizer in oils and frozen desserts. The FDA is conducting further test to evaluate if sorbitol is really safe for use by diabetics. GRAS.

SPICES. See list of "GRAS Spices and Other Natural Seasonings and Flavorings," which follows this list.

STANNOUS CHLORIDE. Used as an antioxidant in soft drinks, canned asparagus, and some other foods. GRAS.

STARCH GUM ... see *Dextrin.*

STEARIC ACID (Octadecanoic Acid). Occurs naturally in some vegetable oils and is also manufactured synthetically. Used in butter and vanilla flavorings for beverages, bakery goods, and candy. Also used in chewing gum as a softener. Can cause allergic reactions in some people. GRAS.

STEARYL CITRATE. Sequestering agent. GRAS.

STERCULIA GUM ... see *Karaya Gum.*

STPP ... see *Sodium Tripolyphosphate.*

SUCCINAMIC ACID. GRAS.

SUCROSE (Sugar, Saccharose, Cane Sugar, Beet Sugar). The primary sweetening agent additive used in food processing. GRAS but nutritionists raise questions about the amount of sucrose consumed by Americans, especially children.

SUGAR ... see *Sucrose.*

SULFAMIC ACID. GRAS.

SULFITES ... see *Sodium Sulfite.*

SULFUR DIOXIDE. Used in processing fruits and vegetables as a bleach and preservative. Used as an antidiscolorant in wines, syrups, jelly, dried fruits, beverages, dehydrated potatoes, soups, and condiments. Currently on GRAS list but FDA has asked for further study.

TANNIN (Tannic Acid). Found naturally in the bark and fruit of many plants and trees and in coffee and tea. It is used in many artificial flavorings such as butter, caramel, maple, fruit, and brandy, which are used in frozen desserts, bakery goods, and candy. It is also used by vintners and brewers as a clarifying agent and as a refining agent in rendering fats. GRAS.

TARTARIC ACID ... see *Potassium Bitartrate.*

TARTRATE ... see *Potassium Bitartrate.*

TBHQ (Tertiary Butylhydroquinone). Used as an antioxidant, frequently in combination with BHA and BHT. FDA will allow a relationship of no more than 0.02 percent TBHQ to the amount of the fat or oil in the food product.

TETRASODIUM PYROPHOSPHATE. Used in dry food packaging. GRAS.

TEXTURED VEGETABLE PROTEIN (TVP). A product of soybeans mixed with various additives to promote color and texture changes. Used in place of meat or as a meat extender.

THEINE ... see *Caffeine.*

THEOBROMA OIL ... see *Cocoa Butter.*

THIAMIN HYDROCHLORIDE, THIAMIN MONONITRATE. Dietary supplements from the B-complex vitamin family. GRAS.

THIODIPROPIONIC ACID. Preservative agent. GRAS at no more than 0.02 percent of fat and oil content and used in accordance with good manufacturing practice.

THYMOL. Found naturally in oil of lavender, origanum oil, and thyme. Used to produce fruit, mint, and spice flavorings in beverages, ice cream, candy, bakery goods, and chewing gum.

TOCOPHEROLS. Preservative agents. GRAS.

TRIACETIN. Multipurpose additive. GRAS.

TRIBASIC CALCIUM PHOSPHATE... see *Calcium Phosphate.*

TRICALCIUM PHOSPHATE ... see *Calcium Phosphate.*

TRICALCIUM SILICATE. Anticaking agent. GRAS.

TRIETHYL CITRATE. Multipurpose additive. GRAS.

TRISODIUM CITRATE ... see *Sodium Citrate.*

TRUE OTTO OIL ... see *Rose Bulgarian.*

TVP ... see *Textured Vegetable Protein.*

UNDECANAL. An artificial flavoring agent used to simulate fruit and honey flavors in beverages, ice cream, candy, bakery goods, gelatin desserts, and chewing gum. No known toxicity.

UREA. Used in food processing by vintners and to brown some baked goods (such as pretzels). GRAS.

VANILLIN (Vanillin Acetate). Found naturally in vanilla extract but more commonly compounded synthetically from eugenol (an extract from cloves) and from waste wood pulp. Much stronger than natural vanilla. Used to simulate the same flavors as vanilla and in the same sorts of food products. GRAS.

VEGETABLE LUTEIN ... see *Xanthophyll.*

WHEY (Milk Serum, Serum Lactis). Whey is the liquid part of milk that remains after the casein has been removed. It is used as an additive in imitation sausage and in soups and stews. GRAS.

XANTHAN GUM. A product produced from the fermentation of corn sugar. It is used as a thickener, emulsifier, and stabilizer in dairy products and salad dressing. GRAS.

XANTHOPHYLL (Vegetable Lutein). A coloring agent that occurs naturally in egg yolks, some flower petals, and some bird feathers. Provisionally listed as being safe for use in food products.

XYLITOL. An artificial sweetener used in preserves and chewing gum. A diuretic so not suitable to be used in soft drinks. No known toxicity but under study as a possible cancer-causing agent.

ZEIN. GRAS at levels not to exceed good manufacturing practices.

ZINC CHLORIDE, ZINC GLUCONATE, ZINC OXIDE, ZINC STEARATE, ZINC SULFATE. Dietary supplements. GRAS.

ZINGERONE. Found naturally in ginger. In its synthetic form is used to simulate nut, root beer, spice, ginger ale, and wintergreen flavorings in beverages, bakery goods, candy, frozen desserts, and chewing gum.

LIST OF GRAS SPICES
AND OTHER NATURAL SEASONINGS AND FLAVORINGS

Common Name	Botanical Name of Plant Source
Alfalfa herb and seed	*Medicago sativa*
Allspice	*Pimenta dioica*
Almond oil	*Prunus amygdalus*
Ambrette seed	*Hibiscus abelmoschus*
Angelica	*Angelica archangelica*
Angostura	*Galipea officinalis*
Anise	*Pimpinella anisum*
Anise, star	*Illicium verum*
Asafetida	*Ferula assafoetida*
Balm (lemon balm)	*Melissa officinalis*
Balsam of Peru	*Myroxylon pereirae*
Basil, bush	*Ocimum minimum*
Basil, sweet	*Ocimum basilicum*
Bay	*Laurun nobilis*
Bay leaf oil, myrcia oil	*Pimenta racemosa*
Bergamot orange	*Citrus bergamia*
Bitter almond oil	*Prunus amygdalus*
Bois de rose	*Aniba panurensis*
Cacao	*Theobroma cacao*
Calendula	*Calendula officinalis*
Cananga	*Canangium odorata*
Capers	*Capparis spinosa*
Capsicum	*Capsicum frutescens*
Caraway	*Carum carvi*
Caraway, black	*Nigella sativa*
Cardamom	*Elettaria cardamomum*
Carob bean	*Ceratonia siliqua*
Carrot	*Daucus carota*
Cascarilla bark	*Croton eluteria*
Cassia, Batavia	*Cinnamomum burmanni*
Cassia, Chinese	*Cinnamomum cassia*
Cassia, Saigon	*Cinnamomum loureirii*
Cayenne pepper	*Capsicum frutescens*
Celery seed	*Apium graveolens*

Common Name	Botanical Name of Plant Source
Chamomile, English	*Anthemis nobilis*
Chamomile, German	*Matricaria chamomilla*
Cherry, wild bark	*Prunus seronita*
Chervil	*Anthriscus cerefolium*
Chicory	*Cichorium intybus*
Chives	*Allium schoenoprasum*
Cinnamon, Ceylon	*Cinnamomum zeylanicum*
Cinnamon, Chinese	*Cinnamomum cassia*
Cinnamon, Saigon	*Cinnamomum loureirii*
Citronella	*Cymbopogon nardus*
Citrus peels	*Citrus species*
Clary (clary sage)	*Salvia sclarea*
Clover	*Trifolium species*
Cocoa	*Erythroxylum species*
Coffee	*Coffea species*
Cola nut	*Cola species*
Coriander	*Coriandrum sativum*
Cumin	*Cuminum cyminum*
Cumin, black	*Nigella sativa*
Curaçao orange	*Citrus aurantium*
Cusparia bark	*Galipea officinalis*
Dandelion	*Taraxacum officinale*
Dog grass	*Agropyron repens*
Elder flowers	*Sambucus canadensis*
Estragon (tarragon)	*Artemisia dracunculus*
Fennel, common	*Foeniculum vulgare*
Fennel, sweet (finocchio)	*Foeniculum dulce*
Fenugreek	*Trigonella foenumgraecum*
Galanga (galangal)	*Alpina officinarum*
Geranium	*Pelargonium species*
Geranium, East Indian	*Cymbopogon martini*
Geranium, rose	*Pelargonium graveolens*
Ginger	*Zingiber officinale*
Grain of paradise	*Aframomum melegueta*
Grapefruit	*Citrus paradisi*
Guava	*Psidium species*

Common Name	Botanical Name of Plant Source
Hickory bark	*Carya species*
Hops	*Humulus lupulus*
Horehound	*Marrubium vulgare*
Horsemint	*Monarda punctata*
Horseradish	*Armoracia lapathifolia*
Hyssop	*Hyssopus officinalis*
Immortelle	*Erythrina nicropteryx*
Jasmine	*Jasminum species*
Juniper (berries)	*Juniperus communis*
Kola nut	*Cola species*
Laurel berries	*Laurus nobilis*
Laurel leaves	*Laurus species*
Lavender	*Lavandula officinalis*
Lavender, spike	*Lavandula latifolia*
Lemon	*Citrus limon*
Lemon balm	*Melissa officinalis*
Lemon grass	*Cymbopogon citratus*
Lime	*Citrus aurantifolia*
Linden flowers	*Tilia species*
Locust bean oil	*Ceratonia siliqua*
Lupulin	*Humulus lupulus*
Mace	*Myristica fragrans*
Mandarin	*Citrus reticulata*
Marigold, pot	*Calendula officinalis*
Marjoram, pot	*Majorana onites*
Marjoram, sweet	*Majorana hortensis*
Maté	*Ilex paraguayensis*
Menthol	*Mentha species*
Molasses (extract)	*Saccarum officinarum*
Mustard, black/brown	*Brassica nigra*
Mustard, brown	*Brassica juncea*
Mustard, white/yellow	*Brassica hirta*
Naringin	*Citrus paradisi*
Neroli, bigarade	*Citrus aurantium*
Nutmeg	*Myristica fragrans*
Onion	*Allium cepa*

Common Name	Botanical Name of Plant Source
Orange	*Citrus sinensis*
Orange, bitter	*Citrus aurantium*
Oregano	*Lippia species*
Origanum	*Origanum species*
Palmarosa	*Cymbopogon nartinu*
Paprika	*Capsicum annuum*
Parsley	*Petroselinum crispum*
Pepper, black	*Piper nigrum*
Pepper, cayenne or red	*Capsicum frutescens*
Pepper, white	*Piper nigrum*
Peppermint	*Mentha piperita*
Pepper tree	*Schinus molle*
Peruvian balsam	*Myroxylon pereirae*
Pettigrain	*Citrus aurantium*
Pettigrain lemon	*Citrus limon*
Pettigrain mandarin	*Citrus reticulata*
Pimenta, pimenta leaf	*Pimenta officinalis*
Pipsissewa leaves	*Chimaphila umbellata*
Pomegranate	*Punica granatum*
Poppy seed	*Papaver somniferum*
Pot marigold	*Calendula officinalis*
Pot marjoram	*Majorana onites*
Prickly ash bark	*Xanthoxylum (Zanthoxylum)*
Rose absolute	*Rosa species*
Rose, attar of roses	*Rosa species*
Rose geranium	*Pelargonium graveolens*
Rose hips (fruit)	*Rosa species*
Rosemary	*Rosmarinus officinalis*
Saffron	*Crocus sativus*
Sage	*Salvia officinalis*
Sage, Greek	*Salvia triloba*
Sage, Spanish	*Salvia lavandulaefolia*
Saint-John's-Bread	*Ceratonia siliqua*
Savory, summer	*Satureia hortensis*
Savory, winter	*Satureia montana*
Sesame	*Sesamum indicum*

Common Name	Botanical Name of Plant Source
Sloe berries	*Prunus spinosa*
Spearmint	*Mentha spicata*
Spike lavender	*Lavandula latifolia*
Star anise	*Illicium verum*
Tamarind	*Tamarindus indica*
Tangerine	*Citrus reticulata*
Tarragon	*Artemesia dracunculus*
Tea	*Camellia sinensis*
Thyme	*Thymus vulgaris*
Thyme, wild or creeping	*Thymus serpyllum*
Tuberose	*Polianthes tuberosa*
Turmeric	*Curcuma longa*
Vanilla	*Vanilla planifolia*
Violet flowers	*Viola odorata*
Wild cherry bark	*Prunus serotina*
Ylang-ylang	*Canangium odoratum*
Zedoary	*Curcuma zoedaria*

Sources for More Information

In addition to the addresses given in the text, these are sources which can provide excellent specific information, brochures, and referrals if contacted:

U.S. Department of Agriculture

Food and Consumer Services
U.S. Department of Agriculture
14th St. and Independence Avenue NW, Room 207-W
Washington, D.C. 20250
202-447-7711

Food Safety and Quality Service
U.S. Department of Agriculture
14th St. and Independence Avenue NW, Room 332-E
Washington, D.C. 20250
202-447-7025

Food Consumption Research Group
Consumer Nutrition Center
U.S. Department of Agriculture
Federal Building, Room 337
Hyattsville, MD 20782
301-436-8484

Human Nutrition Center
Science and Education Administration
U.S. Department of Agriculture
14th St. and Independence Avenue NW, Room 330-A
Washington, D.C. 20250
202-447-5121

Food and Nutrition Information and Education Resources
  Center
National Agricultural Library Building, Room 304
10301 Baltimore Boulevard
Beltsville, MD 20705
301-344-3719

Nutrient Data Research Group
Federal Building, Room 313
6505 Belcrest Road
Hyattsville, MD 20782
301-437-8491

Nutritional Labeling
Meat and Poultry Standards and Labeling Division
Compliance Program
Annex Room 204
300 12th Street S W
Washington DC 20250
202-447-7620

Office of Governmental and Public Affairs
Publications Division
U.S. Department of Agriculture
14th St. and Independence Avenue NW, Room 114-A
Washington, D.C. 20250
202-447-2791

Agricultural Research Service
U.S. Department of Agriculture
Room 111, Building 004 BARC-West
Beltsville, MD 20705
301-344-3572

Dairy Laboratory
U.S. Department of Agriculture
Eastern Regional Research Center
600 East Mermain Lane
Philadelphia, PA 19118
215-247-5800

Food and Drug Administration

Consumer Awareness Project
Office of Consumer Affairs
Department of Health and Human Services
5600 Fishers Lane, Room 1685
Rockville, MD 20857
(301) 443-5006

State and County Extension Services

Check your telephone directory or contact the reference department of your local public library for the address of the service nearest you.

Producer Associations

Almost every food product has its own producer association. One purpose of these associations is to promote the use of their product by the consuming public. Quite often, therefore, they have an active public relations and publications program. There are a great many of these associations already, and every year produces even more. The most complete and up-to-date source for locating these associations is the *Encyclopedia of Associations,* which is a multivolume reference set published by Gale Research Associates Company in Detroit. It is a standard reference source and should be available in almost any library. Entries are arranged by subject and there is an excellent index to the set. If you need assistance in finding or using it, ask the reference librarian for assistance.

Index

Author's Note and Acknowledgments

The information in THE COOK'S BOOK OF ESSENTIAL INFOR-MATION has been gathered over the years from a wide variety of sources both formal and informal. Data generated by the U.S. Department of Agriculture, various state university extension services and county extension services of Washington state have been invaluable. Although our tax dollars pay for the work these extraordinary organizations perform, few Americans fully appreciate the scope and importance of their research. What they do affects the life of each of s every day. As a research librarian and lecturer with a special interest in food and nutrition, my files bulge with notes from literally hundreds of sources I have used over the years. If I could give a separate acknowledgment for each bit of information I would, but it just isn't possible to do so. I hope that all of the people who have contributed in any way will accept my deepest appreciation for making this book possible.